"A clear and accessible journey through the planning and implementation of a coherent English curriculum, from curriculum vision and design to subject-specialist classroom practice, drawing on real classroom experience. I would recommend this book to any English teacher who wants practical, research-led advice to inform and improve their practice."

Michael Conley, CIT Leader, Runshaw Sixth Form College

THE TROUBLE WITH ENGLISH AND HOW TO ADDRESS IT

This essential book will help English teachers to address the challenges and opportunities in creating a powerful, knowledge-rich, concept-led curriculum, which draws on lived experience and engages with cognitive science and other educational research. It explores persistent problems in the teaching of English, why we have struggled to address them and how we can go about creating a curriculum which enables all pupils to achieve.

Written by experienced English teachers and teacher educators, the book empowers teachers to reclaim their subject as one which has the power to change lives, and to deliver it with passion and authenticity. *The Trouble with English and How to Address It* contains:

- A detailed exploration of the challenges English teachers face in designing and delivering a rigorous, coherent, sequenced curriculum
- An overview of the implications of cognitive science research for the teaching of English
- Approaches to building a powerful, knowledge-rich curriculum which encompasses concepts, contexts and content in English
- Suggestions for how to use curriculum design and implementation as a training opportunity in departments
- Practical strategies for English teachers which provide the link between cognitive science research and their classroom practice

To equip leaders and classroom teachers with everything they might need to improve their provision, this book provides a forensic account of what to change, why and how, moving from the big picture into fine details about what we might see in a highly successful English classroom.

Zoe Helman is a highly experienced teacher and Education Consultant from West Yorkshire. She is co-founder of English-Ed which works with secondary schools to transform their English provision. Her main interest is in using Continuing Professional Development (CPD) to improve outcomes for disadvantaged pupils. She was also involved, as an Advisor and Assessor, with the CPD Assessment Pilot set up by the Wellcome Trust.

Sam Gibbs is Trust Lead for Pedagogy and Curriculum across secondary schools in Greater Manchester. She is an experienced teacher educator and coach, who has delivered evidence-informed training on curriculum design and implementation to primary and secondary schools across the country. She co-founded English-Ed with Zoe and was previously an Advanced Skills Teacher and leader in English departments. Sam lives in Leeds with her husband and three children.

THE TROUBLE WITH ENGLISH AND HOW TO ADDRESS IT

A Practical Guide to Designing and Delivering a Concept-Led Curriculum

Zoe Helman and Sam Gibbs

Cover image: Getty Images

First published 2022
by Routledge
4 Park Square, Milton Park, Abingdon, Oxon OX14 4RN

and by Routledge
605 Third Avenue, New York, NY 10158

Routledge is an imprint of the Taylor & Francis Group, an informa business

© 2022 Zoe Helman and Sam Gibbs

The right of Zoe Helman and Sam Gibbs to be identified as authors of this work has been asserted in accordance with sections 77 and 78 of the Copyright, Designs and Patents Act 1988.

All rights reserved. The purchase of this copyright material confers the right on the purchasing institution to photocopy pages which bear the photocopy icon and copyright line at the bottom of the page. No other parts of this book may be reprinted or reproduced or utilised in any form or by any electronic, mechanical, or other means, now known or hereafter invented, including photocopying and recording, or in any information storage or retrieval system, without permission in writing from the publishers.

Trademark notice: Product or corporate names may be trademarks or registered trademarks, and are used only for identification and explanation without intent to infringe.

British Library Cataloguing-in-Publication Data
A catalogue record for this book is available from the British Library

Library of Congress Cataloging-in-Publication Data
Names: Helman, Zoe, author. | Gibbs, Sam, author.
Title: The trouble with English and how to address it : a practical guide
   to implementing a concept-led curriculum / Zoe Helman and Sam Gibbs.
Description: Abingdon, Oxon ; New York, NY : Routledge, 2022. | Includes
   bibliographical references and index.
Identifiers: LCCN 2021035717 | ISBN 9780367470616 (hardback) | ISBN
   9780367470647 (paperback) | ISBN 9781003033158 (ebook)
Subjects: LCSH: English language--Study and teaching (Secondary) | English
   literature--Study and teaching (Secondary) | Curriculum planning.
Classification: LCC LB1631 .H357 2022 | DDC 428.0071/2--dc23
LC record available at https://lccn.loc.gov/2021035717

ISBN: 978-0-367-47061-6 (hbk)
ISBN: 978-0-367-47064-7 (pbk)
ISBN: 978-1-003-03315-8 (ebk)

DOI: 10.4324/9781003033158

Typeset in Interstate
by KnowledgeWorks Global Ltd.

For Mum & Dad, and in memory of Henry John 'Janner' Helman (ZH)
For Lucas, Maya & Elliott (SG)

CONTENTS

Acknowledgements   x
Foreword   xiii

Introduction   1

1   **Persistent problems in English**   5

2   **How do pupils make meaning in English?**   13

3   **Teaching abstract concepts**   32

4   **What are the implications for English curriculum design?**   53

5   **Curating a curriculum**   66

6   **How should the curriculum be assessed?**   78

7   **Evidence-informed approaches to enacting the curriculum**   90

8   **How should we implement change?**   116

9   **Resource design – supporting teachers to enact the curriculum**   130

10   **How can we measure impact?**   147

11   **Sustaining high standards**   153

Conclusion: A Vision for English   168

Appendices   170
Afterword   176
Index   179

ACKNOWLEDGEMENTS

This book is one for teachers, written by teachers. We are neither academics nor cognitive scientists and any errors are our own.

We would like to thank the many teachers and leaders who so generously gave their time, experience and expertise to contribute to this book. In particular, we would like to thank Amanda Wright, Lucy Clark, Judy Webb, Joe Clark, Charlotte Cowles, Olly Mackett and the staff at the West Norfolk Academies Trust for sharing their experiences of implementing a new concept-led English curriculum. It has been both a pleasure and a privilege to be a part of your journey. We're particularly grateful to Jamie Warner-Lynn, whose support and trust in us from the beginning has meant so much.

Our grateful thanks also to the teachers who have helped us to ground this book in the daily work of educators up and down the country, by offering their insights: Daisy Holland Selby, Liz Chillington and especially Louise Gill for her helpful and constructive comments on early drafts.

We are indebted to the work of other education writers whose ideas have inspired many of our own. In particular, we would like to thank David Didau, whose work on threshold concepts in English was the spark for our own thinking around the place of foundation concepts in curriculum design, and for his invaluable feedback during the editing of the book. We have also drawn heavily on Dylan Wiliams' work on teacher education and Mary Myatt's thinking around school improvement. George Lakoff, Efrat Furst and Oliver Caviglioli have also influenced our thinking and we are grateful for their work and their insights.

Zoe

To the great teachers who taught me when I was a pupil, in particular Mr Marston, Mr Priestley and Mrs Butterworth, my eternal thanks for inspiring me to join you in the profession. To the teachers who were there at the beginning, thank you for your patience and guidance: Geoff Gill, Lisa Dearman, Julie Varma, Jason Rees, Jeremy Jones and Gail Howe. To colleagues who championed me along the way, Alex Kent, Karen Horler, Sarah Donarski, Andy Milner, Eileen McCarthy, Paul Yorke and Guy Marsh, thanks for your support and for calling me higher. To the mentee teachers who taught me more than I taught them, Oliver Hurt and Vera Hew, I'm humbled by your talent and commitment to your pupils. And to my students, past and present, thank you for the pleasure and privilege of being your teacher.

Thanks also to the neighbours in the street where I grew up, who had the good sense to tell me that Mr John Pullen at number 18 was so highly regarded by everyone because he was a teacher, 'and a good one'.

Thanks to my parents, Judith and Bas, for teaching me the value of education and to love reading and for allowing me to climb the shelves of the bookcases in the local library as a toddler – I'm sure it helped; to Leila Asoko for her friendship and inspiration and introducing me to oysters; to Nick and Jane Helman for looking out for me always, a thankless task but one they perform brilliantly; to Laura, Sam and Georgina for doing us proud every day; and to Enric Johnson, a great friend of my family, whose work with young people made him a genuine hero in the community.

Finally, I'd like to thank my dear friend and writing partner, Sam Gibbs, who, over the many years we have worked together, has helped me indulge in the joy of thinking so hard it hurts and been a constant support in our joint mission to improve things for pupils both in our own classrooms and in the wider school community.

Sam

I have been privileged to work with many wonderful English teachers who have shaped my thinking and practice. I would especially like to thank Karen Bryant – who mentored me as a new teacher and exemplified the high standards I have worked to live up to throughout my teaching career – Sarah Elliott-Maher, Roz Dobson and Kate Bradley, who all shared their expertise so generously and whose friendship made my first experiences of teaching so joyful. Sam Lawson taught me far more as my mentee than I could possibly have taught her, and our many coffee-fuelled curriculum conversations developed my early thinking around some of the ideas in this book. And to Daisy Holland-Selby and Sophie Halaka, my love and gratitude for your friendship, and for reminding me of the joy of teaching English with truth and authenticity, and the importance of leadership with integrity and courage.

My thanks to Francis Gilbert at Goldsmiths University, who introduced me to reciprocal reading, showed me how to utilise educational research in the classroom and encouraged me to pursue my interests further. Indira Banner at the University of Leeds has given me constant support and encouragement throughout my MA studies, and has driven me to keep the daily work and concerns of teachers at the heart of research. My friends and colleagues, past and present, at Ambition Institute share my commitment to supporting teachers to keep getting better, and my deep passion for tackling educational disadvantage in the North: my love and thanks to Anna Nelson, Alex Reynolds, Lisa Heys, Paul Deay, Yasmin Morris, Omehra Mahmood and to Elen Jones, who taught me the true nature and value of leadership, as well as how to 'manage my tell'. I am also grateful to Anna and her partner, Michael Conley, for their encouragement and feedback on this book. During my time working on Ambition's Transforming Teaching program I had the privilege of working in many schools across the country, and I would like to thank the teachers who welcomed me to their classrooms and allowed me to see so much expert teaching in action.

I am grateful to the many colleagues and friends who have supported and inspired me throughout my career. My thanks to Eileen McCarthy, Sarah Donarski, Sam Powell, Maria Hlabangana, Shona Best, Jackie Bowen, for her inspirational leadership and her faith in me, and especially to my friend Jagdeep Dhaliwal, for the conversations about education, and for pushing me higher.

Every good teacher is inspired by a great one. I would like to thank David Gore, formerly of Bilborough College, Nottingham, who introduced me to *Hamlet* and showed me the power of an inspirational English teacher to open minds and change lives.

To all of the young people I had the pleasure of sharing an English classroom with, who taught me so much.

To my family, especially to Matt and our three wonderful children, and in memory of my grandad, Joseph Cotterill, who shared my love of books. To Laura, Alice and Liz, for the years of friendship, and for being women who cheerlead for each other, and give me the self-belief that makes achievements like writing a book possible.

Finally, this book is the product of twelve years of collaboration, shared experience, much diagram drawing and friendship. I would like to thank Zoe, for making the process of unpicking 'the trouble with English' far less laborious and far more fun than it probably ought to have been.

FOREWORD

Every subject has its troubles and every subject struggles to tame the nature of the discipline: to work out how it can best be sorted and articulated to pupils so that they can learn from it. The struggle to do this work is at the heart of curriculum thinking, and there are no short cuts. However, in spite of the problems, it is a fundamentally interesting, intriguing and rewarding endeavour.

In 'The Trouble with English' Sam Gibbs and Zoe Helman scope the historic, persistent problems in the teaching of the subject: the lack of understanding of the importance of concepts; the infuriating gap between pupils 'knowing' how to do something and their 'actual' doing; scant access to high-quality professional development related to the subject and grounded in evidence; and the lack of a codified body of knowledge. In mapping the territory of past mistakes, the authors open the way for a discussion about new ways of working so that our pupils know more, remember more and are able to do more in their English studies.

In order to do this, the authors call on evidence from cognitive science to inform their model of curriculum planning: they consider how learning happens, its provisional and ongoing development which have implications for curriculum design in general, and for English in particular. So, for example, if the concept of 'symbolism' is important, how is this incorporated into and developed across the curriculum over time? In doing so, the authors identify some of the limitations of previous ways of teaching metaphor and instead point to a richer, more sustainable model.

Next, the authors turn to the curriculum models that have already been tried: topic, language/literature split, themes, chronology and texts. In dissecting the problems and limitations of each of these, they offer instead a concept-led English curriculum:

One grounded in the big ideas of the subject: concepts such as genre and theme, rhetoric, grammar and meaning, structure and representation. These are used as the building blocks to underpin a key stage 3 curriculum. In this way, the authors make the case that pupils will develop rich schema, or ways of interpreting and understanding English and at the same time better prepare them for the exams.

One of the temptations is to privilege the techniques needed for the final examinations: this is understandable for two reasons because they are passports for pupils for the next stage of their careers and schools are held accountable for these results; nevertheless, this temptation can lead to distorted practices whereby exam questions and their answers become the driver for curriculum design, rather than the careful sequencing of big ideas. These big ideas are both more rewarding for pupils to learn and more interesting for teachers to plan, moreover they have a greater chance of improving the results. It is this separation of the rich and demanding content to which all pupils are entitled from the attachment to the rubrics that is at the heart of deep curricular thinking. To turn this aspiration into reality requires a different model of professional development: one where teachers work together to flesh out the principles and to develop their curricular thinking as well as their pedagogy – Sam and Zoe make the case that this is best realised not through one off generic training days, but through carefully considered coaching which tracks back to the curriculum purpose. We are talking here of a fundamental shift in the way that we articulate and realise improvements in curriculum design and delivery: 'The Trouble with English' provides the prompts for that conversation.

M Myatt
030121

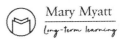

Introduction

This book is borne out of three things: a love of English, a keen interest in research and a frustration with the lack of really good Continuing Professional Development (CPD) that might, were it unleashed, spark a glorious revolution in English, one which would see us enabling many more pupils to develop their understanding, en masse, beyond anything that has been achieved before.

We draw not only on research but also on our own long experience of classroom teaching. We are teachers first and interested students of cognitive science second. Studying people, their brains, minds and social interactions is hardly an exact science and we try to continually bear that in mind. David Berliner wrote a journal article which he titled, 'Educational research: the hardest science of all'[1] where he unpicks the complex nature and potential pitfalls of this scientific field. That said, research has, for us, opened a door into a world where we are more effective with teachers and pupils than we have ever been; seeing them develop and achieve is its own reward. We want to share what we've learned and encourage further debate around our wonderful subject. In particular, we want to focus our attention on those pupils who need great teaching even more than most. We are most interested in trying to understand how we might better serve those pupils coming from disadvantaged backgrounds. They will be our primary focus.

Where are we now? Change without improvement

When the new specifications for English were first introduced in 2015, we both breathed a sigh of relief. Finally, we thought we could be rid of controlled assessment, with all its time-consuming preparation, rules and regulations. Instead of teaching to narrowly focused essay questions, we would be free to teach whole texts again, and instead of hours marking endless practice questions, we would give pupils the knowledge and skills they would need to write analytically and creatively and to tackle challenging unseen texts in a series of final exams. The two-year General Certificate of Secondary Education (GCSE) course suddenly appeared to be a vast void of time to be filled with a multitude of poems, novels and plays. We would have time to discuss and debate, to read and write for pleasure. Our pupils would love English again, because we wouldn't be dragging them through a seemingly endless series of assessments and quantifying their every effort with a cold, hard grade. The marking pile would significantly reduce – we would get our weekends back! Perhaps there would be time for a

DOI: 10.4324/9781003033158-1

new hobby! And then we remembered, we had been here before, only two years previously, when a specification where 40–60% of pupils' grades were determined by coursework, was replaced by the one with controlled assessment. We had felt the same relief, that the hours spent labouring over endless coursework drafts would soon give way to a more rigorous system of assessment, where pupils would surely have to take more personal responsibility for their grades, because the new rules would mean we couldn't give them so much written feedback. All the time we would gain! Perhaps a new hobby?

And that has been the trouble with teaching English. In our combined 28 years of teaching, we've seen specifications come and go, each ushered enthusiastically out of the door by English teachers who hope that the next one will solve the problems the previous one created. The current specifications, which inspired such optimism and hope, are losing their gilded edge. Pupils aren't magically more independent, and worse still, they can't seem to remember things from lesson to lesson, never mind for two whole years. It feels at times like more problems have been created than solved.

Each time we approach curriculum development, and it should be continually revisited, there should be meaningful improvement. We are presented with a great opportunity to re-examine this just now. Ofsted's new framework is deliberately designed to close the disadvantage gap. There is an emphasis on conceptual thinking which sits perfectly with a rich, meaningful English curriculum. The new framework document tells us teaching should be, 'designed to help learners to remember in the long term the content they have been taught and to integrate new knowledge into larger concepts'. But what are the larger concepts in English? How do we exemplify them?

In trying to answer these, and many other, questions about English as a subject, we explore the possibilities that research opens up. We try to navigate a meaningful way to achieving an English curriculum that is fit for both the purpose of allowing pupils to engage with the joy of literature and language and also the purpose of preparing pupils for formal examinations. We don't believe these are mutually exclusive. We also look at teacher CPD, where it might be failing, and how we might better unleash the potential of all of our teachers.

Chapter 1 considers where English teaching might have gone wrong through an exploration of the persistent problems we see in classrooms across the country, particularly where pupils might be disadvantaged. This covers the sorts of problems that pupils have in their learning, such as difficulty writing essays and remembering concepts. It also explores how these relate to, and are a product of, the difficulties teachers themselves face, such as lack of time, lack of effective, subject-specific CPD and difficulties in managing a range of needs. The chapter considers how problems in teacher training and in curriculum design can create a lack of parity for pupils, whose experiences of English may vary widely depending on which school or which class they are in. The chapter presents an argument for referring to cognitive science as a way of improving teacher training and pupil outcomes.

Chapter 2 explores an idea from cognitive science, namely, the notion of schemas. It covers what schemas are and how they might be built over time, particularly within English as an academic discipline. An argument is made that English, long thought of by many as a skills-based subject, is actually a knowledge-based subject. The differences between narrative and disciplinary schemas are considered, as is the importance of organised knowledge. The chapter begins to discuss the function of central organising principles in conveying ideas to pupils.

Chapter 3 explores how we might teach the abstract concepts that sit at the heart of English teaching. It considers the importance of providing opportunities for pupils to make sense of their own learning alongside the use of explicit teacher instruction. The chapter draws on relevant research, exploring dual coding, dialogic talk and generative learning specifically in relation to the teaching of English.

Chapter 4 explores the strengths and weaknesses of a range of approaches to curriculum planning. This shows the journey, a progression, from older models to more carefully sequenced, robust alternatives. It advocates a concept-led curriculum that exposes the, often hidden, conceptual framework within English as an academic discipline. In order to better teach pupils, teachers are encouraged to curate a rigorous, carefully sequenced curriculum that purposefully revisits knowledge to build connections in learning over time.

Chapter 5 makes the case for, and begins to exemplify, a concept-led curriculum that retains a strong sense of chronology but prioritises the abstract concepts that sit at the heart of the discipline of English. The chapter also makes suggestions for when and how teachers might select texts for inclusion in the English curriculum.

Chapter 6 explores how UK examinations in English work and discusses their limitations and the effects they have had on how teachers approach curriculum planning. The chapter examines how teachers currently use assessment and offers suggestions for approaching assessment in a more useful and meaningful way. It considers essay writing to be only one, albeit very important, tool at teachers' disposal. A broader approach that is less reliant on full essays as the only means of assessment is advocated. Assessment portfolios are described, and there is a commentary on how these might be marked within a realistic school context.

Chapter 7 provides explanations and examples of how a concept-led curriculum might be enacted in a classroom so that it has the greatest possibility of 'landing' with pupils. It says more about an overall approach, drawing on pedagogical research to do so, including cognitive load theory and its implications for task-setting in English. The notion of differentiation is explored, and the authors make the argument that much of what we currently do to differentiate for pupils is unnecessary.

Chapter 8 outlines the thought processes and practical steps to take when implementing change in the English department or introducing a new curriculum. The chapter is based on the Education Endowment Foundation (EEF) framework for implementing change in an English department and the Cambridge Schools, 'Cycle of Planned Failure'. This is applied to a particular problem in English to show how deeper thinking around underlying causes of persistent problems is needed to avoid misidentifying and then failing to adequately address problems.

Chapter 9 provides a range of practical suggestions for lesson planning in English, exemplifying how teachers might interpret medium-term plans in ways that are faithful to curriculum intentions and help create parity for pupils without sacrificing teacher autonomy. The chapter draws on aspects of cognitive science research to explore, in practical terms, how long- and mid-term planning might incorporate pedagogy with a strong evidence-base.

Collaborative planning, led by experts in pedagogical content knowledge, is presented as a highly effective way of training teachers in curriculum planning and delivery. A range of specific examples of long-term and medium-term planning in English are provided, all of which attempt to translate underpinning research into real-life curriculum planning.

Chapter 10 considers the inherent difficulties in defining and measuring 'impact' – difficulties such as reliability and validity, cognitive biases, and the fact that learning itself is not visible or directly measurable. Suggestions for how senior leaders might best approach evaluation, including what to do if it isn't going well, are offered for readers' consideration.

Finally, Chapter 11 considers the role of senior leaders and teacher educators in sustaining change. It considers the attributes of effective leadership and a range of useful strategies for sustainable implementation. The chapter advocates subject-specific CPD delivered by experts in current research. Using case studies from practising teachers, it explores how coaching might be introduced and cascaded across a school, or even a large, multi-academy trust. It also recommends Teacher Learning Communities (TLCs) to help embed best practice.

Throughout this book, we will draw on research to explore how aspects of our work, from curriculum design to CPD to teacher training, might be managed more effectively in order to improve secondary English provision. We start by exploring the persistent problems we face in more detail.

Note

1 Berliner, David (2002). Comment: Educational research: The hardest science of all. Educational Researcher, 31, 18–20. 10.3102/0013189X031008018

1 Persistent problems in English

The frequent changes to the way English has been examined, assessed and taught have done little to address the problems many teachers and pupils still experience in the classroom. Ask any teacher with more than ten years' experience and they will tell you that they have seen numerous methods and practices enthusiastically ushered in, only to fall out of favour, and then return in a slightly different guise some years later. In education, ideas and practices tend to eventually come full circle. We repeat mistakes and reinvent wheels, sometimes the wrong wheels, because we are constrained by time and misled into short-term, surface fixes rather than identifying and wrestling with problems at a deeper level. It is also true that most of us only know the history of English teaching from the point at which we joined the profession onwards. We spend little or no time reflecting on patterns of successes and failures over the last century or beyond.

We have not been short of dedicated, passionate teachers who want the very best for their pupils. Like many others, we embraced any new ideas and approaches, attended training in and out of school time, planned new schemes of work, scoured examiner's reports to understand how to improve our teaching and then did it all again when the specifications or frameworks – or both – changed. Unfortunately, passion isn't enough. Sometimes, 'passion' is problematic, if it leads to surety rather than self-doubt, reflection and discussion.

There is little evidence that this constant change has led to any meaningful improvement in outcomes for pupils in English because the attainment gap has increased rather than decreased. According to the Education Policy Institute's recent report on trends in educational attainment and disadvantage, the most disadvantaged pupils in England have fallen further behind their peers and are now on average over two full years of learning behind non-disadvantaged pupils by the end of secondary. In general, the gap between disadvantaged pupils and their more advantaged peers is closing but it is closing so slowly, it will take a full 50 years before we reach any kind of equity.[1] This does not include predicted further widening of the gap due to the current coronavirus pandemic. That disadvantaged pupils have fallen so far behind is such an important metric because it tells us we're letting down those pupils who need us most. These issues are tied up in complex social problems that we cannot hope to fully unpick in this book, and some of them are not specific to English, but clearly there is much work to be done to turn the tide.

While it may feel controversial to say so, socio-economic status is still the biggest determinant of academic success. Those who have more advantages at home might still need us, but they usually need us less than those pupils from low-income households. The advantaged are often successful **despite** what schools do. This enables leaders and teachers to kid themselves that what they're doing is effective. If we want to know whether a school is truly effective, we should prioritise looking at data pertaining to the most disadvantaged cohorts. If those pupils are not progressing well, then probably no pupil is doing as well as they really could.

Within this context, English inhabits a space which for teachers can feel particularly pressurised. Sometimes it seems that we are expected to achieve far more than is specified on the General Certificate of Secondary Education (GCSE) syllabus – not just to develop our pupils' reading and writing literacy (which sometimes means actually teaching them to read and write in the first place) but to also give them enough conceptual and contextual knowledge to close the disadvantage gap, to help them to become lifelong readers, to communicate with and make meaning from the world around them. We want all of these outcomes for our pupils, as well as the grades at the end of Year 11, but sometimes it can feel overwhelming when we consider what we are expected to achieve in only five or six periods a week, or fewer. There is even greater pressure on English teachers because of the importance of pupil outcomes to schools, and because our subject is especially well placed to improve outcomes in other subjects too. And some of that pressure we put upon ourselves, because we want our pupils to see so much more in our subject than can be measured by an exam. We know that English offers powerful and meaningful ways to interpret the world, to find joy and beauty in language, to broaden our human experience. Many of us know these things because we were taught them by an inspiring teacher ourselves.

Constant change has been driven by a quest for improvement, but most of these changes have at best made little difference, and at worst, exacerbated the problems further. At the heart of the trouble with English sits a number of persistent problems – those tricky, knotty issues with which many pupils seem to struggle, and that we teachers habitually encounter but often fail to resolve. With such complex problems, there are rarely simple answers, although far too often we make the mistake of applying sticking plaster solutions.

What are the persistent problems in English?

To address these endemic problems, we need to first identify the key things that create the struggle. Let's start by examining the main things many pupils find difficult before we dig deeper to uncover some underlying causes.

Many find it difficult to think conceptually

Like all academic subjects, English is full of conceptual abstractions. We have thematic concepts such as power, betrayal and love, as well as more foundational disciplinary concepts such as genre and characterisation. Pupils often write about characters as if they are real people. It's not as if they don't know that these characters are constructs – if you ask them, they can tell you that Scrooge isn't a real person – but because a good book mirrors something about real life so convincingly, this essential underlying concept gets lost. To be immersed in a good book is to be immersed in a different world; real life is left behind. That can be a good thing in helping pupils engage with and enjoy texts, but it can also be a barrier to seeing English as an academic subject. If pupils can't 'see' characterisation, for example, as a conceptual tool to create meaning, then their ability to understand texts is limited, which spoils the experience for them and might hold them back in their examinations.

Pupils struggle to make connections

As well as being conceptual, English is also full of interconnected information. For example, when studying *Of Mice and Men* pupils need to be able to connect Steinbeck's characterisation of Curley's wife with his bigger ideas about social injustice, and to make further connections with the real world. And it is helpful for pupils to see that texts relate to one another as well. Many other texts explore the theme of social injustice, such as *An Inspector Calls* and *A Christmas Carol*, for example. Seeing connections between texts, themes and concepts in English helps pupils understand the subject as a discipline. And, as we will demonstrate later in this book, all pupils have the potential to develop a disciplinary schema, to study English as academics, if we expose them to those insights.

Pupils lack creativity and struggle to think of ideas

Pupils often produce stories that are entirely plot and have little description or characterisation. Or they might struggle to come up with a meaningful thesis statement for an essay. Rhetorical writing might be reduced to a box-ticking exercise where pupils try to use 'lists of three' (known technically as tricolons) and rhetorical questions without really understanding why or how to employ them effectively. And a possible reason for this lack of creativity is insufficient knowledge about underlying concepts and about the real world. Sometimes it can feel that, as English teachers, we are expected to teach everything about human experience.

Pupils struggle to write in enough depth and detail to fully articulate their ideas

Pupils often stop short just at the point that their essay was becoming interesting. It might feel like they will never be ready to do the thinking for themselves. We try to support them with scaffolds and acronyms such as Point, Evidence, Explanation (PEE), but it doesn't seem to work and the scaffolding can never quite be removed. And how often do pupils say, 'I know what I mean but I don't know how to write it down'? Too often they become dependent on the scaffolding we provide. We explore models of writing with pupils but they don't necessarily apply any of what we have discussed. Sometimes we might attribute this to poor behaviour and sometimes it might be, but often there is something else going on that causes a disconnect between how we hope our pupils will write and what actually happens when they try to apply our teaching. Often, we simply have not modelled clearly enough. There were too many disruptions and interruptions, or too much happened inside the teacher's head rather than out loud, for pupils to clearly follow our thinking.

Pupils forget

Many are the lessons when we have been tempted to scream, 'But we did this yesterday!' And they forget all kinds of things as well. Below is a list of some of the things pupils seem to forget:

- names of characters
- what a metaphor is
- relevant context
- effective ways of starting an essay
- how to use basic punctuation
- a decent explanation of why writers use settings (they fall back on 'it sets the scene' or, 'it paints a picture' with alarming predictability).

Sadly, willing pupils to remember and believing that they should has never manifested in any actual improvement in pupils' retention. There is certainly an argument that they didn't grasp it in the first place but we often recall the exact same pupils being able to articulate these things at one time, usually right after we've just explained it. So why doesn't stuff, 'go in' over the long-term? The move to linear courses has exacerbated this problem because there is so much more for pupils to remember.

When writing essays, we want pupils to remember everything about the text, work out an effective way to organise their ideas and then get on with it without even thinking about asking us for a sentence starter or an essay plan. They should, eventually, be able to do this on their own. But often, they don't seem to move beyond needing teacher support. The stabilisers never really come off.

And we would also really like our pupils to be able to work effectively and independently in groups, rather than one person doing all the work, or the whole group getting stuck unless we're constantly directing them, or the pupils turning in a response that is just disappointing compared to what we had been hoping for. There is a gap between knowing and doing in that pupils have understood something about these models, or at least they appear to have understood, but they are not applying that knowledge.

If we are ever to address these problems, we need to look at why they exist in the first place. This means digging more deeply into the underlying causes so that we avoid any further change without improvement.

Why have we not been able to resolve these persistent problems?

There is a lack of time and headspace

The culture of high pressure and constant change with its emphasis on data and performance, coupled with our spending too much time on marking, has meant there is little space left for genuine reflection or research. English is a vast subject and most teachers have knowledge gaps that require time and opportunity to address.

CPD is lacking and sometimes irrelevant

Where we have had opportunities to engage with professional development, it has rarely had much impact because of a lack of subject specificity and a lack of evidence-informed approaches to teacher training. These generic approaches and fads often leave us with little we can really use. Lack of effective Continuing Professional Development (CPD) leads to a lack of parity for pupils, which we explore further below.

There is a conflict between our desire to teach English authentically and a ruthless assessment system

We informally measure progress intuitively through our relationships with pupils, but the school data machine requires constant performance checks and data collection which often seem inaccurate and impede real learning. There is a conflict between our wanting to teach authentically and our wanting to prepare pupils for examinations.

To explain what we mean by this, it might be helpful to consider how different teachers approach poetry. The same probably applies to novels and plays but it is poetry where the tension is often at its most intense. Some teachers prioritise teaching pupils to experience and enjoy poetry. Others focus on preparing them for an exam question. Of course, we mostly try to do both but we will each tend to lean slightly to one extreme or the other. This choice, often unconscious, determines the approach we take. But do we realise how different, and how at odds, these two approaches might be? Appreciating a poem might require very little instruction, or none at all. Our appreciation might be instinctive, it might not make sense, it might be 'wrong' in the sense that how we've responded is unlikely to be an accurate interpretation of what the author was really thinking. This is rather beautiful. Our strange instincts and the somewhat inexplicable and deeply personal connections we make are the reason many of us love literature and especially poetry.

However, this approach doesn't fit well with passing an examination in which we will need to identify an important meaning, a thread that we can follow and illuminate through careful exemplification. We want pupils to be exploratory without undermining their overall interpretation, to know when an 'alternative interpretation' might be appropriate and meaningful and when it is actually deeply helpful because it conflicts with the overall argument. We need to be purposeful and our argument needs to be valid if we are to achieve the highest grades. By valid, we tend to mean there has to be an internal logical consistency to our argument and (usually) it should feel like the author would be on our side – our interpretation might not be exactly what they intended, if they even know what exactly they intended, but it would not jar or cause offence. There are occasional exceptions to this, especially if an author's representation of a group is problematic.

Of course, the best essays are a mixture of those shared meanings we will all recognise within a particular poem, carefully elucidated and the personal insights of an engaged individual. In truth, teaching poetry probably takes both approaches. There needs to be a willingness to engage with and explore an instinct wherever it might lead, and an ability to know when and how to tame that instinct and develop it into an academically framed analysis. A balance should be struck between the teacher using their expertise to support and guide pupils, and space for those pupils to find their own nuances in the poem.

It helps us as teachers to acknowledge this consciously and explain to pupils that there is more than one way to respond to a poem depending on whether or not we are preparing for an examination. This allows us to enjoy those personal moments while also reminding pupils that some of our ideas wouldn't necessarily work in an actual essay because they wouldn't allow us to create a consistent interpretation or 'story' of the text for the examiner. While teachers have some sense of this, of course, that balance is a difficult one to strike and many of us would like to collaborate more and discuss ways forward with other like-minded colleagues. There is usually little time for this, sadly.

Top-down approaches stifle autonomy and creativity

School leaders may not have received much, if any, training about how pupils learn in English, which might lead to them misdiagnosing problems or micromanaging departments. It is difficult to work outside your own subject. Leaders might struggle to know how to interrogate department decision-making or challenge a curriculum if they lack in-depth knowledge of important underlying subject concepts. They might also struggle to know what a good one looks like in a subject that isn't their own – a good exemplar, a good pupil response and so on.

Teachers may lack expertise

Some teachers may have been poorly taught themselves, lack experience of the subject discipline or work in a culture that does not facilitate deep subject knowledge and therefore might not have developed **conscious** competence in our subject. Even where teaching is highly effective, because of the constant changes in English, the numerous fads and fashions, and the lack of a codified body of knowledge that we can all agree on, successful teachers can struggle to know or articulate how and why they are effective. This is a particular problem for novice teachers, who need to be coached by an expert who is able to break down effective pedagogical, planning and assessment strategies into clear and manageable components they can practise.

Teachers have been encouraged to see English as skills-based, rather than knowledge-based

By 'knowledge-based', we are not reducing English to a bunch of facts or lists of subject terminology, far from it. We are talking about rich, complex conceptual knowledge, emotional understanding and empathy, instinct, knowledge in its broadest possible sense. The notion that English teaching is skills-based has led teachers to prioritise doing things, creating products such as essays, for example, rather than thinking and learning. One notable example would be an overemphasis on teaching the 'skill' of essay writing. Essay writing is far more dependent on knowledge of the subject matter than an understanding of the procedures we might follow to actually construct an essay. Though we do need both, of course, too much time has been spent on creating essay products over and above thinking deeply about the texts we are exploring. We return to thinking about crafting essays at several points in this book but particularly in Chapter 2.

Curriculum is often poorly constructed and sequenced

The lack of time and headspace and lack of effective, research-informed CPD, coupled with assessment-driven practice, leave many teachers ill-prepared to design and implement the kind of curriculum that will lead to secure understanding of the subject. As a result, many teachers spend hours creating their own resources and even spend their own money on resources from English teaching websites, but often without a clear sense of the big curricular picture they want their pupils to experience. This leads to a curriculum design which does not address pupils' persistent problems. The recent national emphasis on curriculum planning has gone some way to alleviate this problem but there is still a long way to go and a new problem has reared its head. Many schools and academies are moving to centrally planned curricula that are completely inflexible and/or poorly understood by staff.

There is a lack of parity of experience for pupils, even where the curriculum they follow is the same

A potential consequence of all these problems is a lack of parity across or within schools. Pupils can end up having very different experiences of curriculum even in the same school for a variety of reasons. Sometimes it is because teachers' own schemas differ and therefore it can be hard to follow someone else's planning. It can be a consequence of a lack of sufficient detail which results in individuals planning the detail on their own and coming up with very different interpretations of the topic. Teachers can also struggle to adapt their teaching to their specific class so that all pupils can get the most out of the content.

Some teachers have access to CPD which can address some of these persistent problems and others do not. One of the most frustrating things for leaders is knowing how to create parity for pupils in a department likely to have teachers with a range of subject knowledge and experience. English is vast. We need to know everything from how to use relative embedded clauses for impact to how to analyse a rhetorical speech, how to comment on Shakespeare's use of prose in the sleepwalking scene from *Macbeth* and how to unravel Priestley's intentions in *An Inspector Calls*. Nobody knows it all and for those who have recently qualified, working out what to teach can be an overwhelming task. Even if we know we are to 'teach *Romeo and Juliet*', what exactly should we teach? And how do we, in our isolated classrooms, know what other people are teaching and whether we are in alignment? We both prefer to teach that *Romeo and Juliet* isn't really a love story. This came as some surprise to a Head of Department (HOD) who, despite agreeing that the text isn't the love story people usually presume it to be, had never actually taught it that way. We were not in sync and we only found out by chance when our pupils compared notes. It's not that either interpretation is more valid than the other, it's more that pupils had very different experiences and this sometimes led to confusion during any intervention or revision sessions where classes were mixed. There is a fine balance to strike between some level of centralisation that develops teacher expertise and ensuring that teacher autonomy is not sacrificed and teachers are not deskilled. Neither extreme – teachers completely isolated or teachers restricted by an overly prescriptive, centralised approach – is ideal for pupils. Both of these are a form of isolation because collaboration and shared input do not routinely occur.

The other obvious problem is that curricula are often not consciously and conscientiously designed to address the sorts of specific persistent problems pupils face, which we identified in the introduction. They are not thoughtfully responsive enough to pupils' struggles and misconceptions.

Many English teachers have a great deal of subject knowledge, although the range of content and the concepts involved are extremely varied so it is particularly difficult for anyone to have mastered the whole of English as an academic discipline. Pedagogical knowledge varies widely because teacher training routes vary greatly as do CPD systems within schools. Added to this, what pedagogical knowledge teachers do possess may be out of date or not particularly well informed by research. Improving teaching and learning might rely on teachers having to do more in their own time than is realistically possible. Knowledge of how to teach our subject specifically (pedagogical content knowledge) is often lacking because of a lack of subject-specific CPD, which would otherwise enable teachers to make sense of research and pedagogical constructs within their own subject discipline. This essential sense-making ensures that abstract theories are made more concrete via direct reference to subject examples that teachers can relate to.

Throughout the history of English teaching, that marriage between experience and research knowledge, particularly of pedagogical practices supported by research, has been difficult to come by and there has been a disconnect between universities and classroom practitioners. To make matters worse, there has often been an emphasis on quick fixes and short-term planning and interventions that is reactive, often reacting to poor results, rather than comprehensive, proactive, long-term strategic planning. Our accountability culture has much to answer for. We explore this later in the book and suggest that the majority of issues could be addressed through better, more consistent CPD. Deciding what matters most, developing expertise and then sharing it can address the problems that teachers have and therefore the experience the pupils have.

In summary

- Despite frequent changes to the way English is taught and assessed, persistent problems remain which create difficulties for pupils and teachers.
- CPD is often poor quality and lacks subject specificity and/or a robust research base.
- Curriculum design is not often geared towards addressing persistent problems in English.

To further explore how we might start to address persistent problems, we need to look at how pupils learn, and how this applies to English. Once we have some sense of what we need to understand to succeed in teaching our subject, we can then think about how to train and support teachers to actually do it. In subsequent chapters, we'll look at how we might address problems in a comprehensive and sustainable way.

Note

1 Education Policy Institute, *Closing the Gap? Trends*, viewed 10th February 2021, https://epi.org.uk/publications-and-research/closing-gap-trends-educational-attainment-disadvantage

2 How do pupils make meaning in English?

To start to understand some of the problems discussed in earlier chapters in more depth, we need to briefly step away from English and look at what current research tells us about cognition and memory. We seek to cast a wide net and explore learning as broadly as we can, not just in terms of our own experience, so that we might better support pupils.

Our primary role as teachers, besides making children feel safe and valued, is to facilitate learning, and learning happens in the physical brain as well as our conscious mind. It seems logical then to spend time exploring current research in neuroscience and cognitive science. Neuroscientific research, which focuses on exploring the physical brain itself, has provided some support for cognitive models which attempt to describe the mind and have been developed to try to understand learning in particular. This is a wide and ever-developing field but we feel that there are particularly useful ideas that we can benefit from, which already seem to be having an impact in real school contexts around the country where work is based on research. Dixons Academies are a good example of this. Their work is strongly research-informed and their recent results show great improvement among cohorts that have historically underperformed.

Recent insights from cognitive science on how we learn are useful but it has been tricky to make sense of them in relation to English. How do we apply a scientific approach to a subject full of abstractions and emotions? This has deepened the divide – some teachers feel it is an attempt to reduce English to a series of facts and knowledge, to drill pupils, Grandgrind-style. We are all too aware that some of this research has been poorly explained, poorly understood and poorly implemented as classroom practice, and that as a consequence, lethal mutations of key concepts, misunderstandings that lead to poor application of research are common. This can undermine the idea that research has value in English.

However, we see a way forward in which useful strategies, properly explored, can enhance our classroom practice, make us more consciously competent and improve curriculum design. It's about working out what the significance and usefulness of research might be in our own unique subject.

To begin this conversation, we might need some (broad) definitions. Firstly, how might we think about intelligence? We draw upon the cognitive model, first introduced by Cattell[1] that suggests that intelligence might be divided into two categories: fluid and crystallised. Cattell described fluid ability as a general ability to discriminate and perceive relationships between

DOI: 10.4324/9781003033158-3

things. This sort of ability is **not** based on any prior learning or experience. An example of it might be the ability to perceive patterns in shapes or numbers, perhaps even to spontaneously realise that a fork can make a good back scratcher.

He suggested that crystallised ability consists of all the things we can do that once required fluid intelligence to some degree but no longer rely on it. This is the sum of everything that we have learned. It is all of what we might now call our learned, accommodated prior knowledge.

This might suggest that much of what we think of as 'intelligence' might be learnable, collectable over time, rather than immediately heritable. In other words, children's ability isn't necessarily capped at a particular level when they are born. They can become cleverer, more intelligent, through what we teach them. The jury may still be out on this idea but if this might be true, we owe it to our pupils to teach them accordingly.

And what about learning? Ofsted derive their definition of learning from cognitive science, and frame it as, 'a permanent change in long-term memory' an idea they borrowed from Kirschner, Sweller & Clark.[2] While there is some debate about the nature of long-term memory, the important word here seems to be *change*. We're less interested in what long-term memory is and more interested in the idea of creating change by introducing new connections. For learning to have happened, something presumably has to have changed. Some new idea, or extension of an old one, has to have begun to attach itself to pre-existing knowledge. By knowledge, we don't just mean facts. Knowledge is sometimes reduced to something basic – a list of dates of historical events, for example. But this is of little use unless we can also grasp the significance of those historical events, how they interrelate, and what they say about us as a nation. For this reason, we include conceptual understanding and the understanding that comes from experience as well, and knowledge of feelings and instincts. An instinct might not feel like knowledge depending on how you relate to that word but analysis begins with instinct. We see it as a type of knowing that might be partially formed, hard to articulate, but it has value and counts as a form of knowledge in our opinion.

This implies that English is more about thinking than doing. Although reading and writing are the vehicles we use to communicate and explore ideas, our subject is primarily about noticing, gathering, organising and articulating thought.

What are schemas?

Investigation into cognitive science has enabled researchers to develop useful models of how learning happens. At the most basic level, learning might be thought of as taking what we know and then adding something new to it. This is how each individual human builds schemas. A schema can be thought of as a neural network, although it is not just a static entity sitting in the brain. Humans develop schemas in relation to a knowledge domain. A knowledge domain can be thought of as everything it is theoretically possible to know about a topic. Of course, nobody can really know everything about a specific knowledge domain (language is infinite so knowledge is also infinite). Instead, we build up our own personal schema. This is an entirely dynamic entity that is slightly different each time we reconstitute it. For example, the schema we activate when we think about *Macbeth* is personal, reconstitutive and slightly different each time. And, really, there are multiple schemas overlapping to help us understand this specific play. This gets complex but we can use a simplified model to help us to teach effectively. We can usefully think of a schema as a complex web of interconnected knowledge in relation to a specific topic. It is our personal understanding of, say, *Macbeth*, or algebra, or photosynthesis.

Schemas develop over time. The first time we are exposed to new learning, we might consider that it leaves a sort of shadow. There is enough 'learning' to recognise the information if we were to see it again; we have familiarity with it. We might even be able to make some predictions using it. But we don't really have anything more than that yet. Through repeated exposure to a concept, and through pursuing further examples, case studies, related concepts and so on, we build a deep complex web of understanding as represented in Figure 2.1.

So, a schema can be loosely thought of as a 'mental model' or 'cognitive network' pertaining to a particular knowledge domain. It is not a fixed entity to be added to in the way one might add an extension onto a house – it is fluid. It is a range of possibilities, potential connections we can make based on the pre-existing knowledge we can draw upon.

We might think of the development of a schema, or mental model, associated with driving a car. Our early experiences of a car might be falling asleep on the back seat while an exhausted parent drives us around as a last resort to settle their child. We might not even know the word, 'car' but we will probably have some sense of what it's for – moving, falling asleep!

Over time, we add to this. We add words and phrases associated with travel, we add movements and gestures associated with driving, we add metaphors associated with travel (going *off the beaten track*, having a *crash course* in something). Eventually we learn to drive ourselves. When we first learn to drive, we have instruction to support in this process. We learn some of the procedures in isolation (e.g. changing gear) before we apply them. We learn background knowledge, such as what a clutch is for, and we practise skills (procedural knowledge, knowledge in action) such as a three-point-turn. Through building up language, experience, abstract metaphorical connections, knowledge and practice, we develop a schema

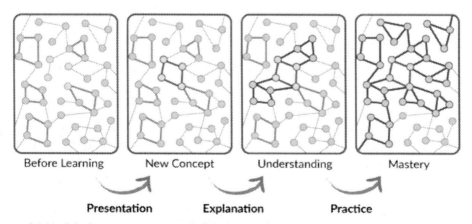

Figure 2.1 Model of memory representation in long-term memory store
Image from the website of cognitive neuroscientist, Efrat Furst (https://sites.google.com/view/efratfurst/home)

around driving that will eventually be automatised. Much of the work will then be done pre-consciously and we will achieve independence. We have moved from having a novice schema to having a more expert schema in relation to driving. This will allow us to drive without really thinking about it. It reduces the cognitive load involved in the task and allows us to think about other things instead, like listening to an audio book. And because we have more headspace to think with, we can make better predictions and react more quickly to hazards. Driving has become effortless and feels intuitive.

How knowledge informs schema building (why English isn't skills-based)

When we perform a 'skill', whether that is driving a car or writing an essay, we do so by drawing on our schemas. It is the knowledge we have already stored that enables us to do these things. Without knowledge, there can be no skill, and the extent of knowledge helps to determine the level of skill. When our driving instructor corrects us, they are imparting more knowledge, helping us to refine our understanding of actions and procedures. We might think of a skill as *procedural* knowledge – knowledge of how to approach a task. There are procedures when it comes to writing essays or even holding a basic conversation – turn-taking, adopting the right level of formality, and so on – but without sufficient knowledge of different levels of formality and how they relate to context, it would be pretty hard to strike the right tone. Without knowledge of the subject matter, even the most skilled conversationalist will come unstuck. For example, neither of us can sustain a conversation on quadratic equations for very long despite having very good command of the English language.

But how do schemas develop in English, and why do some pupils seem to build them more easily than others?

Some years ago, the inner-city school where we were both working at the time organised a day trip to a nearby stately home. On the trip, we found ourselves in conversation with a group of pupils who were aged around 14. They were walking around the farm attached to the estate and the conversation that unfolded could easily have been in a scene from Willy Russell's *Our Day Out*. It started with a pupil pointing at a cow and asking, 'Is that a sheep?'

He wasn't joking and none of his friends were laughing because, despite living 10 minutes away from the stately home by bus, they had never visited it before, or anywhere similar, and so they weren't sure how to tell a cow from a sheep either.

And later the same day, the same pupil misunderstood a key relationship on the farm. He thought the gardener was the owner of the many-bedroomed property and he thought the actual landowner was the gardener's dad. It occurred to us that this pupil not only lacked quite basic knowledge, but he also lacked conceptual knowledge about social class, about the relationship between clothing and identity, about how to recognise something about power relationships from people's interactions.

Now, we might think that it's good that he doesn't know, that he has some kind of freedom to operate outside of our still-too-rigid class system. But that might be naïve. It certainly won't help him to understand texts that explore the relationship between class and individual power and status. That might make mastering *An Inspector Calls* rather difficult. This lack of knowledge about the world forms a significant barrier to the development of schemas. A lack of knowledge about the world is a major barrier to pupils being able to add new knowledge to what they already know because what they already know is so limited. By extension, coming up with independent interpretations of a text will also be more difficult. If we need to co-construct a text using our background knowledge and experience, it stands to reason we won't be able to do this if we don't know enough.

Other pupils have greater access to the world than those from disadvantaged backgrounds. Recently Sam's seven-year old daughter, Maya, proudly presented her with the 'Star Writer' certificate she had been awarded at school for her story about a young Victorian girl. When asked about how she had come up with the ideas in her story, she recollected a visit to a National Trust property in Yorkshire, where she had the opportunity to take part in a reconstruction of a typical Victorian lesson, taught by an actress who played the part of a strict Victorian teacher. In her story, she had described in detail the costume worn by the teacher, the slate board and chalk she wrote with, and what it felt like to sit in silent rows. Although she was being praised for her writing, her writing was an expression of her thoughts and experiences. Other pupils didn't 'fail' at writing, they just weren't able to capitalise on an enriching experience that they had never had. Extracurricular experiences are, of course, not the only way to build this knowledge, but the differences in our experiences go some way to explaining why there can be such a knowledge gap.

The logical consequence of this is that what has historically been thought of as a disadvantage gap, or an ability gap, is probably primarily a knowledge gap. Disadvantaged children like the one in the earlier anecdote are not cognitively 'lesser' than their peers.

Some pupils from low socio-economic backgrounds may also have a working memory deficit but that doesn't mean they can't learn complex ideas, it just means their cognitive load, which we'll explore a little later on, might need to be even more carefully managed.[3] And anyone can present with a working memory deficit – it is not a function of being poor.

In *Make it Stick*,[4] the authors also describe some pupils as 'low structure builders'. Low structure builders find it more difficult to organise knowledge and identify the most salient ideas. This would seem to have huge implications for how we teach. We should consider how we help pupils to build schemas and think about incorporating central organising principles that are explicitly, and regularly, communicated to pupils. We should continually ask ourselves and our pupils, what those central organising principles might be. What is the most high value thing to know about x and how does other knowledge attach itself? What connects to what? We return to this idea throughout the book.

Where pupils have been exposed to far less knowledge, this has dramatic consequences for the new knowledge they can acquire because there is less cognitive architecture for new learning to attach itself to. Figure 2.2 is helpful in considering this idea:

In order to go some way to resolving this knowledge inequity, we, as teachers, need to try to fill gaps and provide as much access to high quality, organised knowledge for all pupils as we can. If schemas in English require richness, depth and complexity, which they do, we need to ensure all pupils are exposed to relevant conceptual thinking. 'Dumbing down' work to make it more accessible, or over-simplifying learning, can actually make it harder to learn anything because the deeper connections aren't there to make. To unravel further what this might look like, we need to take a look at what schemas might look like in English.

18 *How do pupils make meaning in English?*

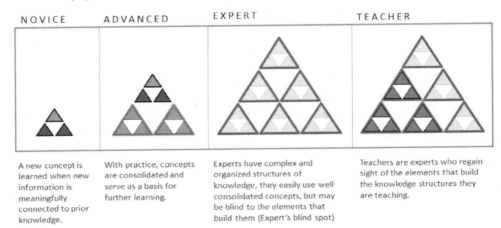

Figure 2.2 New learning builds on prior knowledge
Image from the website of cognitive neuroscientist, Efrat Furst (https://sites.google.com/view/efratfurst/home)

Narrative schemas

Let's think first of all of a schema about a single text, in this case, *Macbeth*. Firstly, we can have a *narrative* schema – one that allows us to be immersed in the play and understand its story.

We build *narrative* schemas by immersing ourselves in the story, co-creating it moment by moment with the author, and using our own prior knowledge and real-world experiences to co-construct meaning. This gives us a sense of the world of that story, its setting and characters, almost as if they are real. We use the same neural networks to 'watch' the story unfold as we would to watch real-life scenes in our lives play out in front of us. And by the time we have finished reading, the text will probably have taught us something. It will have revealed truths about the world.

If a pupil is to understand a text, the opportunity to build such a schema is essential. Pre-reading (or cold reading) a text prior to analysis is so important because it allows the book to teach us, and pupils, relatively uninterrupted and unmediated. Pre-reading simply means reading a text all the way through without really analysing it as we go along. We then go back to various parts of the text, or even re-read the entire work, for further analysis and study. With some texts, Shakespeare, for example, it might be preferable to watch the play, or a filmed version, or perhaps read an abridged version, than to cold read the entire text. Any of these approaches could fulfil the purpose of giving pupils an overview. Bear in mind that key parts of the text, at the very least, should be read in their original, unabridged form. We do not want to deny any pupil the right to experience Shakespeare or any other great author just because the language might be tricky. Later analysis should also be based upon the original text as much as possible. We can always prime pupils to understand important meanings through what we do *before* we read an extract. We can share images; front up dilemmas; draw on personal anecdotes; discuss important concepts pupils will encounter; tell pupils the central principle we want them to recognise in the text and then help them to explore its nuances; make links to other texts, films, art or media that might be relevant and many, many more.

How do pupils make meaning in English? 19

The analytical process that comes after pre-reading is about the teacher helping pupils to see how the text worked its magic – we show them how the book taught them and what they gained from the experience. With this second pass of the text, we might build a related but slightly different schema. This is a *disciplinary* schema. It goes beyond one text. It is the beginning of conquering the whole of English as an academic subject.

Disciplinary schemas

If we imagine Figure 2.3 contains everything it is possible to know within a particular domain of knowledge[5] (let's say, *Macbeth*), then the network below might represent everything that we personally know about the play; it is a schema, a mental model of *Macbeth*.

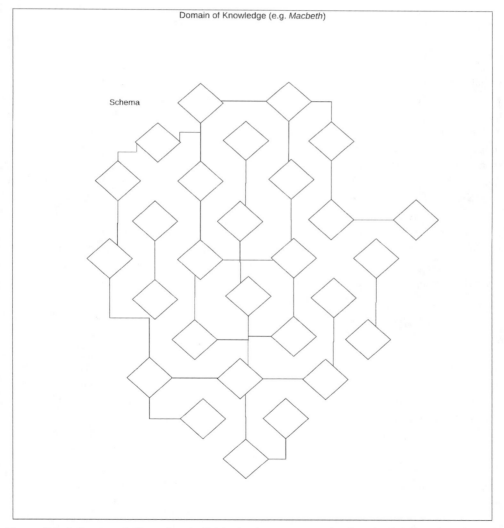

Figure 2.3 A representation of an individual schema mapped onto a knowledge domain

Within an individual schema resides all sorts of information:

1. Details of the content of the play: character names, places, etc.
2. Some sort of historical 'sense' of the past, its social structures, its hierarchies, etc.
3. Deeper concepts that Shakespeare was exploring: ambition, gender, etc.
4. Concepts that might be considered deeper still because they go beyond this specific text and help explain English as an academic subject: the concept of characterisation, the idea that groups within society are represented in texts, sometimes unfairly, etc.

A narrative schema will have elements of the first three, but a disciplinary schema requires more conscious awareness of these elements and also incorporates number four, where there is the strongest sense of English as a subject.

The text can teach us, under the right conditions

To really comprehend the play and have both an intellectual and an emotional, personal response to it, we need to understand something about all of the above. While it may seem possible that we can have thoughts and feelings about something we don't understand, we would tentatively argue that there is some kind of knowledge lurking underneath those thoughts and feelings, even if we can't articulate it. We can certainly have feelings and not understand them, we can have instincts and not know where they came from, but can we really respond with anything other than confusion to something we genuinely have no understanding of at all, instinctive or otherwise? We need to have some sense of all the above and it should really be more than just a passing familiarity with these ideas. We need a schema that stores and connects all of this knowledge.

It also reminds us of the truths behind the disadvantage gap: pupils with lots of life experience (holidays, trips, books and so on) have pre-existing schemas about all sorts of things that new knowledge can easily attach itself to. But what about the boy who couldn't accurately identify a sheep or notice apparent differences in social class?

The text itself, if allowed to do so, might teach some of this in and of itself. But it requires further discussion and exploration in order to make connections and meanings clearer and more vivid, as well as provide useful academic vocabulary. Teaching is, in part, the ability to judge how much to add and when to do it. In our opinion, many teachers start analysing the text too early. If we consider the opening of *The Hunger Games*, we can see that the protagonist, Katniss wakes up in a bed she shares with her sister. The cover on the bed is made of 'rough canvas'. It seems obvious, then, that the writer is establishing that Katniss and her family are relatively poor. But one pupil who encountered this text really couldn't see poverty in that opening. Unfortunately, she lived in a very deprived area and was expected to share a bed with her four siblings. They slept under their coats. She thought Katniss's experience was pretty normal. By the end of the novel, however, she, and others, could 'see' poverty because by that time, the book had compared the districts with the Capitol and revealed its most important meaning. Attempting to analyse the text too soon simply wasted time and led to unnecessary confusion.

Figure 2.4 exemplifies just a few of the knowledge domains we would need to draw on to understand another text, one many teachers will be familiar with, *A Christmas Carol*. Pupils

How do pupils make meaning in English? 21

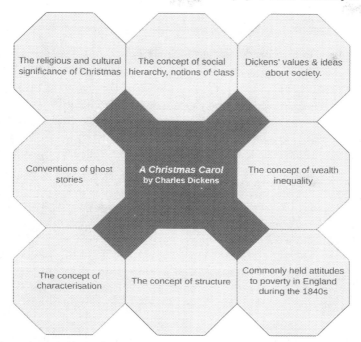

Figure 2.4 A representation of some of the knowledge domains that underpin an understanding of Dickens' *A Christmas Carol*

would need a schema representing each of these domains, and many others, in order to fully grasp concepts in this novella. That doesn't mean that we have to pre-teach everything. It means we have to be aware of potential gaps and how we might best go about filling them. We will explore later the ways in which the text itself might teach pupils, and ways in which that process can sometimes fall down.

And to understand Dickens' craft as an author, we need to add subject-specific concepts such as *characterisation* and *structure*. These ideas may be somewhat graspable quite quickly by many pupils but to understand and articulate them thoroughly is much more difficult. We need many examples to draw on as well as explicit teaching of what they mean. There is potentially a huge amount of conceptual knowledge involved in understanding a piece of literature, or indeed, non-fiction writing, for which the same principles apply.

From internal schemas to external production: writing essays

Eventually, we build up our own schema in relation to a given knowledge domain. It is unique to the individual. The schema becomes *flexible*. That is, we can adapt our thinking to new situations, effectively bringing our knowledge with us. For example, a pupil with a truly flexible schema about *A Christmas Carol* can answer a wide variety of essay questions about the play because they have enough conceptual knowledge and enough corresponding concrete examples to do so independently. Their knowledge is coherent and organised enough to *flex* to fit the question. This ability to apply their knowledge to different contexts is what allows pupils to be truly independent. But, as we discussed in the previous chapter, developing such independence is difficult. That might be, in part, because we attempt to find quick fixes to this and encourage pupils to be too independent too quickly.

For example, we have often attempted to fix the problem of pupils' lack of independence by providing structures such as Point, Evidence, Explanation ('PEE') paragraphs or similar writing frames. But these have typically failed to solve the problem because they do not address the underlying issue. Such structures are an attempt to address the *specific* problem of pupils not being able to write in depth and detail but we focus so much on the specific problem we can see – pupils struggling to write analytically – we might fail to consider the underlying *causes*. As we have explored, writing analytically is heavily dependent on knowledge rather than skill. The procedures (skills) for writing an essay are probably not that complex. We might think about introductions, driving an argument, including quotations and providing a conclusion, for example. These are not particularly hard concepts to grasp, although we will need suitable models. The real reason pupils are struggling is more likely to be a lack of sufficient, organised internal knowledge of the actual subject matter on which each pupil can draw. Superimposing writing structures onto pupils' thinking to try to guide them in how to think through an essay is unlikely to help because there is not enough foundational knowledge sitting underneath for pupils to think with, or think about, in the first place.

As English teachers, we are reasonably good at writing essays. We may have pretty well mastered the 'skill' part of essay writing. But despite our relative proficiency at putting pen to paper, if we were asked to write an essay entitled, 'The Economy of the Mongol Empire in the 13th Century', we wouldn't get very far. And if we were to ask Google for help with the research, we would bring to bear all of our knowledge and understanding of related knowledge domains to guide us and help us make sense of what Google told us. Figure 2.5 exemplifies this idea. It covers just some of the different domains we might draw on.

The implication here is, when preparing to write essays, we need to be mindful of how much prior knowledge is required. We might need to focus on that much more than the procedural knowledge of how to put an essay together. We also need to strike a careful balance between providing a jumping off point for pupils who lack prior knowledge, or whose knowledge is disorganised, while also avoiding anything that might stifle those pupils who already have sufficient knowledge to go it alone. We don't want to tell them what to think. But we do want to ensure each pupil has enough support to *be able* to think with increasing independence over time. That is a tricky balance to strike and making it work is far from an exact science but it begins with careful modelling by an expert teacher. We discuss the idea of modelling further in Chapter 6. Here, we will focus on exploring what an independent, personal response to a text really is.

How a disciplinary schema can inform a personal response

Pupils often struggle to make their own spontaneous observations and connections. As well as recognising the need to impart knowledge to our pupils in order to create connections and fill gaps, we must balance this with space and opportunity for pupils to develop personal responses. This is the art of English teaching!

How do pupils make meaning in English? 23

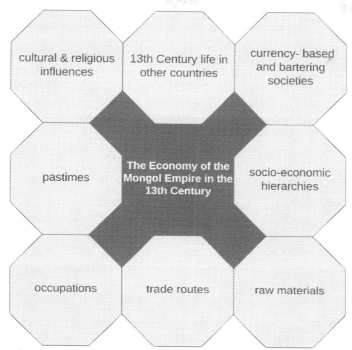

Figure 2.5 A representation of some of the knowledge domains that underpin an understanding aspects of a historical period, in this case, the Mongol Empire in the 13th Century

But it's worth pausing to consider what else goes into a personal response and how truly 'personal' it might be. The answer might seem obvious – of course, a personal response to a text is a response, both emotional and intellectual, in which we make very individualised connections to it, and also carry out our post-hoc rationalisations of what it all meant. The text might conjure up specific memories, feelings and thoughts that are unique to the individual. It is certainly true that we co-create our own meanings with, and in response to, texts. This is something we want to preserve and exploit.

However, it is easy to overlook how often meanings and responses are actually very similar for a whole range of people [look at how many of us cried when Lennie died!]. The truth is, we are often moved by the same things. There is good reason for that. We have established story conventions and patterns of communication over millennia that allow us to recognise and respond to narrative cues and react in a somewhat predictable way.

Of course, we can only do this if we are made aware of that rich narrative history. Many of us, especially those of us who teach English, are often so good at 'seeing' metaphor – we don't even realise it is metaphor. We seem to process such things as being somehow inherently true or obvious. For example, how often do we stop to think about the fact there is nothing inherently obvious in using a heart shape, which doesn't much resemble an actual heart anyway if we're honest, to symbolise love? Now, we might be able to see some kind of logic: love makes the heart beat faster perhaps? The symbolism has its origins somewhere. But we weren't born with this association. We learn it from a society that negotiated its meaning long before we were even born. Yet, we now accept it as a natural assertion and we don't question it at all.

While those of us growing up in the United Kingdom will almost certainly recognise that a heart shape symbolises love, there are so many more conventions and patterns that we haven't necessarily been exposed to, or we didn't understand when we were exposed to them. It is hard to join in the co-construction of meaning and develop a personal response to a narrative if we're missing most, or all, of the narrative clues because we just don't 'see' them. Inference is not really a skill. There is no part of the brain that does our inferring for us. We either have sufficient prior knowledge for a connection or meaning to reveal itself, or we do not. We would suggest that reading a great work of literature is trickier, and more like a complex task such as doing a crossword puzzle than many of us might realise.

Zoe's mum, Judith, is Queen of the Crossword Puzzle. On many occasions, she has tried to unlock for her the secret wizardry of the tricks used in creating and interpreting crossword puzzles. For example, Judith knows, via years of study and practice, that certain clues come around quite often. The clue 'it turns into a different story' produces the solution, 'spiral staircase'. She has automatised this so that she doesn't seem to use conscious thought at all to conjure up the answer to what I believe is quite a clever and tricky play on words.

She knows that if the clue is abbreviated somehow, the solution will also be an abbreviation. And that if the clue uses slang, the answer will also be slang. And she knows many other baffling and marvellous things that allow her to complete a puzzle in ten minutes that Zoe might not work out in ten years. But the most wonderful thing about all of this is that she really does believe that it's all quite obvious. She suffers from the 'curse of knowledge'.[6] So, when Zoe complains that she doesn't 'get it' Judith tuts quietly and rolls her eyes and wonders how her English-teacher daughter can be so utterly useless at crosswords.

We have realised that, in our own teaching of English, we have been guilty of the same curse of knowledge. For example, we have assumed that it's obvious that in *A Christmas Carol*, the jet of light issued by the first spirit is primarily used to symbolise truth and realisation. And when pupils didn't know this automatically, we thought that giving them the answer, 'it symbolises the light of truth and realisation' was enough of an explanation. We seemed to think they'd all agree: 'Oh yeah, that light, we remember now'.

But why should they know that light symbolises anything? Or even that there *are* symbols in literature, unless we've carefully and explicitly taught them about symbolism? To do this successfully requires unpicking many examples and explaining English Literature as a body of knowledge, as an academic subject. There's no way all pupils will have a personal response to the symbolic use of the light in *A Christmas Carol* unless they already have the shared knowledge that literature uses symbols, light is one of them, and it can mean various things, including truth and realisation.

And shared knowledge is also how we measure the validity of a personal response. We touched on this idea earlier. Some responses are more valid than others and as teachers, we can spot the difference. We know that, in *Of Mice and Men*, Curley's keeping his hand, 'soft for his wife' is a vulgar and misogynistic euphemism, but one or two pupils over the years have tried to argue that it's a sign he's very gentle and kind!

We ascribe validity by comparing a pupil's response to our perception of the author's intention. That seems to be a very reasonable way of going about it. After all, it is the writer's creation we are trying to explore, so thinking about their intention(s) seems pretty central to our understanding although this, of course, might be debatable. There are times, for example, when a writer is deliberately being ambiguous or obfuscating meaning, but that in itself, we would argue, is still an intention. Not all intentions are entirely conscious or deliberate but all elements of a story (or poem) have to work together to create meaning somehow, even if the meaning is, paradoxically, 'this is meant to be meaningless'. In that sense, even unconscious details can be said to carry the broader intention of making meaning.

So, when we talk about a personal response, we really mean one which is personal but also acutely aware of the potential intentions and motivations of another human being: the writer. And because literature allows us to 'tune in' to the intentions of another human being, through its symbols and conventions, the meanings we make are often similar. For example, assuming we have enough prior knowledge of British history and concepts of social class and hierarchy (those are big assumptions by the way, especially of disadvantaged 15-year-olds), we can't really read or watch *An Inspector Calls* without noticing that it is about the class system. And if someone said that Priestley was exposing flaws in that system, nobody would argue. Or if they did, we'd rightly consider their argument invalid.

So, personal responses are hugely important. But we can only have them if we have enough knowledge of:

- the world itself, in order to comprehend the text independently, and
- English Literature as a discipline, in order to spot its codes and conventions independently.

When we think of our responses as being instinctive and visceral, let's not forget that instinct doesn't occur spontaneously. Our instincts are based on knowing enough about something for us to experience an automatic response. Even if those instincts and feelings are sometimes hard to articulate, they happen because we have understood something, even if we can't explain it yet.

So, the implication for us as teachers of English is that we need to recognise how much shared and background knowledge it might take for personal responses to emerge. We must beware the curse of knowledge and avoid making assumptions about our subject or assuming things are obvious. They often aren't. While books can, of course, teach us, they can only do so if we have enough pre-existing awareness and understanding of the world in order to meet them halfway.

We do want pupils to develop independence, of course, but there is nothing wrong with the teacher being the expert in the room and guiding them through this incredible journey. Teachers should enjoy the opportunities they have to share their expert knowledge. Over time, pupils can find greater and greater independence so that eventually, they won't need us. But in the beginning (and the 'beginning' might take years), most pupils need us to hold their hands.

It's also OK to tell a pupil that their response is interesting but ultimately not valid in terms of preparing for the specific requirements of a discipline and an examination – we will obviously choose our words carefully in conveying this. It's also OK to give them a 'big idea' of the probable over-arching theme of a text so that they might begin to develop a schema in relation to that text around a clear central organising principle. This might me phrased as an enquiry question that we returned to throughout the course of study. Often, if you're waiting for pupils to tell you that Shakespeare's *Macbeth* has a lot to do with the destructive power of unchecked ambition, or is a fascinating exploration of the supernatural and human worlds, which raises questions about free will and the nature of reality, well, don't hold your breath. Tell them. Help them explore how it ripples through every moment of the play. Pupils will always go on to define their own big idea about a text over time anyway, and rightly so. It may start with them thinking about the power of unchecked ambition but they might end up exploring where ambition comes from and those deeper ideas around fate and free will.

And there's nothing wrong with teaching children to recognise certain symbols. Pupils might even benefit from having this knowledge automatised to some extent so that when they see a light source mentioned in a literary text, they ask themselves if it is a symbol of something, and what that symbol might mean. The shared meanings we have negotiated over centuries imply that the light probably represents one or more of the following: truth, realisation, hope, life, goodness. We work out which it might be by marrying it with wider knowledge of other aspects of the text. Something will hopefully click and make sense. (Or else, it really is just a light.)

That list of possibilities is one that, to some extent, can be learned. We must ensure that we hand down our great literary heritage to all our pupils, explicitly and carefully, so that even the most disadvantaged are given the knowledge they need to develop personal responses. They have as much right to develop a true connection with the power of great literature as anyone.

Building a disciplinary schema around central organising principles

Currently, it is the nature of assessment in our subject that in order to achieve the highest grades at GCSE, pupils' thinking needs to be coherent, organised and conceptual. Academic knowledge of English has to eventually emerge in the form of an essay and at this point we might need to offer some sort of thread that readers can follow. There are plenty of people who might disagree with this idea but it might be that we are really disagreeing on what we understand by a 'thread' that people can follow. That thread can certainly take many forms, and might evolve or emerge over the course of the writing, but if there were truly nothing coherent, the essay would be incomprehensible to other people. Essay writing as it is currently assessed at GCSE does require a clear conceptual lens that frames the essay.

In order for the knowledge we teach to be learned as required by such an assessment framework, we might need to see that knowledge as being, at least loosely, hierarchical, even if it isn't really. That sounds a little bizarre and is probably quite controversial so let's think about why we say this. If we're simply reading a text, it might not be necessary to identify central organising principles. Knowledge can bubble up in all sorts of ways and meanings can coalesce without our needing to clarify or explain our ideas to anyone else. But if we are going to create *analytical essays* about texts, we need to sort through all of this wonderful 'noise' and think about what pieces of it would help us to create, or curate, an effective essay – easier said than done!

Unfortunately, many pupils think that the thread they need is either the plot of the story, or the arc of some key characters and relationships. But if pupils then write about nothing but plot, or talk about characters as if they're real people, they're not thinking conceptually enough to achieve the highest grades. It's a conceptual thesis, repeatedly exemplified and explained, that drives the most well-rewarded essays. Some concepts are indeed richer than others and therefore knowledge might be considered to settle into a hierarchical structure once we think about transforming what we have learned so that it meets the requirements of a coherent essay structure. Knowledge might be considered *powerful* if it predicts, explains and enables us to envisage alternatives. Some knowledge facilitates more potential connections and a more developed schema than other knowledge. Which leads on to a rather fundamental question: of all of that rich, complex understanding, what matters most? What golden nugget of understanding might sit at the heart of a schema about a given text – *Macbeth* or *A Christmas Carol*, for example? And how might this schema relate to an even bigger one – the domain of English as an academic subject? Knowing a lot about one specific text probably will not help us much in developing an overarching schema about English as a whole.

It would seem sensible to suggest that the pieces of knowledge that will underpin or connect to lots of other pieces are the highest value. The value is in their readiness to receive a wide range of new information which can extend a neural network. These ideas might form central organising principles for a schema to wrap around.

Figure 2.6 is an attempt, albeit a woefully simplistic one, to think about the types of knowledge we use in English and how they might connect in some sort of disciplinary schema that captures the whole of our subject. Of course, our subject is vast, so this is just an exemplifying piece of what is really a substantial puzzle.

So, how can we achieve this in relation to understanding a particular text? Take a look at this list of things we need to know about *Macbeth*:

- Details of the content of the play: character names, places, etc.
- Deeper concepts that Shakespeare was exploring: ambition, gender, etc., some sort of historical 'sense' of the past, its social structures, its hierarchies, the relationship between the human and supernatural worlds.
- Concepts that might be considered deeper still because they go beyond this specific text: the concept of characterisation, theme, the idea that groups within society are represented in texts, sometimes unfairly.

If we consider which of the above might sit closest to the centre of a developing schema about *Macbeth*, we can see that knowing who is king before Macbeth seizes power (Duncan) is a pretty important detail in the play. But it isn't as high value in becoming a great student of English as having a secure grasp of the concept of ambition because this idea probably runs through the entire text and will allow us to explore patterns and make more connections. Thematic knowledge connects to every scene and every character whereas the name 'Duncan' is only occasionally going to be relevant. We could even get around it completely

28 How do pupils make meaning in English?

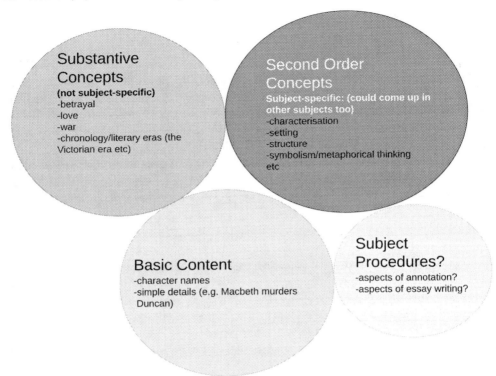

Figure 2.6 A representation of the types of knowledge that underpin English as an academic discipline

by simply referring to the character by his title rather than using his name. Hence knowledge of an underlying theme like 'ambition' has added value because it is knowledge we can constantly reuse. And it may help us understand texts that draw on a similar theme. And the concept of theme itself is of higher value still because it allows us to recognise and map other themes across the same and other texts.

Immersion in the Jacobean period might deepen understanding of *Macbeth* and a great many texts. In this way, a knowledge of history can be extremely beneficial. But even this is arguably still less important to being successful in the subject of English than understanding the concepts which underpin every single text we will ever encounter. These might be the highest value concepts of all. Concepts like characterisation: we need to know that characters and narrators are constructed (even when they are based on real people, they are still, inevitably, constructs) and that they are a way of capturing something about people in real life: about human emotion and behaviour, about relationships, about wider society. These concepts are central to analysing any text. They go far beyond the study of Shakespearean plays or works of the Jacobean era.

We have to be really careful here because we're not suggesting that learning and being able to recall basic details isn't important. It is. Knowing texts matters. These concrete details are examples that will reinforce the more abstract concepts we are exploring around them.

Themes emerge through those specific details. This is not a manifesto for ignoring knowledge of the basics. But how much time do we spend on explicitly teaching the more valuable disciplinary concepts?

Pupils need to learn two major things in parallel. They need to learn those underlying concepts such as characterisation and setting, *and* they need to learn the big thematic concepts that hold a specific narrative together. When teaching *Macbeth*, what big idea might we employ to guide pupils' study and enable them to make the connections we so want them to see?

Consider this: how would pupils answer the following question?

Q. What is the highest value knowledge to understand about *Macbeth* when **studying** English?

1. Lady Macbeth is evil (Too over-simplistic to be true but so many pupils write this in exams!).
2. Macbeth kills King Duncan and seizes the throne.
3. Lady Macbeth is (arguably) different to the typical stereotype of femininity.
4. Shakespeare might be said to use his play to explore the relationship between the human and the supernatural world, a popular theme in Jacobean society.

Would you agree with your pupils' answer?

Number four seems to be a particularly powerful candidate for a central organising principle because we can explore any moment within the text through that specific lens. (It isn't the only lens, of course!) None of the others achieve this aim to quite the same extent but we often spend a lot of time talking about them. It seems we often hide, or do not prioritise, the deepest, most valuable knowledge. We conceal it under waves of storytelling and (shallow?) analysis that don't always make deeper knowledge explicit, perhaps because we are preparing pupils for an upcoming assessment deadline? But if pupils are 'not getting it' then we should acknowledge that we haven't made it clear enough exactly what it is we want them to get.

When it comes to curating an entire English curriculum, we argue that we need to pay much greater attention to subject concepts and share them explicitly with pupils. When it comes to deciding what those concepts should be, the only thing we'll guarantee is that no two teachers are likely to agree exactly on what should and shouldn't be included. However, the discussion itself is an important one.

In summary

- As pupils learn, they develop schemas.
- In English, pupils need to develop both narrative schemas and disciplinary schemas.
- Often, too little attention is paid to the development of pupils' disciplinary schemas and this underlies many of the persistent problems they go on to encounter.
- Subject concepts need to be explicitly defined and taught to help develop those disciplinary schemas.

In the next two chapters, we introduce our own selection of Key Stage 3 subject concepts and explore how we arrived at them and what else we would hope to weave around them.

Teacher Insight

Daisy Holland-Selby, Lead Practitioner for English, Dixons Trinity Academy

Daisy is an experienced English teacher and Key Stage 4 lead who is working to embed evidence-informed approaches across the department.

On numerous occasions I have ended a lesson confident that the knowledge I imparted had been absorbed by my pupils, only to return to the same content soon afterwards to discover they had little to no recall. While mildly deflating my ego – I am not the maverick teacher I was yesterday who could cultivate knowledge by passionate, creative delivery alone – I was also falling foul to one of the major misconceptions regarding how students learn. Just because they could understand the content of the lesson in the moment, it did not mean that they had learned it.

And what knowledge should they be learning? One of the main problems facing English teachers today is the sheer volume of content that needs to be covered; this has been made more challenging since the introduction of more rigorous examinations in 2016. And we don't just want our students to be successful in exams, but also to be flexible thinkers who can use knowledge in differing contexts to understand and enjoy the world they live in. For students who come to secondary school with lower levels of prior knowledge, teaching this content becomes even more challenging.

Deciding what knowledge to prioritise is not an exact science; there is no way of predicting accurately what even the most able student does or does not know. Recently, I taught Wordsworth's poem, *The Prelude*, to a group of students who are low prior attainers. I had attempted to compensate for gaps in knowledge by creating a vocabulary glossary. But still I had underestimated what I knew and overestimated what they knew. I had not predicted that the group would struggle with vocabulary that I had considered basic. This became apparent when one student raised their hand to ask a question regarding the simile 'heaving through the water like a swan'. One might think that it would be either the concept of a simile that the student struggled with, or possibly the more complex word 'heaving'. Rather, the student had no idea what a swan was.

I now understand that my pupils' knowledge deficit would have caused cognitive overload in this lesson. But moments like this are not confined to lower prior attainers. A high achieving A-Level pupil who is learning new English Language terminology could experience the same, if presented with new material without activating and consolidating prior knowledge. It's important that teachers take into account that how pupils encounter new material depends upon their existing schema when planning lessons. Worked examples, where a novice can emulate an expert's response, can reduce cognitive load and help pupils to develop their schema. Understanding the implications of cognitive science for English is having a huge impact on my own practice and that of the teachers I work with, helping us to deliver the best outcomes for our pupils.

Notes

1 Cattell, R. B. (1943). The description of personality: basic traits resolved into clusters. *The Journal of Abnormal and Social Psychology, 38*(4), 476-506. https://doi.org/10.1037/h0054116
2 Kirschner, P. A., Sweller, J., & Clark, R. E. (2006). Why minimal guidance during instruction does not work: an analysis of the failure of constructivist, discovery, problem-based, experiential, and inquiry-based teaching, *Educational Psychologist, 41*(2), 75-86. www.cogtech.usc.edu/publications/kirschner_Sweller_Clark.pdf
3 Evans, G. W., & Schamberg, M. A. (2009). Childhood poverty, chronic stress, and adult working memory. *Proceedings of the National Academy of Sciences of the United States of America, 106*, 6545-6549. https://doi.org/10.1073/pnas.0811910106
4 Brown, P. C., Roediger, H. L. III, & McDaniel, M. A. (2014). *Make it stick: The science of successful learning*. Belknap Press of Harvard University Press: Cambridge, MA.
5 In truth, knowledge domains cannot be boxed off like this. Domains are always infinite because language itself is infinite. In other words, even if I know the play very well, there will always be many other ways of explaining its details and nuances that I have never heard and never will hear.
6 Willingham, D. T. (2010). *Why don't students like school?: A cognitive scientist answers questions about how the mind works and what it means for your classroom*. Jossey-Bass: San Francisco, CA. [The term was originally coined by economics Colin Camerer, George Loewenstein and Martin Weber in 1989, in an article for the Journal of Political Economy.]

3 Teaching abstract concepts

We discussed how pupils might build schemas in Chapter 2. As we think about the kind of connections we make in English, one of the interesting things we become aware of is just how many of those connections are abstract. For example, themes like betrayal and revenge are somewhat abstract. In a sense, the historical periods in which we immerse our pupils are abstract too – we can't actually visit them so we have to reconstruct them internally. And then there are the subject concepts we have outlined in previous chapters. Of course, we can observe all these abstractions in the examples that we draw from texts. Texts are much more concrete but even this is tricky because a written text is, in itself, an abstraction of reality; a world made of words. We're not really in the world that the writer has created, we are visiting it in our minds. And the feelings that come up while we're there are also abstract; they are often loose, perhaps fleeting and hard to articulate. Thus, English is full of abstraction.

Teachers can see these abstract ideas; we weave easily between these differing levels of abstraction, often without even noticing we're doing it. We seem to know what to feel too, sometimes imposing our feelings about characters, relationships or situations on our pupils, again without necessarily realising it. It's not that those feelings aren't valid, or even that they wouldn't be shared by pupils once they understood the text better, they probably would. And it may be that we need to explain our feelings first, in order that they might get better at expressing theirs. But it's also true that if we share our conceptual with pupils and make our own thoughts and connections explicit, their emotional responses might grow more naturally out of the learning process.

How do we currently handle abstract concepts and why is it problematic?

With so much abstract thinking in English, it is no wonder that pupils sometimes struggle to keep up! Research within cognitive science draws attention to the idea that the human brain understands abstract concepts by attaching them to concrete examples. The best way for us to learn an abstract concept is to alternate between the abstraction and its exemplification in order to build a coherent schema around a concept.

It's useful to look at an example here of what we mean by conceptual thinking and about why our teaching sometimes isn't conceptual enough, why it might not land quite the way

DOI: 10.4324/9781003033158-4

we had hoped. Let's take a look at the teaching of metaphor, a particularly useful example of abstract thinking.

Firstly, we often teach *metaphors*, not metaphor. We teach examples without ever really referring to the underlying abstract concept of one thing representing another. Or when we do, we simply refer to this as the *definition* of the word 'metaphor', without really unpicking what it means or why it is important, meaning a key part of the schema is missing.

We might teach a series of connected or random metaphors with the definition, like in the example below:

Definition: A metaphor is a type of comparison where one thing represents another.

Some Examples (these are often made up and decontextualised rather than taken from great literature so we've deliberately followed that format here):

- The moon is a giant golf ball in the sky.
- The classroom is a zoo.
- She is a night owl.

Many teachers also prioritise learning the distinction between a metaphor and a simile because they focus solely on metaphor as a rhetorical technique. We might provide tasks where pupils have to separate out the two from a mixed list of examples.

But this probably makes it even harder for pupils to spot the abstract concept of metaphor underpinning both metaphor and simile, because we are teaching pupils to *separate* when it would be much more beneficial to *connect*. The ability to distinguish between a metaphor and a simile seems low down on the list of priorities in understanding English and yet we make it very important. Why? Probably because it is easily testable. They either know or they don't. We can 'prove' progress, if we can show they know the difference. That's a feeling that is quite rare in English compared to other subjects and we tend to latch onto it. It is also probably how we were taught when we were pupils ourselves, so it seems somehow obvious to do the same thing.

Teaching the concept (even though it might be hard to pin down)

We tend to rely on reductive definitions because we think they serve as a shortcut for explaining something complex. Metaphor is quite a hard concept to pin down but that is sort of the point of abstract concepts – they go beyond simple definitions.

But what if we taught the concept of metaphor more deeply instead? What is it? It helps us understand by transferring meanings about one thing onto another. It's understanding and experiencing one kind of thing in terms of another. For example, we understand controlling a pandemic as *flattening a curve*. It's about a meaning that takes us beyond the literal, beyond the obvious. How about we teach pupils that idea using all sorts of examples, not just from texts? We might use works of art, idioms from real life, sports commentary, the euphemistic language of death (e.g. he's 'passed away'). We can encourage pupils to think about why we use metaphor: the brain processes visuo-spatial information much more quickly than words. We're actually very good at this type of thinking and a lot of our verbal metaphors contain spatial references (*I'm feeling down; the whole world turned up-side-down* and so on). It can help us articulate things that are complex, multi-layered and hard to explain. George Lakoff has written extensively about this topic.[1]

It can also help us socially; we can avoid saying things that might be socially inappropriate (e.g. by using euphemisms at a funeral), and by helping us build a shared identity. We can learn to, quite literally, 'talk the same language' as those around us in our family and community. We might use the example that, in France, if someone says, *'les carottes sont cuites'*, it literally means 'the carrots are cooked'. However, it is used to imply that a situation cannot be changed. It's a bit like the English saying, 'there's no use crying over spilt milk'.

And we can teach metaphorical language in a way that encourages synthesis rather than separation. All the examples below are metaphorical in the sense that they reflect the concept of metaphor in its broadest sense: we can use similes, personification, etc. [We can also refer to it as *figurative language*, but the link between metaphor as a concept and this new vocabulary would need unpicking explicitly with pupils. We might choose to avoid this terminology until they have a secure grasp of the concept.]

- She was as pale as a pearl.
- The microwave roared quietly in the corner of the kitchen.
- The youngsters stomped in like a herd of elephants.
- The man stared into me, ice cold, biding his time.

We might discuss:

- How these are examples of the concept of metaphor: one thing is symbolising another.
- What they have in common; the patterns we see.
- The images or feelings that come up.
- How many different ideas might each one convey.
- This kind of explicit practice becomes even more powerful when we use it to explore patterns in a particular writer's composition.

Metaphor is such a fundamental concept in English. But if we only teach an abstract concept as 'definition + examples', we are picking at nuggets on the surface when we really should be mining the deep core (now, there's a metaphor!). More generally, when we explore abstractions with our pupils, we need to bear in mind the brain's propensity to latch onto the more concrete example rather than the abstraction underneath. This can lead to misconceptions that can be hard to unpick later on. To really understand a concept, we need to delay our understanding until we have gathered a range of concrete examples that is broad enough to offer insight into the abstract idea being exemplified. To develop a rich personal response takes careful exemplification of an abstract idea but this doesn't always happen and explains why pupils can struggle to generate meaningful personal responses.

Two teachers talking about betrayal over coffee: a worked example of how we use concrete examples to express abstract ideas

Some time ago, while enjoying a brief repose in a local coffee shop, we tried a little thought experiment. We both tried to picture the abstract concept of *betrayal* in our minds' eye. Then we compared notes. Sam pictured the word *betrayal*, written in red, being slashed through with a dagger. Zoe pictured two people in a space, one with their back turned on the other. Why are they so different? Well, Sam studied revenge tragedy at university so the idea of betrayal as violent and blood-soaked sort of makes sense. Her conceptualisation has come from the examples she has been exposed to. The same is true for Zoe, except the examples were different. The texts and experiences she drew on were much more concerned with relationships, with feelings and reactions, than with acts of violence.

But we had enough broad experience to appreciate the others' point of view. Neither of us were surprised by the others' ideas because the schemas we have offer many different examples beyond the one we each focused on. For pupils that don't have such a range of examples of a knowledge domain, only narrow definitions of abstractions are available.

For some pupils, they might think of being betrayed in terms of their own playground arguments with former friends. That might be all they have to draw on. They might then struggle to see the concept of betrayal in a play where a woman murders her cheating husband until someone points out that it is, at least on some level, the same sort of experience. How they are introduced to the word *betrayal* will also influence how they understand it. Ideally, we would explore a range of examples with pupils so that their own ability to conceptualise betrayal is rich and varied. As a side note, we've found that sharing conceptual drawings like the ones above with pupils, and asking them to create their own, can be an extremely powerful way of generating discussion. If we build these abstract concepts and examples over time, a pupil might arrive at a point where they can truly have an authentic personal response, which is also deep and articulable.

Organising abstract concepts

Central organising principles in concept-led learning

For pupils to understand abstract concepts, they need concrete examples. They need us to alternate between the abstraction and the examples until they have a broad enough range of examples to be able to extrapolate the underlying concept. Very few teachers are proficient in explaining an abstract concept off the top of their heads. This is because they're too good at English! The abstraction is so deeply buried and so well understood that it has become hard to put into words. It's more of a sense of something. For example, you have a sense, a very good sense, of the concept of structure. But how well can we explain it? Which of the following comes up, and which are the better explanations? Do we share them, or some version of them, with pupils?

- How texts 'unfold' (whatever that may mean).
- How texts are organised
- How texts are broken into chapters.
- Beginning, middles and ends and their contribution to meaning.
- How texts are laid out.
- How patterns and associations are established within texts? These patterns and associations contribute to meaning, helping a writer present a particular theme or themes in a particular way.
- Writers draw on literary conventions to create patterns and associations which influence how we understand characters and events.

Are any of these 'right'? And which versions would be sufficiently coherent to pupils? It's probably important for teachers to have something like the last two versions in the list above firmly established in their mental models. It might look different for pupils but that's because they need to be fed part of this 'story' of structure one piece at a time. For some groups, it might be shared simply as: *texts are organised*.

Once we've established a usable definition, we need to keep returning to it with more and more examples. We might find a short story or poem with a cyclical ending, refer to *An Inspector Calls* or *Of Mice and Men* (or some other relevant text that pupils already know) and explore cyclical endings, we might find a non-fiction example of a writer referring back to the start in a feature article or some travel writing. Each time, we would attach the new example to the idea that *texts are organised*.

And then we might branch out to look at other patterns such as character arcs or foreshadowing perhaps. In this way, we might slowly and carefully build a sense that *texts are organised* and we might even extend this to something like: *texts are organised to create meaning*.

We might read one fiction text and work with whatever comes up, using that text to exemplify the concept of structure. The important thing is that we do it knowingly and deliberately, and **every** time we discuss structure, in any way, in any text, we can explicitly remind pupils of the central organising principle and help them refine that principle into something that helps them as an individual to express its meaning. It helps to ensure that the learning is *connected* to other relevant learning, that we are developing a discipline schema and not just a narrative schema, and it can enable pupils, eventually, to articulate their own personal understanding of the concept in their own unique way.

Central organising principles or 'big ideas' in understanding literary texts

We would love every pupil to become able to make their own valid interpretations of texts without teacher interference or assistance. There are two words in that sentence that are really important: the first is 'become'. It takes time to develop the capacity to recognise patterns and conventions in English literature and to master the nuanced intricacies of language. Sometimes the lack of independence has come from our unwillingness to accept that learning complex ideas takes time.

The second important word in that sentence is 'valid'. Although there might be no, 'right answer' in English, most responses are variations on a theme, although there are notable exceptions to this. For example, we'd all agree that *An Inspector Calls* critiques the British class system. In fact, on the 'big ideas' of what a text is about, there is usually a great deal of consensus. Disagreements tend to brew around the subtleties of particular images or moments in the story, or in the extent to which we perceive something to be true. For example, we might disagree on how much responsibility Lady Macbeth bears for how things unfold in the play.

These differences are very welcome; they make our subject interesting. Texts do not impose particular meanings on a reader, rather, the reader constructs their own view of the text bringing to bear all of their own experiences and preconceptions. In essence, we each create our own personal version of every story.

But, as we said, these differences are usually subtle. Many of the greatest stories we tell act as vehicles for a world-view that it is pretty easy to spot and so we notice when interpretations are just wrong. And they can be wrong. We want pupils to have a sense of what is valid in terms of a writer's intention so they can spot the difference between that and a rogue idea that is no longer based on the text. We might return briefly to the example of a pupil trying to argue that the vulgar joke Curley tells in *Of Mice and Men* about 'keeping his hand soft for his wife' is evidence of what a loving, gentle husband he is. We need them to realise they are wrong.

Returning to the example of *Macbeth* from the previous chapter, in order to build a valid, independent interpretation, pupils need a coherent thread to build their learning around until they are ready to formulate their own thesis about a text. Without this central organising principle, ideas can become fragmented and incoherent. It isn't that we want our pupils to only ever see *Macbeth* as a tale about the power of unchecked ambition – it's much more than that. But in order to get them to those deeper conversations about fate and free will and time and the nature of evil, we need them to start somewhere. Building around a graspable but still abstract notion of ambition or deception or actions having consequences, etc., so that pupils see how everything in the play can be tied to that single idea, is a good way to teach them that texts are coherent. They have 'big ideas' and these are what we are really striving to understand, and will be examined on. A central thread helps pupils remember the text in a way that is both concrete and abstract simultaneously. They see the abstract being continually exemplified in important moments, e.g. how Lady Macbeth's unchecked ambition ultimately leads to her fate in the sleepwalking scene. And then, later, when pupils are increasingly ready for it, we can push these ideas into new and more complex abstractions – *is that Lady Macbeth's fault or is it her fate? How much control do we have over who we become and so on?*

Dual coding (making the abstract more visible and facilitating dialogic talk)

Another way we might help pupils to see abstraction is to use dual coding. Dual coding involves utilising different, compatible components of working memory – visual and verbal – to help bolster processing capacity. What follows serves only as a brief introduction to dual coding but we invite teachers to consider its potential benefits in our subject – a subject we might naturally associate more with words than with images or diagrams. In his book, *Dual Coding for Teachers*,[2] Caviglioli explains that there appears to be a 'strong neuroscientific case' for thinking that, 'the brain maps out ideas and memories like spaces'. We have specialised neurons for real-life navigation, and 'a similar system is thought to help us navigate the mental spaces of abstract knowledge and memories'. Symbols and spatial relationships can be mapped and read just like real objects and spaces. It's easier for the brain to process than verbal information alone. Figure 3.1 is an expression of how this process might happen.

As with so many things in education, there is always the possibility that dual coding will be too loosely understood. This has sometimes led to teachers spending a lot of time creating infographics which might be of little benefit, or even counterproductive, for a variety

38 Teaching abstract concepts

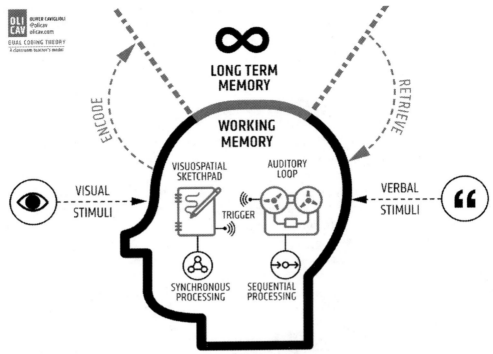

Figure 3.1 Oliver Caviglioli's representation of a model of dual coding from his website olicav.com

of reasons. Cluttering a presentation or document with unnecessary or unhelpful images might well increase the cognitive load and make learning more difficult. Likewise, a poorly constructed diagram will only add to pupils' confusion. Dual coding has many functions but we think that, used to its fullest potential in English, it allows us to explore concepts using visuo-spatial metaphors. We try to provide some suggestions for potential uses of dual coding in Chapter 7 but would also suggest reading *Dual Coding for Teachers* for a fuller exploration.

One practical application of dual coding which might be of particular interest in English is its ability to help foster dialogic talk. Of course, it isn't the only way to foster dialogic talk, but it can be useful.

Dialogic talk

Dialogic talk refers to pupils talking *to each other* in order to make sense of and/or apply their learning in some way. It allows pupils themselves to explore, question, articulate and generally wrestle with their learning. It can be considered a generative activity (see below for what we mean by generative learning if you are unfamiliar with this term). It is the type of talk that might be stimulated by an image or visual metaphor of the kind we use in dual coding. For example, we could present pupils with different images of actors portraying Dickens' Miss Havisham on stage and screen and ask them to explore which one captures the

Teaching abstract concepts

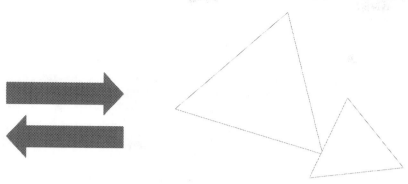

Figure 3.2 Concept drawings of conflict

characterisation more effectively for a modern audience. Or we might share two visual metaphors of the concept of 'conflict' – perhaps the ones in Figure 3.2 – and ask pupils which is the most appropriate for representing the relationship between Romeo and Tybalt, or Juliet and her father, Capulet.

Extensive research points to the role of talk in improving student outcomes: the Education Endowment Foundation reports that oral language interventions are moderate impact for very low cost.[3] Alexander cites a 'critical mass of robust evidence' which confirms that 'the quality of classroom talk has a measurable impact on standards of attainment in English, mathematics and science'[4] and argues that 'we need a different kind of talk from *teachers* in order to extend the repertoire of *pupil* talk and raise the standard and cognitive impact of classroom talk overall'. He argues that dialogue and discussion are not employed enough and that children need to experience them much more frequently, as 'we seek to empower learners both cognitively and socially'.[5]

A caveat to this is that introducing dialogic talk does not mean abandoning teacher talk or doing away with direct instruction. It is about building in opportunities for pupils, once they have a sufficiently developed knowledge-base, to perform a structured task in which meaningful dialogic talk will naturally be employed. 'Discuss in pairs' is not enough. There needs to be modelling and scaffolding of purposeful discussion with specific examples. That means setting up carefully constructed activities that foster that kind of talk. It might even mean that pupils are directed to use certain words or phrases in their discussion – words and phrases they already know.

Incorporating pre-reading

What is pre-reading?

As we said in Chapter 2, pre-reading, or cold reading as it is sometimes called, is an approach to teaching longer texts, novels and plays, where the text is read in full without stopping to analyse as we go along. If reading a full text might be a problem, which is probably the case with a Shakespeare play, then watching the play or a filmed version should work just as well. Analysis of the text takes place via a second reading, either re-reading in full or partially re-reading using extracts.

Why haven't we done it before?

Time. Accountability measures and the focus on frequent assessments have put teachers under pressure to read and analyse texts simultaneously in order to save time.

There has also been an understandable nervousness around requiring pupils to sit and listen for long periods. Studies around concentration are often cited with claims being made that there is a specific length of concentration span that pupils of a certain age can cope with and we shouldn't go beyond it. Often, the figure quoted seems to be about 15 minutes. However, in their 2007 literature review, psychologists Karen Wilson and James H. Korn concluded there is little evidence to support this belief.[6] Storytelling, in particular, is such a fundamental aspect of being human, something we have probably evolved to do, that it should usually be possible for the vast majority of students to sit and listen to someone reading, especially if the text is challenging and thought-provoking.

Why should we do it?

There are probably three main reasons for pre-reading. These reasons are not truly discrete – they are all routes to developing pupils' understanding of the individual text being read and its wider relevance to English literature as a whole.

- **Challenging texts read at pace provide pupils with a powerful, immersive experience**

    If pupils' experience of a text is constantly being interrupted, this seems likely to impede their understanding to some extent. In other words, reading should be as immersive an experience as possible, which fits very well with what we understand about attention and cognitive load. Where reading is immersive with few or no interruptions, pupils' attention is focused on what we actually want pupils to think about. Processing power can be dedicated to capturing and synthesising the unfolding events of the story. So, well intentioned though it may be, interrupting to explain parts of the text or ask multiple questions might be problematic.

- **Analysing a text is much more difficult, and sometimes impossible, when we don't know the whole story**

    Texts are holistic. Different aspects work together to drive towards one or more overarching, abstract ideas. It's hard to make sense of all this when pupils only have partial information to work with because they are still only on the first page and do not know the full story. It's like asking pupils to see the full image of a jigsaw puzzle, and how all the pieces relate to one another, when they have only been given a handful of pieces to look at.

    Concrete exemplification of abstract concepts is one of the 'Strategies for Effective Learning' recommended by Smith & Weinstein in their 'Learning Scientists' blog. We need multiple concrete examples from across a domain (i.e. across a text) in order to draw out the different aspects of an abstract concept. For example, if the thematic concept running through the novel is something to do with *social injustice*, there must be multiple occasions where events in the novel exemplify this. Characters manifest these themes. To 'get' the thematic concept, pupils might need to be exposed to most or all of those examples. It also needs to be made explicit each time. Trying to get pupils to analyse texts too early means they are working with too few examples to be able to properly approach the learning.

- **Before we can use a text to develop a disciplinary *schema*, we need to build a coherent narrative *schema***

    Reading a text is not the same as studying a text within an academic discipline. Though a slightly crude description, schemas can be thought of as networks of understanding in a human brain. For example, all of the things we personally can know, feel, think about, etc., in relation to *A Christmas Carol* might be said to constitute our schema, our mental model, of the novella. Other readers will have their own mental models of the text, although there will probably be a lot of overlap between us.

    What has been described thus far, knowing about one text, constitutes a *narrative* schema. This is the mental model we create about the story itself. It's the world we imagine and inhabit as we learn about Scrooge and the other characters. To just read and enjoy a text, this is all we need.

    But studying English demands that we go beyond one individual text and develop an understanding of literature as a whole. What is it? What are its parts? What do we study? Building our understanding in this, much bigger, domain will, over time, develop a *disciplinary* schema. This is our individual mental model of the whole of English as an academic subject. It will not just be full of examples of texts but also of underlying concepts that come up in every text, such as structure or characterisation. These disciplinary concepts are extremely abstract, much more so than the more imaginable world of the text itself. They need to be made explicit and exemplified to help pupils grasp them.

    Pupils will build their own individual *narrative* schemas as they listen to the story all the way through for the first time. It's through receiving this more 'concrete' storytelling that they will later build outwards to more and more abstract disciplinary knowledge.

    Pupils also need their own narrative schema to begin to develop their own personal responses to events and characters. Where texts are read too slowly, or in a manner that is disjointed, many pupils struggle to build these schemas.

Generative learning

As we've explored, we don't really want to break up reading with lots of tasks. However, to help pupils remember important meanings and stay on track, short generative exercises at the ends or beginnings of lessons *might* be useful. Of course, they might also be useful within other aspects of teaching English as well. There is an important caveat here, which is that how teachers carry out these strategies matters enormously. Generative exercises could easily mutate into a poor quality, poorly thought through tick box exercise in which a task is done but little or nothing is actually learned. There is a fine line between a meaningful exercise which draws on imagination and facilitates sense-making, and an exercise where little consideration has been given to the actual *thinking* we want pupils to do. And the thinking behind a product is always more important than the product itself. We'll proceed with caution as we explore these ideas and remember that whatever product pupils might be called upon to create or whatever task they might do, our true focus is really on the thought processes happening underneath.

Fiorella and Mayer[7] describe generative learning as a set of strategies, 'in which learners actively make sense of the material so they can apply their learning to new situations'. They proposed eight strategies which were summarised by Enser and Enser[8] in their recent book. Writing in the foreword of that book, Fiorella uses the example of being in an airport. We are asked to imagine that someone sprints past with their luggage. On seeing this, we naturally generate the meaning: *they must be running late for their flight*. We have therefore *generated* a plausible explanation of the person's behaviour based on our pre-existing knowledge of airports. He points out that, 'you didn't just observe the behaviour; you made sense of it – you generated a plausible explanation of the behaviour'.

In English lessons, we want our pupils to develop plausible explanations of characters, relationships and authorial intentions. Generative learning, then, might help.

Eight strategies

All of these approaches involve **Selecting, Organising and Integrating** new knowledge with prior knowledge. This comes from Mayer's 'SOI' model of memory. The thinking within each activity has to be explicitly modelled. The modelling of **thought processes** takes priority. If we approach these tasks as being about modelling rather than thought processes products (e.g. we're more worried about creating a pretty drawing than the thinking associated with drawing) they are likely to be less effective and may spawn misconceptions. The eight strategies are:

- summarising
- mapping
- drawing
- imagining
- self-testing
- self-explaining
- teaching
- enacting

What follows is by no means exhaustive. It's just an attempt to exemplify a little further what these approaches might look like in practice.

Summarising in English: what and how?

To do this, we need to model how *we* summarise. This might bring up more questions than answers, but they're worth asking! Imagine summarising *A Christmas Carol*.

Do you focus on plot, characterisation, authorial intention? What do we leave out? What matters most? What comes first? Does anything change when we remind ourself that we have to work towards writing an *essay* – just knowing the plot will not be enough?

And we need to think about pupils. What and how should they summarise? Should pupils focus on plot, characterisation, authorial intention? How might we help them integrate all three? Which would most benefit pupils at a specific point in their learning? There is a summary question on the language paper. Can we use this opportunity to build towards that too?

Let's go back a step. Rightly or wrongly, the current GCSE examinations require students of English to be able to frame their understanding of meaning according to authorial intention - we ask ourselves what the writer might have wanted to achieve and why. Perhaps, in summarising anything, this always needs to be in there. Perhaps it should always come first. This provides pupils with a consistent central organising principle around which schemas can start to build. We might suggest that everything in *A Christmas Carol* (representation, symbolism, etc.) centres around *changing to become kinder*. This is inevitably an oversimplification. But it is only a starting point. We can build complexity as we go along.

How to approach summarising

Early on in the pre-read, summarising the entire plot is impossible, but pupils might usefully summarise events so far. Integrating it with what we will have told them **from the outset**, that *A Christmas Carol* holds the really important meaning of *changing to become kinder*, will make it the summary even more useful. We probably wouldn't include quotations at this point because it adds an extra layer of complexity. As ever though, it's a matter of choice and depends where pupils are in their understanding of English as a subject.

So, summarising the opening of the novel might go something like this example below. It is written live and in note form to help pupils see us capture the important fragments of our own thoughts before we model writing it up:

Central theme - Dickens explores the idea of *changing to become kinder*
How we see this in chapter 1 (written as fragments):

- establishes Jacob Marley is dead
- significant because
- Marley will be the initial catalyst that helps Scrooge *change to become kinder*.

Our summary is then, *in* chapter 1, *Dickens starts by establishing that Jacob Marley is dead, which is significant because Marley will be the initial catalyst that helps Scrooge change to become a kinder man.*

It's worth mentioning things we don't want to include too, as non-examples of appropriate summarising. For example, we don't need to mention the part where it says the registry of Marley's burial was signed by the clergymen, the clerk, the undertaker and the chief mourner. Why? Because the most significant meanings for **understanding the whole story** are that:

- Marley is dead
- Marley's ghost is a catalyst for Scrooge to change.

We might ask pupils to use quotations or we may not. We might ask them to incorporate more examples or select one or more pivotal moments.

We might summarise chapters or extracts from other texts, as practice for the language paper. We can build up to summarising two sources rather than just one. But we practice summarising in a similar way each time and we model frequently, not just once!

Dual coding via mapping and drawing

If English is full of abstract concepts, dual coding lends itself to helping our pupils demystify those abstract concepts and begin to articulate complex thoughts. So, how might we use this in English? There are so many ways to use images and diagrams it might feel hard to know where to begin. It's important to choose the right task for the thinking you want to encourage pupils to do, or want to try to capture on paper. As we'll see, a traditional mind-map is pretty useless for making comparisons.

Mapping in English

Mapping is about capturing important details and, most of all, *making connections*.

Often, people do their mapping quite badly. Their maps are spontaneous, have no framing, lack detail and are disorganised. They might not be appropriate for the thinking required by the task. A concept map, for example, is useless for making comparisons; a bubble diagram or Venn diagram might be more appropriate. Starting with simple ways of capturing and organising information (a Venn diagram might be a good example but they're rather limited for space) is a useful introduction to thinking about thinking using a visuo-spatial frame. Creating ambitious maps requires practice, just like writing requires practice.

Imagine the map as the beginning of an expert schema. Provide a framework to help pupils get started and, as with anything, model it many times.

How to approach mapping

Chapter 6 contains an example of a concept map (see Figure 6.5). Inevitably, you will find flaws in this diagram. It is not the diagram you personally would have made. But that is probably acceptable, as long as the approach encourages a type of thinking that is useful and provides a framework for thoughts to form around, we can be reasonably content. We can also go back in and add to, re-word or reconfigure the diagram later. We shouldn't let perfect become the enemy of good.

Concept maps are useful in enabling pupils to be aware of what they know about a particular concept or text. We might then want them to organise their thoughts in preparation for an essay. We might ask pupils to write down everything they can remember, and then in a separate stage, consciously organise or sequence their ideas in some way. Perhaps they could decide which idea is the most important, number the items, or just notice meaningful connections. This needs modelling, as do all of the other approaches, and can take time to master. Starting with a simple range of the most important connections is a helpful beginning.

Drawing in English

Pupils will need an introduction to what we might call concept drawing. This is where we draw representations of an abstract concept in order to facilitate dialogic talk where we

- explore the meanings that lie within it
- reconnect those meanings with the text that originally inspired the drawing.

How to approach drawing

We've heard many English specialists dismiss the idea of concept drawing as a waste of time but those who claim that often haven't tried it as a way to clarify their own thinking because they simply don't need to. We have found that giving pupils several different visual

Teaching abstract concepts 45

metaphors as focal points for discussion helps some pupils explore abstract notions about texts with greater confidence. It takes seconds to create the actual image because it is simple and intuitive, and the actual discussion itself is about symbolic meanings in the text being studied. It also helps pupils see the connection between an instinct and a more thorough, articulated analysis. The drawing is the instinctive sense of something – our processing of semantic meanings and visuo-spatial relationships is much faster than our processing of language – and the analysis is the discussion and the vocabulary we build around the image.

Of course, like anything, it can be done badly. Drawing and labelling literal images is probably always a waste of time. But a genuine visual metaphor that mimics a truth within a written text can be very useful.

Consider the following scenarios:

Afternoons, a poem by Phlip Larkin, is mainly about the way motherhood changes women. It focuses specifically on working class women and the responsibilities they have. We come across the line, 'behind them, at intervals, stand husbands in skilled trades'. This spatial relationship has meaning and a visual representation unpicking this might help pupils see those meanings more clearly and spontaneously. We might discuss with pupils the significance of the spatial detail that the men are 'behind' the women. We might ask, why not *beside* the women? And even, how do we see the distance between them – are they very far apart and what might this mean? Writers often use spatial relationships and it can be useful to visually represent them. Figure 3.3 is one way in which this might be achieved.

Pupils need to understand and compare different possibilities with an abstract domain. We might ask them:

- Which of the icons in Figure 3.4 best symbolises Macbeth's ambitious nature?
- Or, what can we learn about ambition from exploring these icons and how might that help us understand the characterisation of Macbeth?
- What else might we draw?

[Images were downloaded from nounproject.com following a search of the site using the search term: ambition. Actual pupil comments from a class discussion are underneath the icons.]

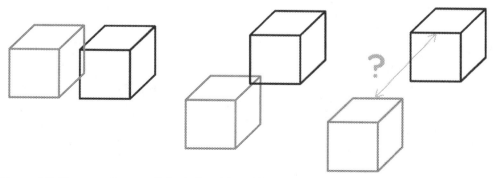

Figure 3.3 Representing spatial relationships within a poem

46 *Teaching abstract concepts*

What Macbeth wants is unattainable	Macbeth is consumed by the goal of becoming king – it fills his head	He sees the danger but ploughs on anyway – he must be really overwhelmed by wanting the crown	He is deceitful - he's mostly deceiving himself
He doesn't understand himself – he's reaching for things he doesn't truly value	He doesn't realise he is sabotaging himself – he is his own target	He can see risk but he can't manage or resist it	'Look like th' innocent flower but be the serpent under't
He is completely distracted – alone with his ambitious craving	Macbeth is a target too – of the witches – but he is unwilling to see it	He's paranoid – remember he thinks the stones 'prate of my whereabouts'	He no longer reflects his own high values of loyalty and honour

Figure 3.4 Exploring representations of Macbeth's ambitious nature

Pupils have a sense that they know what they think but can't properly articulate it. We might let them reflect on these images out loud and simultaneously track useful fragments of what they say:

In this exercise, a Year 8 pupil, who happens to have a dyslexia diagnosis, was asked to comment on R.C. Sherriff's perspective of war by thinking about his characterisation of Stanhope in *Journey's End*. He initially couldn't find the words and was frustrated that he couldn't answer the question because he felt like he did know. He was shown a few sketches similar to the ones in Figure 3.5. Inevitably, this gave the pupil a few extra moments of thinking time, which might have made the difference, but the images did seem to help. He had

-a leader -he must show strength -has to inspire people	-inside, he feels confused and insecure -sense of disbelief	-the real struggle is inside him -forces himself on -he's disillusioned; he was supposed to become a hero but doesn't feel like one

Figure 3.5 Exploring representations of the characterisation of Stanhope in *Journey's End*

Teaching abstract concepts 47

already had a lot of thinking time. His own feeling was that they helped him 'see his thoughts'. As soon as he saw the images, he started talking and spoke quite fluently about his ideas. There was no need for any further verbal prompting or questioning.

When pupils are familiar enough with concept drawing to be able to have a go themselves, we might ask them to draw 'human nature' based on their understanding of Lady Macbeth.

We might want to draw sketchnotes, as in Figure 3.6. This was referred to periodically during a period of study into the theme of identity, which was explored through a range of poems. Sketches like this can also be co-created with pupils. It is not an idealised example but a realistic, quick sketch created by copying small images from Google. Sketches don't have to be perfect to be useful. Again, we do not advocate spending a lot of time on this, unless you intend to keep and reuse the images.

The number of ways in which we might employ dual coding in English seems infinite. It is an area definitely worth exploring. It has revolutionised our ability to communicate and share complex abstractions with pupils and it has given struggling pupils more of a voice in the classroom. It has enabled us to draw attention to the highest value ideas in whatever we're teaching so that we can direct the development of a discipline schema and, hopefully, avoid extraneous cognitive load.

We use these discussions to focus our abstract thoughts onto something tangible that we all can all literally see. We label the images with useful vocabulary and make notes together. We invite pupils to draw their own abstract images of all sorts of things: emotions, relationships, themes, etc.

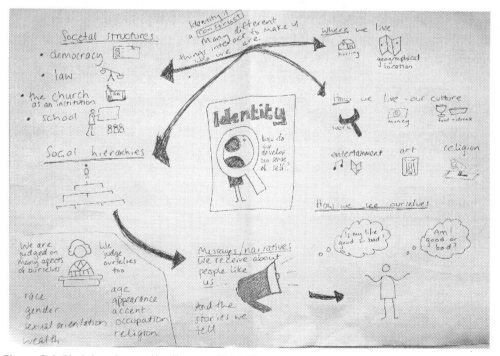

Figure 3.6 Sketch notes on the theme of identity

Imagining in English

We might think pupils do this all the time in English and that it is automatic. But sometimes we might be doing the work for them and just passing on what we, or other pupils, have figured out ourselves. We might also assume that how we should react to unfolding situations in a narrative is just obvious. For example, for many of us, the notion that we should sympathise with Eva Smith when she is fired by Mr Birling for taking strike action seems obvious. We assume everyone feels the same, but not everyone does. Some people think Birling, as a successful businessman, had to do what he had to do. That's fine. But it doesn't help them understand Priestley's overall authorial intention and it therefore makes it harder to see connections across the text. For example, they need to connect his criticism of Birling with his criticism of Mrs Birling and Gerald in order to see the picture of a wealthy class exploiting its power being presented.

How to approach imagining

So, we might ask them to imagine being Eva Smith. But how we do this matters. This type of task has often been turned into a writing task. *Imagine you are Eva Smith. Write a diary entry...* This changes the focus from imagining to writing. We might want to avoid complicating a task unless it's appropriate and necessary. Don't get pupils to *produce* anything; just give them space to think. We might combine this activity with another, enacting or self-explaining perhaps.

Make imagining as authentic as possible. Some pupils won't connect much with Eva Smith. It might be better to ask them to imagine someone they know being fired, at least to begin with. But bear in mind that pupils need sufficient knowledge and understanding to imagine *with*. Being fired might be too abstract. What about being excluded from school for demanding better dinners?

Self-testing in English

Research consistently shows that low stakes quizzing is an effective and important way to help pupils remember. Multiple choice questions with one right answer, and at least one plausible distractor, a question designed to identify potential misconceptions, is a well-supported approach to crafting questions. But we might have to provide the tools for self-testing because pupils might struggle to come up with their own relevant questions and their own plausible distractors. Instead we could take a different approach.

How to approach self-testing

If pupils are concept drawing and mapping, we might show them how to form quizzes around these. We sometimes see teachers trying to demonstrate the sorts of questions that facilitate the highest value answers. The suggestion is that *why* questions are better than *what*, etc. But this might be problematic. Knowing *why* is often the result of knowing a lot of *what*. And questions that start with *what* often feel more accessible for pupils, even when they're quite thought-provoking. It might be more useful, therefore, to create streams of questions and show just how powerful *what* can be:

> *What did the character do?*
> *What was her/his motivation?*
> *What was the consequence – what happens next?*
> *What was the writer trying to say about [insert big idea – e.g. changing to become kinder]?*

We can repeat these sorts of questions and help pupils build a meaningful, if simple, starting point for exploring texts.

We can also use free recall, inviting our pupils to write down everything they can remember. But this needs to then be organised in some way or useful connections may not materialise.

Self-explaining in English

Self-explaining is really just teaching yourself about what you've just read. It helps to frame this process with some thinking questions. It also relies on pupils having sufficient knowledge of the subject matter and some practice in building deeper explanations.

How to approach self-explaining

We might ask pupils to self-explain Scrooge's reasons for not wanting to donate to charity early on in the novella. Or to self-explain how Scrooge is described at the beginning of the novel. We might ask pupils to think about the following:

- What led Dickens to set the scene in Scrooge's counting house, as opposed to his kitchen or bedroom?
- What does Dickens want to achieve by setting the novella at Christmas time?

These questions are generative because the answer is not straightforward. We can't just look it up in the text. We have to make sense of the material.

It's a small point, but inviting pupils to *think about* questions has quite different implications to inviting them to *answer* questions. In both cases, we might want pupils to write their answers down, but the former phrasing puts the emphasis on thinking, the latter on production of short answer pieces of writing.

Sometimes we might frame this as an imagining task: *imagine you're Charles Dickens and you want to tell a story about a man who changes from miserly to kind and generous. Why might you decide to set the story at Christmas time?* And we might usefully offer prompts where pupils struggle. *Think about the significance of Christmas. What do people think about or feel?*

Pupils teaching each other

Teaching requires pupils to select, organise and integrate knowledge sufficiently well that they can explain it to someone else. Knowing you will be responsible for teaching someone can also be motivating.

Teaching abstract concepts

How to approach teaching

We're not sure how well this works within English. English is such a complex subject that it might be very difficult for a pupil to teach it adequately. It might be impossible to provide sufficient guidance to enable a pupil to do this well enough, and it is unlikely to be time well spent by a busy teacher.

If we were going to try to break it down, it might look something like the list of ideas below. This probably just shows how tricky it might be in our subject.

- A series of words or phrases (3 to 5) that might accurately describe different aspects of this character. [Lennie is...]
- Examples of moments in the text where we see those characteristics [at the start, he...; at the end, he...; in the fight scene with Curley, he...]
- One thing about how the character changes from the beginning to the end of the text [Lennie probably *doesn't* really change. How can he?]
- Two things about their most significant relationship with another character [Lennie & George ...]
- The significance of at least two other relationships [Lennie & Curley; Lennie & Crooks; Lennie & Curley's wife]
- How this character's inclusion in the text helps the writer achieve their goal of ... [Steinbeck uses Lennie to explore the idea of...]

Enacting in English

It might seem obvious that drama is a useful tool for exploring ideas in English. Like any tool, though, it depends how it is used. Vague tasks in which pupils re-enact a scene might lead to misconceptions unless there is sufficient understanding of characters and authorial intention. The knowledge doesn't initially from the enacting process itself. Pupils need knowledge first to then *make sense* of it through enacting.

How to approach enacting

So, we might pre-read and then study the text in some depth before asking them to enact it themselves. We might remind them of the general characteristics that underpin a character – say, *Jane Eyre* – AND the particular aspects we most see rising to the fore in the scene we've chosen. It might be Jane at her most outspoken or Jane at her most submissive, which is still less submissive than some other characters. I like to work with a couple of pupils a little more, in front of the class, to workshop the scene and get even more out of it, just as in a real rehearsal.

Pupils might enact part of a story they're writing themselves. Again, clear direction helps. They might imagine they are a character in a given scenario and then write and/or perform a monologue based upon it. They will need to have studied the form and have access to examples to help them. This could be tweaked to help them craft a story, perhaps written in the third person, from it. Again, the process needs to be modelled.

Pupils might also practice the gestures and movements they intend to use in a rhetorical speech. Ask them to imagine the sound is turned off so that they focus solely on their use of their body and the physical space.

Teaching abstract concepts 51

The list of possibilities with all of these approaches is endless but we hope this is a useful starting point! Whatever we do, we should do it with conscious competence, knowing why the approach might be useful and how to get the most out of it.

In summary

- There are useful evidence-informed strategies that might help us to teach abstract concepts effectively, such as dual coding and generative learning.
- These strategies can easily become meaningless tasks, if we are not clear enough on the intention of the strategy and how best to carry it out.
- Sense-making is an important part of assimilating abstract concepts and involves, selecting, organising and integrating new learning.

We've thought deeply about what to teach and why and begun to explore how we approach teaching the abstract ideas that lie at the heart of our subject. In Chapter 4, we consider the implications of choosing to put concepts first within curriculum design.

Teacher Insight

Amanda Wright, Head of English, Smithdon High School

Amanda is an experienced HOD supporting her department to introduce a concept-led curriculum.

Usually when a new strategy or initiative is introduced, buy-in from the department varies, but when we started talking about moving to a concept-led curriculum, it didn't take long before all were on board.

English is a challenging subject for many reasons and rewriting the curriculum can feel like an impossible task. For every text on the syllabus, there are hundreds of texts not taught. Meaning is complex; there's more than one right answer. Marking and assessment are victims to subjectivity. These factors are inherent to the nature of English. After Sam and Zoe explained the 'foundation concept' framework, re-writing the curriculum began to transform into a manageable endeavour. We take the abstract and make it concrete through exemplification. Not only does it make the intangible tangible, but through revisiting concepts and exploring how writers use a range of tools to create meaning, our students develop a deeper understanding and appreciation of the choices writers make.

We use texts: extracts from fiction and non-fiction, poetry, lyrics, images, you name it – to exemplify the concept we are teaching. Knowledge is carefully sequenced so that it is layered, making connections between and amongst concepts with constant reference to the foundations: the big ideas.

The ethos of the department (and the wider, cross-trust department) has transformed: we are a team of teachers who plan, teach, assess and reflect together. This is crucial to good practice: the concept-led approach has revolutionised our teaching and, more importantly, our students' learning. The concepts are the thread that binds the curriculum and students are equipped to follow the narrative.

Notes

1. Lakoff, George, & Johnson, Mark (April, 1980). The metaphorical structure of the human conceptual system. *Cognitive Science: A Multidisciplinary Journal, 4*(2), 195-208. https://doi.org/10.1207/s15516709cog0402_4
2. Caviglioli, O. (2019). *Dual coding with teachers*. John Catt Educational Ltd: Woodbridge, UK.
3. Education Endowment Foundation. *Teaching and learning toolkit: An accessible summary of the international evidence on teaching 5-16 year olds* [Accessed 1 December 2017]. Available at: https://educationendowmentfoundation.org.uk/evidence-summaries/teaching-learning-toolkit/
4. Alexander, R. J. (2012). *Improving oracy and classroom talk in English schools: Achievements and challenges* [Accessed 3 November 2017]. Available at: http://www.robinalexander.org.uk/wp-content/uploads/2012/05/DfE-oracy-120220-Alexander-FINAL.pdf
5. Alexander, R. J. (2008). *Dialogic teaching essentials* adapted from *Towards dialogic teaching: Rethinking classroom talk*. 4th Ed. Dialogos: London.
6. Wilson, Karen, & Korn, James H. (June 2007). Attention during lectures: Beyond ten minutes. *Teaching of Psychology, 34*(2), 85-89. https://doi.org/10.1080/00986280701291291
7. Fiorella, Logan, & Mayer, Richard E. (2015). *Learning as a generative activity: Eight learning strategies that promote understanding*. Cambridge University Press: New York, NY.
8. Enser, Zoe, & Enser, Mark (2020). *Fiorella & Mayer's Generative learning in action*. John Catt Educational Ltd, UK.

4 What are the implications for English curriculum design?

Like many teachers, we received very little robust training in curriculum design. Lack of training and guidance mean that a teacher's planning might end up being an ineffective mix of the previous planning of colleagues, schemes of work from other schools or the Internet and their own ideas. Many teachers simply lack sufficient experience in planning and sequencing learning across key stages. They might not see themselves as curators of curriculum.

We would argue that getting to grips with curriculum should be a very high priority for classroom teachers, because it should form the basis of their planning. Lesson plans, rather than coming from the Internet or a colleague's hard drive, should be an iteration of learning intentions from a coherent long-term plan which sequences pupils' learning over time. Ideally, all department staff are involved in its design, but the work should be spear-headed by expert teachers with the experience and pedagogical content knowledge – a combination of subject knowledge and the knowledge of pedagogical approaches that might best help pupils learn – to plan and sequence learning in English, to pre-empt and plan to address pupils' misconceptions and to design meaningful assessment which would best help teachers to capture what had been understood.

The purpose of a curriculum is to provide a map of the journey we wish pupils to make in our subject. It should show how and when they will acquire the most important knowledge and skills, and how they will connect those together. In essence, it is a manifestation of the mental model, or schema, we want our pupils to develop. At the same time, it provides a clear mental model for novice teachers, who may lack the content and pedagogical knowledge of more experienced colleagues, and so provides parity of knowledge across a department. Even more importantly, it provides greater parity for pupils too. Research tells us that an expert teacher has the largest effect on pupils' outcomes and life chances, and this effect is magnified for disadvantaged students.[1] Every child deserves to be taught by an expert teacher, and it shouldn't be the case that a young person's experience of and outcomes in a subject depend on which teacher they are placed with. It is, in part, through curriculum design that we can develop the expertise of all teachers.

Where to start?

In curating an English curriculum, the National Curriculum is our starting point. From it, we can see that pupils need breadth and depth and the canon is specifically referenced.

DOI: 10.4324/9781003033158-5

54 *What are the implications for English curriculum design?*

Of course, we need to balance this with text choices that reflect diverse voices and experiences. We explore the idea of text choices further at the end of this chapter.

But we also need to think about how we teach pupils about the nature of our subject itself – how it is constructed and contested. For example, whether the canon maintains its high status or whether it should give way to something more representative of a modern society. Choices we make about what to include also determine what we choose not to include, and an important consideration is how we expose pupils to those choices, and enable them to critically evaluate the inclusion of knowledge.

Crucially, we need to acknowledge the tension between curating an experience for pupils that gives them rich knowledge and prepares them for a formal examination, while also facilitating an emotional and social experience of enjoying and sharing literature and the English language.

With the introduction of the new specifications in 2015, and the new Ofsted framework shortly afterwards, more attention is now rightly being given to curriculum design. By taking an evidence-informed approach and incorporating what cognitive science tells us about learning as we curate our curriculum, we might start to address the persistent problems we habitually encounter in English.

We will begin by reflecting on what we have already tried, and why it can be problematic.

What curriculum models have we already tried?

By topic

Teaching a topic – for example, poetry, non-fiction or creative writing – over a term or half-term seemed to lend itself to the modes of assessment prevalent at the start of our teaching careers. Pupils completed written coursework, and later controlled assessment, worth a large proportion of their overall grade, and so it seemed to make sense to start our planning by considering what the assessment was going to be. Of course, we now know this is the wrong way around. As Ruth Ashbee[2] says, 'in curriculum, the methods of assessment should not be the starting point for curriculum'. The important word here is *methods*. Planning backwards from assessment, and other wider curriculum goals, ensures our teaching is clearly focused towards what we hope to achieve. But an over-focus on the specific things pupils need to be able to do in an end-of-topic assessment will inevitably narrow the curriculum, and deny pupils their entitlement to experience the breadth and depth of the subject.

In this topic-based model of curriculum, there were several pieces of written coursework to complete, and so doing each one in turn in Year 10 seemed the most logical way of structuring the course. The exam content could be covered in Year 11, closer to the final examinations, so pupils would be more likely to remember what they had been taught. The other advantage of doing the coursework first was that pupils could 'bank' their marks, which meant that teachers could make reasonably accurate predictions about their likelihood of achieving target grades at the end of Year 11. Teachers could give feedback on drafts, and pupils could keep re-drafting until they achieved their set target, so this aspect of the General Certificate of Secondary Education (GCSE) course was more controllable, and the constant re-drafting provided a stream of ever-improving data to those who needed it.

One of the intended benefits of designing the curriculum by topic was that pupils would be able to begin Year 11 feeling that a significant proportion of the course was already under their belt and could use their success so far as a springboard for further success with the exam-related content. In principle, this sounded appealing, because it offered the opportunity to free up plenty of teaching time for exam practice and feedback. The reality, however, was somewhat different. Many pupils didn't actually complete their coursework in Year 10, or if they did, it wasn't quite at the standard needed for them to have a chance of achieving their target. The result was a flurry of interventions – after-school, before school, in the holidays – where pupils were re-taught texts or topics and asked to redraft written pieces again. Sometimes, with the benefit of a year of added knowledge and maturity, pupils would be successful. This seemed to be especially true of the creative writing pieces. Sam remembers a Year 10 pupil who proudly handed in her Original Writing coursework – a story she called 'My Lovely Horse'. It was sweet, and she wrote well, but the piece was nowhere near the grade criteria for 'sophisticated' that would help her achieve her A* target in Year 11. She was heartbroken when gently told it was Grade C standard. The following year, she produced a second attempt, a beautifully crafted short story about a fictional post-apocalyptic society, for which she achieved full marks. The transition to Year 11, the exposure to more complex texts, the extra year of teaching, and her growing maturity had resulted in her writing with the 'flair' to achieve in the A* grade band, towards the end of her GCSE course.

Why might a topic-based approach be problematic?

This highlights one of the problems the topic-based curriculum created: pupils will not have the cumulative knowledge and skills to achieve their potential at the very start of a course, so why would we ask them to complete high-stakes coursework at this point and expect it to be anywhere near the standard they could potentially produce towards the end? It seemed entirely predictable that we would end up spending time in Year 11 going back to texts and topics we had taught in Year 10. Of course, revisiting important subject content is important – it's essential for making connections and for remembering. But that's not what many of us were really doing. We weren't revisiting – we were reteaching the same content, in the same way, and then wondering why pupils' work didn't get any better.

And of course, some pupils, despite their very best efforts, do not make the grade gains that the pupil with her horse story made. We would argue that the pupils who do make such rapid progress are almost certainly the ones with higher levels of prior knowledge to begin with. As we saw in Chapter 2, what we already know determines how much we learn and how quickly we can process new learning, because we use our existing knowledge to make connections to new information. For pupils who are already keen and fluent readers, are exposed to increasingly sophisticated texts at school and at home, and have the benefit of additional experiences that help them acquire knowledge, their ability to write creatively will tend to improve more quickly. The school where the Year 10 pupil was taught was in an affluent suburb of North Leeds; she came from a family where both parents were lawyers, and she had the experience of owning a horse to base her story on.

It is humbling to think that our successful teaching of higher set pupils is at least partly down to our being the icing on their already large and well-decorated cake – they were likely to have succeeded, regardless of who taught them and how well they did it. Faced with pupils

56 *What are the implications for English curriculum design?*

who were incredibly de-motivated, did not enjoy English because they did not believe they could be successful, and in many cases lacked the basic literacy skills to even access the texts, it was a struggle to make improvements.

Why, then, did the topic-based curriculum model not work? Modular approaches don't marry with what we know about how we learn. Rather than planning around the knowledge and skills we wanted our pupils to gain over the course, we narrowed our curriculum to modular assessment, and each assessment became an end goal. The problem was, teaching by module led teachers and pupils to see English as a set of separate topics – the coursework was a set of texts and tasks, and the exams a series of questions. But we learn through forging connections; this is how flexible, durable schema develop. All pupils, and lower attaining pupils in particular, need opportunities to recall and revisit knowledge, to build on it over time, and to have explicit links and connections between material made for them. If, for example, we point out that Dickens' characterisation of Scrooge at the start of *A Christmas Carol* shares some of the same techniques Priestley uses to characterise Mr Birling in *An Inspector Calls*, pupils can understand that all writers utilise a similar 'toolkit' of techniques. However, where a curriculum is not rigorously designed, the connections were somewhat left to chance. The subject of English is full of these connections and seeing them is vital for pupils to develop a rich schema in the subject, but a curriculum planned by topic is not often planned around making them explicit.

By completely separating literature from language

The introduction of the new specifications for English in 2015 seemed to offer an opportunity for a fresh approach. Written coursework has been replaced by terminal examinations, and this has forced a re-think about the way we organise English curricula. The modular approach we used previously isn't relevant anymore, because we can no longer 'finish' a topic and put it aside. Instead, pupils need to be able to remember and apply everything they have learned over their GCSE course in four high-stakes exams, two each in English language and English literature. Tiered papers have also been removed and along with them those difficult decisions about which tier each pupil is best suited to.

When the new specifications were first introduced, teachers had a choice between continuing to teach literature and language as separate subjects or attempting to weave them together in some way. Across schools, most examples continued to highlight the split, either by having pupils taught by separate teachers and treating the subjects as distinct GCSEs, or by weaving between the two. A typical curriculum model looked something like Figure 3.2.

However, along with terminal examinations, the new specifications brought with them another significant change, which was to the relationship between English language and English literature. Previously, the distinction between them had mostly seemed obvious. The literature syllabus comprised poetry, plays and novels, while language assessed creative writing, speaking and listening, non-fiction and aspects of media studies. Essay questions on *Lord of the Flies* seemed to require a markedly different set of skills to an analysis of presentational devices in a leaflet. It was because of this distinction, perhaps, that the Department for Education (DfE)[3], further education institutions and employers, and therefore schools, prized English language above literature, and every effort was put into ensuring as many pupils as possible achieved the magic 'C' grade. Often it resulted in some strange distortions of the curriculum, with literature becoming a subject only the top set could study, or being dispensed with altogether by the end of Year 10 under the early entry system.

Under the new specifications, English language and literature have undergone an apparent role reversal, with language now having a very literary focus. Examinations now require students to write about unseen literary fiction and non-fiction texts from different social and historical contexts. While each is still assessed separately, assessment objectives have much overlap. Examination boards are currently required to have similar assessment objectives for both language and literature study.[2] Separating them no longer makes sense, if it ever did.

Why might a lit/lang split be problematic?

The language paper, particularly in its current iteration, is not that different from the literature paper. There are many underlying connections between these two subjects. All texts make use of language; they are all structured in some way; reading and writing are connected – they are two sides of exploring the same entity – the written word. If we disconnect language from literature, or reading from writing, the likelihood is that students will come to see English literature as a series of texts, and English language as a series of exam questions – and thus the problems created by the topic curriculum model are repeated.

By theme

An increasingly common way to sequence an English curriculum is by themes. By theme, we mean an overarching idea that runs through a text and that is somewhat specific. For example, we wouldn't necessarily class *war* as a theme. One word is not enough to really understand this topic as a theme because there are too many different ways in which it might be interpreted. The brutality, or futility, of war, are themes, according to our definition. That is because these short phrases go beyond merely naming a topic area and begin to present some sort of emotional resonance or broad roadmap for considering that topic. It would be a very different conversation from one exploring wartime *propaganda*, for example. Organising the curriculum content under an overarching theme is a possible way to show pupils the broader connections across the discipline of English while still treating each GCSE separately underneath that theme, and lessening any confusion about the requirements of each of the examinations. It also provides an opportunity to teach English in a more holistic way, one which brings together language and literature and potentially resolves some of the problems with the topic/text approach.

Why might a theme-based approach be problematic?

There are merits to a thematic approach. It's certainly a step in the right direction away from teaching exam questions. Immersing pupils in themes offers them a broader, more conceptual lens through which to approach the discipline. But it needs to be handled with caution. For instance, how do we go about choosing which themes pupils will study? Selection involves subjective choices, which necessarily prioritise some themes while relegating the importance of others.

We might want to choose themes which we think our pupils will be able to relate to most, but we also need to consider themes they find less relatable, not just because any theme could be a focus for the final exam, but because through teaching English we have the great privilege of being able to enlarge our pupils' worlds and broaden their horizons. If we stick only to things that are 'relatable' we deny them so much of the world.

And we also need to consider what we want them to know specifically about each theme and how we move beyond thinking simply in terms of topics. If we are teaching 'power', for example, what exactly are we teaching about this subject? What might the themes be and how do we give pupils a broad understanding of 'power'? Without careful thought and planning, there is a danger that pupils develop schemas around power that are so attached to the texts they study – that they think, for example, that conflict is always war, that power always corrupts, that they can't see other themes, other possibilities, within that domain of knowledge.

By text

This method relies on teaching a wide range of literary texts and weaving in poetry and language elements – articles, travel writing, perhaps an autobiography, as we go along. Using texts as a jumping off point to explore themes and concepts can work very effectively, particularly during primary school. It might seem to many teachers to be the most instinctive approach and we believe that it certainly can be done very successfully. It is a joyous and straightforward way to pass on our literary heritage, one text at a time.

Why might a text-based approach be problematic?

Secondary English isn't *just* about using texts to explore the world or a range of other subjects, it is about immersing pupils in an academic discipline in which texts themselves are components of a broad disciplinary schema. Sometimes we focus so strongly on texts themselves, we treat each one as a very separate entity from all the rest. Of course, every text is unique, but this approach might mean that connections between texts are not made explicit. The story of literature itself as an evolution of writing and the story of how we have tried to make sense of our lives might get lost. So, this approach might not always be as successful as we might hope.

Some teachers inevitably lack the relevant deep subject knowledge to teach a broad range of texts to a sufficiently high standard, especially if there is little time to collaborate with peers. Sometimes when they do try to collaborate with peers, their colleagues assume prior knowledge that the teacher requesting help might not have.

Some teachers may not have been taught English particularly well when they were at school themselves and might still have some misconceptions. Others don't necessarily believe that teaching challenging texts is what English is for. An interesting sidenote – in a recent survey we carried out of English teachers at a large trust in the south of England, around third of English teachers thought their primary job as English specialists was to teach exam skills. They thought this came over and above teaching a conceptual framework and teaching challenging texts. These teachers want the best for their pupils, just like we do, and they hope that by prioritising exam skills, they'll help pupils pass exams and improve their life chances. But we would argue that because, as we have already discussed, English is not primarily skills-based, this approach is flawed.

Where a teacher does have excellent subject knowledge, the nature of teaching through texts makes it inherently difficult to organise pupils' learning. Instead of starting with the easiest ways of understanding the underlying concepts in our subject, concepts like structure, or representation, or characterisation, and building complexity over time, the teacher tends to go with whatever the text offers up. Sequencing becomes muddled. In Chapter 1, we might teach pupils about one concept, then Chapter 2 might offer up a particularly sophisticated example of an entirely different concept. In trying to capture and teach everything, we can end up teaching nothing at all.

This lack of coherent sequencing can be mitigated somewhat by doing a cold read of the text first and then choosing examples very carefully as we dive back in for the analytical phase of the learning process. But selecting what to focus on and when requires an eye on a much bigger picture, a longer learning game, than most teachers can hold in their heads while they go about their day-to-day work.

Chronologically

Organising an English curriculum chronologically can be a way to promote pupils' understanding of change over time because it immerses them more deeply in the history of texts and shows them the 'story' of literature itself. Part of this is a sociohistorical story – shifts in attitudes to women, for example, can be identified, so that pupils can understand why Sheila in *An Inspector Calls* is able to speak more freely to her parents than Juliet is to hers in Shakespeare's play. But much of it is about teaching pupils to recognise the conventions of writing of a certain period and what it might tell us about how people saw themselves and the world around them. We can teach them the outliers that broke with the conventions of the time, perhaps Austen, for example, and we can teach them how later works of literary art were informed and shaped by previous ones. We can explore the evolution of the written word, of language itself; we can explore the stories that we have held onto and what patterns might underpin them. There is so much to dive into and so many connections to be made both between texts and with our pupils understanding of history and the wider world.

Why might a chronological approach be problematic?

While there is value to pupils gaining historical, social and political knowledge, and to immersing them in the chronology of literature over time, it's worth coming back to the question of what we want the developing schema of pupils to be based around. English is not History. A curriculum which foregrounds chronology might not lay bare or make explicit the most fundamental knowledge in English – the concepts which come up over and over again. Of course, it can do but we would argue this needs to be carefully managed and many chronological curricula still aren't particularly explicit about the conceptual knowledge of the subject that pupils need. This lack of conceptual understanding might prevent pupils from responding meaningfully to the texts they read. It is possible, we think, to weave the two together somehow – chronology and concepts – and this is what we've tried to do in our the latest iteration

60 What are the implications for English curriculum design?

of our own curriculum. To get there, we also needed to explore a concept-led curriculum, one which prioritises foundational subject-specific concepts such as characterisation or setting.

By concept

Finally, we began to explore a possible way forward with a style of curriculum that is rather different from any of the traditional models we've explored, one which would *foreground subject-specific* concepts. We felt that encouraging teachers to think and teach conceptually would mean that important understanding in our subject that sometimes remains hidden or only half explored, would be made explicit, sequenced carefully and taught *deliberately* rather than opportunistically. Of course, it is impossible to completely separate each one from everything else and we never wanted to. We were also not suggesting that we only refer to a concept within one specific term. That would be madness. Rather, we felt **that each concept could be foregrounded and used as a conceptual lens** for a period of time so that pupils could spend time immersed in each specific part of the overarching conceptual framework: the discipline of English as a subject. It would give all pupils, particularly those from disadvantaged backgrounds or presenting with Special Educational Need or Disability, an opportunity to explore rich, abstract ideas – there would be no 'dumbing down'. Providing a conceptual framework enables deeper exploration and appreciation of texts because we are giving them the knowledge that we ourselves have as experts. Our own ability to construct meaning is enriched by the conceptual framework we, and some of our pupils, have developed ourselves, sometimes by osmosis. Unless we explicitly teach such a framework, some pupils will never acquire it. The door to a genuine and profound connection to literature, to 'humanity talking to itself', will likely remain firmly closed

Before we go into detail, let's just explore what we mean by a concept and why they are important. In referring to different types of concept in English, we recognise the need for a shared language and so we are using the Cambridge Assessment glossary of terms.[4] They describe these concepts as follows:

- Threshold concepts are those concepts which, when fully grasped, will modify learners' understanding of a particular field.
- Second-order concepts can be used across all aspects of a subject to organise the substantive knowledge. They form the heart of the characteristic questions asked by a discipline.
- Substantive concepts form part of the substance or content within a subject.

However, we're less interested in the labels and more interested in how we might think about English.

We are going to preface this by saying that we don't present our final outcome here as the 'right' answer or the 'only' answer. We hope it is useful to explore it and to work through the thinking behind it. We have arrived at a curriculum which combines an element of being 'concept-led' while maintaining a strong chronological sequence. It has three parts:

1. Five 'deep' concepts that we think lie at the heart of understanding our subject. These might be considered threshold concepts. We will share these explicitly and frequently with pupils and staff.

What are the implications for English curriculum design? 61

2   The insertion of a week-long mini-scheme each term, which explores an important aspect of creating meaning within texts. We think of these aspects as the second-order concepts rather than a list of 'techniques'. The distinction matters because we hope for these concepts to be intimately tied to meaning-making, offering pupils a broad range of examples of these concepts in action, doing their work in allowing writers and readers to co-construct sophisticated meanings. In other words, not just the 'how' but also the 'why' or why not.
3   A chronological approach to planning which sees pupils study different *literary* (not historical) eras throughout Key Stage 3, which will allow pupils to make better sense of the concepts they explore.

The five deep concepts which we think might underpin English are listed below. We made a few notes on them and we include them here in Figure 4.1.

These 'deep concepts', or at least one of them, will typically be referred to (at least vocalised by the teacher!) in every lesson – these might be the most important and abstract ideas in studying English as an academic discipline.

Then we have our second-order concepts. These are taught explicitly at the start of year 7 and then each one is foregrounded again during transitional units that sit between and inform longer units. We did this because we think these key concepts are often hidden and not made explicit or exemplified carefully enough. It's not that we're completely separating concepts out (that would be impossible anyway) or that we don't talk about them together or revisit them. We do. It's just about trying to explicitly foreground important abstract concepts to help pupils build a coherent schema of English as an academic discipline.

Our original list of second-order concepts that might be included, since amended, contained all of the following. Some of the pairings are somewhat arbitrary. We had reasons for

Texts are constructs	Texts make use of patterns, all of which are conveyed through language.	Texts are informed by the contexts in which they are written	Every text is an argument - texts can influence us (thoughts, feelings, sometimes behaviour)	Readers construct meaning as they read
Meaning is constructed through texts. *Meanings can be ambiguous or texts might be deliberately nonsensical – that in itself is meaningful. reflect ideas about human condition reflect ideas about wider society reflect ideas about human interaction	structural patterns (motifs, cycles, foreshadowing etc); thematic patterns, genre patterns, patterns in characterisation (e.g. archetypes, stereotypes) sometimes typical patterns are subverted	social historical – wider culture and relevant subgroup culture literary personal how groups are represented critique history – challenge the mistakes we have made as a society explore knotty problems	argument rhetoric social and political change personal empowerment redemption hope empathy and connection inform decision-making	We interpret texts differently (at least to some degree – often there remains some overarching agreement.) Those interpretations are informed by many things, including our own social-historical context; our personal experiences: what and how much we have read before.

Figure 4.1: A table outlining five deep concepts that sit at the heart of English

62   What are the implications for English curriculum design?

pairing them this way, but those reasons probably don't hold up well to too much scrutiny. In the next chapter, we open with a more refined list:

Yr 7
Narratology and Context (to convey the idea that texts are constructs – perhaps we should just have said, 'texts are constructs')
Characterisation and Setting
Genre & Theme
Yr 8
Perspective
Rhetoric
Symbolism
Yr 9
Grammar (to create pace, emphasis, association, contrast, etc.)
Structure
Representation

We also tried to break down what we meant by each of these second-order concepts. We include below our notes on the concept of setting. As always, these ideas are debatable. We were trying to break down what an experts' schema around setting might include, acknowledging that it would not be necessary to teach all of them during the specific scheme of work on setting. It might be that the most significant – perhaps the first four? – were focused upon and reinforced so that other ideas could be explored later. It is the foundation we were trying to build.

All of these can apply to both fiction and non-fiction texts.

1   Settings establish genre.
2   Settings establish mood.
3   Settings reflect character.
4   Writers present places, even real ones in a non-fiction text, through a particular lens. Few, if any, descriptions of places are objectively real.
5   Settings can establish a context (e.g. social class).
6   Settings can function as an extra character in a story.
7   Settings help create allegory.
8   Settings evoke a sense of place that orients readers.
9   Settings are evoked through a writer's choice of words and their arrangement.

Teaching these as explicit concepts, with exemplification, is intended to help us avoid generic responses such as, *the setting paints a picture in the reader's mind* which, while they may be true, tend to lack any further explanation or clarification of how or why this has been achieved.

Once this knowledge had been broken down, we can select core texts that will be particularly helpful in exploring them, as well as carefully curated extracts, articles and poems to support this process. Almost every text has a setting of some kind, although this may not be the case with poetry. Pupils' own written work would also piggy-back on this deeper understanding of how settings reflect authorial intention.

What are the implications for English curriculum design? 63

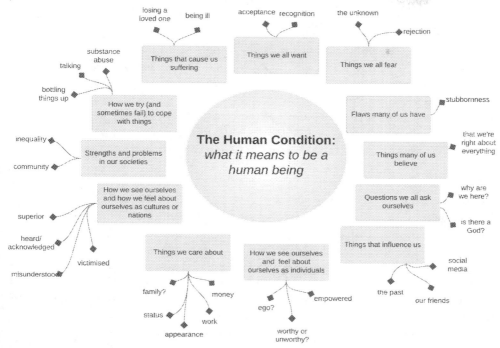

Figure 4.2 A map of some of the core ideas at the heart of English

Ultimately, English is about human beings communicating, sharing and, in the process, trying to understand themselves. This means that some of the substantive concepts in our subject, if we were to begin to map them, might look something like Figure 4.2.

How might a concept-led, chronological curriculum address persistent problems in English?

Any curriculum plan needs to work backwards from some sort of goal. Our goal is not just to pass an exam, even though that's a very important part of what we want to achieve. Our goal is to enable all pupils to have confidence in themselves and their ability to engage with the world at any and all levels. To us, this isn't necessarily about every pupil going to university; there might be good reasons why they do not want to. It's more about making pupils consciously capable of making choices and ensuring all options are available to them.

As curators of English curriculum, we need to ask ourselves these questions:

- What schema/mental models are we trying to build?
- What kind of learners do we want to create?
- How will we know if we have achieved these goals?

In Chapter 2, we explored how schema development is a useful way of understanding the learning process and we considered how we might apply this to how learning happens in English.

We know that schemas might be most usefully formed around central organising principles, and that a flexible, durable schema consists of highly organised knowledge. One of the main issues is that, in our broad subject community, there is no codified body of knowledge for what the study of English looks like at secondary level beyond the broad strokes of the National Curriculum. There is therefore no agreement about what the central organising principles of a detailed English curriculum should be. This might be because many teachers largely believe English to be skills-based and think that it is impossible to define the specific knowledge pupils need to be taught. Some resist the idea of defined knowledge altogether because they believe it restricts personal interpretation of texts. It might seem to be something more suitable in Science or Maths.

This has prompted us to consider what the central organising principles might be in English and we offer them here as the beginning of a conversation about what knowledge might sit at the heart of our subject. We hope that this will then allow us to curate a curriculum that will build the complex web of understanding all pupils are entitled to explore.

We bear this in mind as we think about what might be the highest value knowledge in our subject. Which knowledge underpins all texts, comes up again and again, and therefore makes up the foundational understanding of our subject?

Let's think about characterisation. Characterisation is not the same as writing about a character. Sometimes pupils write about characters without much consideration of the writer behind them, saying things like, *Macbeth is an ambitious general in the King's army*. However, what we want from them moves beyond describing Macbeth almost as if he is a real person towards describing his characterisation, which includes the meanings that the writer creates using this character. A better response would be more along the lines of, *Shakespeare uses Macbeth, a general in the King's army, to explore his ideas about...* We can prompt this kind of writing by giving pupils a sentence starter – e.g. *Shakespeare presents...* but this focus on tweaking a product tends to result in the same poor quality thinking. It's the same thing but with a tagged-on opener. That's because the pupil hasn't understood the concept of characterisation. This might have been because it was not explicitly taught in the first place. We suggest that, because it comes up again and again in every text (even a narrator in a non-fiction article or travel blog, or the voice in a poem might be said to be characterised in some sense) that characterisation is a foundational concept that requires explicit teaching. Once pupils make the shift from writing about characters to writing about characterisation, we are building the disciplinary schema that pupils need in order to consciously apply that conceptual lens to every text they encounter.

Why might a concept-led approach be problematic?

Like other curriculum models we have explored, this one is also in danger of becoming reductive. English is more than a list of abstract concepts that we might ask pupils to learn by heart. It would also miss the many opportunities afforded to us by a chronological curriculum. It could feel dry, depending on how it was approached by a teacher (although that would be true of any curriculum, some might be more prone than others). Though it might help teachers to think more explicitly about some aspects of English, it would probably not address some of the gaps in subject knowledge that teachers might have or help them to deliver a rich experience of exciting texts.

In summary

- There are many different ways to construct an English curriculum.
- In the past, these have often been assessment-driven and have not prioritised the development of pupils' mental models.
- Teaching English as a skills-based subject has denied pupils sufficient opportunity to develop conceptual thinking in English.
- A concept-led curriculum might improve teacher subject knowledge and help address persistent problems, thus improving pupil outcomes.

In the next chapter, we explore what a concept-led curriculum, developed with a keen awareness of chronology, might look like.

Notes

1 Chetty, Raj, Friedman, John, & Rockoff, Jonah (September, 2014). Measuring the impacts of teachers II: teacher value-added and student outcomes in adulthood. *The American Economic Review*, 104(9), 2633–2679.
2 Ashbee, R. (2021) *Curriculum: Theory, Culture and the Subject Specialisms*. London: Routledge
3 Department for Education (November, 2013). GCSE English language: subject content and assessment objectives, DFE-00232-2013, viewed on 10th February 2021, www.gov.uk/government/publications/gcse-englishlanguage-and-gcse-english-literature-new-content
4 Cambridge Assessment International Education, viewed on 14 October 2021, //cambridge-community.org.uk/professional-development/gswkey/index.html

5 Curating a curriculum

We can now start to explore what a curriculum might look like in more detail. This might mean looking at what a department already has in place and thinking about possible tweaks. It could mean a carrying out a complete overhaul. Before introducing the current iteration of the Key Stage 3 (KS3) curriculum itself, we would like to walk through our thought processes in curating it. This is far more useful than the curriculum itself.

Which deep concepts will allow our pupils to understand English as a discipline? How can we shape their thinking in relation to texts?

We need to preface this with the understanding that we teachers, diverse group that we are, will never all agree. That doesn't matter. What matters is the thinking process behind the decision-making, and that any individual department involves its teachers in a similar discussion, whatever the exact outcome might then be. Nevertheless, we offer some suggestions.

These deep concepts are the tools that allow us to step back and see English as a body of knowledge and a way of thinking about that body of knowledge. For example, it is essential for pupils to realise that *texts are constructs*. There are four other statements included in our example. However, we encourage departments to consider what *they* think pupils need to know and think about in order to be functioning as successful disciples of English. These concepts should be referred frequently with both staff, in department meetings, and with pupils in lessons.

What over-arching ideas should we base the curriculum around?

For this, we have considered the kind of rich, interesting discussions we want to have with pupils. We want to use literature and language study to help pupils explore and make sense of themselves and the world they inhabit. To this end, we have a series of enquiry topics that pupils move through. They will explore the canon and a range of diverse voices outside it. They begin by thinking about early human storytelling and why humans tell stories. Their studies culminate in a final term where they bring their knowledge together to consider the nature of the literature itself and what it means in modern Britain.

Our curriculum explores texts that would be considered canonical but also attempts to move beyond the canon. Focusing on the canon is controversial because, by its nature, it excludes many different voices. However, there are two important reasons why exploring the

DOI: 10.4324/9781003033158-6

canon remains important. Firstly, the true story of how literature unfolds in this country is that the canon has dominated our landscape for many decades. This means that it forms, for better or worse, the heart of a great many patterns and conventions in our subject. To deny pupils that, might be to deny them the patterns and conventions of our culture's storytelling, making it harder for them to recognise those patterns. And the thing is, we need our pupils to recognise those conventions, even the racist and sexist stereotypes that blight many a novel, so that they can **critique** them. We want to teach pupils to *contest* what has been written, to contest the way we think about literature. The canon needs to be covered to some extent, alongside other diverse voices, so that we might deeply challenge aspects of it. At every turn, we will explore the outliers, the unexpected voices, the challengers to convention that have sought to express diversity and contest power throughout our history. That too, is an essential part of our story and one that has not been explored fully enough. For each of these, we explore with staff what the most important ideas about each literary era might be. Then we think about outliers, other voices that we want pupils to be aware of. Some brief notes are given here but we accept that we are certainly not experts on every period of literature. That said, we will inevitably have to reduce an era to some of the defining things about it in order to be able to teach it. We would include a key text each term to be read in full. Where pupils might struggle with that, the use of film or play versions, or abridged texts might be employed alongside some use of the original text studied *without* an accompanying modern translation. A side note – teaching original texts side by side with their modern translations probably only serves to ensure the original text is largely ignored. This is how pupils manage the cognitive load of having so much to process all at once.

To further explore what we might cover, we include in Figure 5.1 an example of a long-term curriculum plan covering KS3.

The longer units explore those interesting 'juicy' ideas, ideas that have been important in our developing understanding of ourselves and each other over time. Obviously, we won't all agree on what those ideas are but that's ok. That pupils have some sense of many different voices asserting themselves within time and throughout time probably matters more. These are ideas that may or may not be posed to pupils in the form of an enquiry question.

We weave oracy, literacy, literature, language, original writing, etc. together around it. Some units will focus more deeply on certain forms but there will always be a mixture – it's about helping pupils make connections in order to build beautiful and complex schemas. We would, of course, need to consider where we would cover particular techniques and subject terminology but as techniques are only ever a means to a communicative end, we haven't foregrounded them. We hope to prevent teachers from focusing on techniques over meaning, which is a problem we've both encountered frequently.

The longer units feature a pre-read of a text and then revisiting that text with a particular focus. In other words, we're using the text to explore a subject concept or concepts, rather than just exploring *everything* in the text. It's to help present knowledge in a more organised and coherent way than just 'let's analyse everything and hope some of it sticks!' It doesn't mean tangents are forbidden but it does mean they have to be handled knowingly and with caution so that low structure builders don't get lost.

It also means that we can explore a wider variety of texts, and therefore more examples of the subject concept, within a single term because we're not spending eight weeks analysing

Year	Term 1	Term 2	Term 3
7	Title: **The Story of Storytelling** *includes a three-week transition unit - a literary timeline is introduced; there is lots of immersive reading for pleasure and the introduction of the **five deep concepts**. This is followed by an introduction to some or all of the **second order concepts** over the rest of the term. The main **eras** focused on are early storytelling (myths and legends), contemporary texts and something inbetween - perhaps Chaucer.	Transition unit: **setting** Title: **The Places Writers Go** The **five deep concepts** are referred to frequently and help teachers steer discussion. **Content** might include: -why place and landscape are important to us - how writers *use* settings, studied across forms -how writers *create* settings, studied across forms - original writing focusing on describing places within one or more forms. The main **eras** focused upon might be 19th and 20th Century, to allow for a wide range of travel writing to be explored alongside fiction and poetry texts.	Transition unit: **theme** Title: **Shared Hopes, Fears & Big Ideas** The **five deep concepts** are referred to frequently and help teachers steer discussion. **Content** might include: -common needs and concerns that we all have and have had throughout history, perhaps studied as contrasting aspects of who we are. *E.g. the need to belong vs the need for freedom.* -how writers convey those feelings through their language choices Any **era** might be suitable.
8	Transition unit: **characterisation** Title: **People, Real & Imagined** The **five deep concepts** are referred to	Transition unit: **symbolism** Title: **Patterns & Symbols** The **five deep concepts** are referred to	Transition unit: **representation** Title: **Language & Identity** The **five deep concepts** are referred to

Figure 5.1 An overview of a possible KS3 curriculum

Curating a curriculum 69

		frequently and help teachers steer discussion.	frequently and help teachers steer discussion.	frequently and help teachers steer discussion.
		Content might include: - characterisation as a method - how do writers make choices from infinite possibilities? - archetypes and stereotypes - how characters are created - body language, background history, dialogue etc - character vs caricature The main **eras** focused on might include the Victorian era (Dickens especially) and Shakespeare, perhaps looking at Shakespeare's greatest heroes and villains through their speeches.	**Content** might include: - an overview of symbols both in real life and within texts - a symbol can conjure multiple meanings simultaneously, some of which might be deeply personal, some of which is culturally negotiated - symbols help writers to manifest themes, characters and relationships - we can track symbols across a text (e.g. the conch in *Lord of the Flies*) Any **era** might be suitable. We might look across eras to see how meanings were established and how they have stayed the same, or changed.	**Content** might include: - language acquisition - language change - idiolect and dialect - Standard English and non-standard English - e.g. poetry written in Jamaican patois) - historical speeches of social significance (e.g. civil rights) - newspaper articles that misrepresent groups in society The main **eras** studied would probably be those with the greatest and most obvious social change and interest in identity - the 20th and 21st centuries.
9		Transition unit: **structure (fiction, including poetry)** Title: **Complex Characters & Complex Feelings** The **five deep concepts** are referred to frequently and help	Transition unit: **structure (non-fiction)** Title: **Influence & Protest** The **five deep concepts** are referred to frequently and help teachers steer discussion.	Transition unit: **contesting the canon** Title: **What is British Identity?** The **five deep concepts** are referred to frequently and help teachers steer discussion.

Figure 5.1 (Continued)

| | teachers steer discussion. **Content** might include: - contrast and juxtaposition create complexity - multi-faceted characters vs caricatures - comparing characters - nuanced characterisation / humans being flawed rather than evil - how settings reveal character and mood - characters are a product of their time - we might see them differently

In terms of **eras**, we might choose to study famous characters from across history. E.g. Magwitch, Jekyll & Hyde, Jane Eyre, Frankenstein & his creature, Shakespearean characters, the poetry of Robert Browning to explore characterisation Carol Ann Duffy's poetry invoking famous characters. Questioning historical portrayals of social groups (e.g. women) in fiction and non-fiction | **Content** might include: - language and thought – how thinking is based on analogy - language & power - propaganda - protest poetry - modern speeches - social media

The main **eras** studied would probably be those with the greatest and most obvious social change and interest in identity - the 20th and 21st centuries. | **Content** might include: - what is the canon (do we even agree?) - why is it problematic? - what other voices are there? - how has the representation of social groups (e.g. LGBT) changed over time? - are some groups still misrepresented (e.g. Gypsy, Roma & Traveller communities? - are some groups still underrepresented (e.g. indigenous peoples)? - do texts drive or merely reflect social change?

In terms of **eras** - mainly very modern texts but some examples of the canon and a historical framing of why it exists will be important. |

Figure 5.1 (Continued)

every single page of one book. But we also don't have to sacrifice the reading of whole texts to achieve this – pupils are still having that immersive experience.

In Chapter 7, we explore more about how our ideas might be translated into curriculum materials for teachers. Here, we will continue to focus on the reasoning that has informed the model.

Which second-order concepts should we include?

In the current iteration of our curriculum, we have selected quite a long list of concepts and used them to help us construct a three-year KS3 programme of study, which can form the intellectual powerhouse for later General Certificate of Secondary Education (GCSE) study. Each section would therefore last about one term and what you see below covers all of Years 7, 8 and 9.

This is a little different to the approach taken by David Didau, who also identifies a series of underlying concepts, namely metaphor, argument, story, pattern, grammar and context[1]. We don't disagree with his list, and it might even be possible to boil it down still further. Perhaps everything is essentially a pattern of one sort or another, for example? But this analysis might not convert easily into a practical approach to teaching concepts that makes sense in terms of curating a three-year KS3 curriculum because there are only six concepts. And it might be harder for pupils to take on the important vocabulary that helps them navigate the subject if we don't explicitly include words like 'representation' and 'genre', depending, of course, on how it is done. It is certainly possible. Equally, it could be argued that, if Didau might have too few concepts, we might have too many. There is no right answer. There is only what works for the staff and pupils within a specific department.

The sequencing of such a curriculum is inevitably problematic but worked examples are useful. Our approach has been to think about which concepts might be easier, or more important, to grasp early in order to build understanding later on. We also hope this approach to curriculum will offer breadth and depth, allow us to revisit key concepts over and over again in relation to different texts, and allow us to carefully increase complexity.

The list of second-order concepts we have chosen, which is a somewhat reduced list, is given here. Our brief explanations are intended to give a sense of our thought process without becoming dictatorial about what ideas ought or ought not to be conveyed when teaching them. Again, it isn't about expecting everyone to agree. It's about a conversation that can be extremely productive!

Context – For example, texts are a product of a particular context. They are also read in a particular context. Texts relate to real-life observations, questions and concerns.

Author's perspective – For example, authors write with intention, even if their intention is to write something ambiguous or nonsensical. They always have, at the very least, an intention to communicate. Understanding that a text is a construct written by a person who is real and has agency helps us to reflect upon meanings we encounter.

Influence – For example, texts can influence our thoughts and feelings and our behaviour. They can help form, or challenge, our sense of identity. They can also create cohesion among groups who find shared meanings with a text.

Theme – For example, themes often explore common concerns and help us to explore the human condition. They manifest in the language, structure, characters and symbols in the text. It's particularly important in the study of English to consider texts at the thematic level.

Symbolism – For example, symbols are representations of, manifestations of, ideas. We use them in real life. Symbolic meanings might be seen in the structure of a text, or in the language, or in the characterisation.

Characterisation – For example, characters are not real (even when they're inspired by or based upon real people) but they do attempt to reflect, perhaps exaggerate, truthful characteristics of our human nature.

Setting – For example, settings might reflect themes, genres, characters. Any setting is a representation of a place, as it is viewed or imagined by a writer.

Structure – For example, how we organise and sequence information influences the meanings a text might generate.

Representation (of groups within society) – Texts can misrepresent groups. Some social groups are underrepresented. Historical texts often offer problematic representations of social groups for a modern reader. Texts can also help to change attitudes towards social groups and can reflect and/or manifest social change.

We simplified the list to make it more manageable and avoid teaching concepts as somewhat arbitrary pairs. We invite you to consider what would be achievable for a pupil who explicitly understands these concepts and can apply them with increasing independence to texts they encounter.

In terms of chronology, we consider eras we might most want our pupils to be immersed in but we shy away from the notion that chronology must be taught *in chronological order*. This seems unnecessary and rather restrictive. As long as pupils are introduced to a timeline early on, and explicit reference is made to it each time a text is introduced, and pupils are taught to make connections between texts, there seems little need to actually teach each literary era in date order.

How might the KS3 curriculum link fiction and non-fiction reading?

We often focus on the differences between language and literature but there are also many similarities or areas of overlap that provide us with an opportunity to help pupils make connections. To give one example, narrative voice in a non-fiction article, while not a form of characterisation in a fictional story per se, still bears strong similarities. There is a sense of someone within, or behind, the writing, a sense of personality. Attitudes and values, explicit and implicit, can be expressed through narrative voice and they can be expressed through characterisation in a fictional text. In both cases, on some level, we are responding to people's stories, whether those people are real or imagined, and whether or not those stories are true, imaginary biased, reliable or unreliable.

These similarities naturally dictate that literature, language, oracy, reading and writing all need to be taught together. They need to be allowed to feed into each other.

Usually, the greatest starting point for learning anything is story. Stories are a powerful tool that humans have nurtured to allow them to learn and understand all sorts of things. Therefore, a concept-led curriculum driven by well-chosen, high-quality literary texts taught roughly chronologically might form the basis of a curriculum which then spirals out to include all the other elements that we want our pupils to explore.

We might use Figure 5.2 as a guide to thinking through the tricky process of curating a curriculum.

Curating a curriculum 73

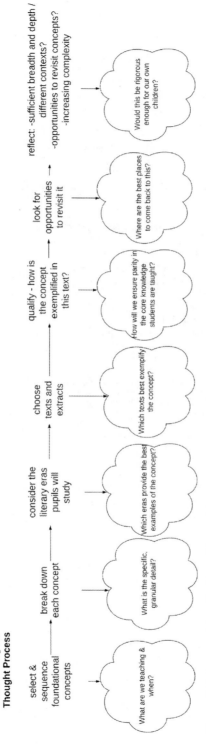

Figure 5.2 Summarising the thought process

How is the curriculum a progression model and how does it link to other Key Stages?

- The five deep concepts, the most over-arching and abstract ideas about our subject, are referred to frequently. They are constantly being revisited with more complex or nuanced examples and greater relationality with other concepts.
- The second-order concepts are all introduced in Year 7 but are then frequently revisited. Each concept can be broken down and mapped so that more complex or nuanced examples are introduced over time, and second-order concepts are interwoven more intricately.

Each individual English department will need to consider how best to build complexity over time through the texts and extracts they select, and what they choose to say about them.

Making a seamless transition from Key Stage 3 to Key Stage 4

A KS4 curriculum would use the examination specification as a framework, but would refer back to and draw upon the concepts studied at KS3. The (GCSE) texts would enable pupils to apply their KS3 study and complexify their understanding of the concepts, thus making a seamless transition between the key stages. Having studied a concept-led, chronological curriculum at KS3, we hope pupils will be better prepared to tackle, with greater independence, GCSE study at KS4. Pupils can bring their conceptual understanding and their familiarity with different historical periods to KS4 in a way that connects the two key stages with greater coherence than has perhaps happened in the past. Although the GCSE course requires us to cover certain content, that content is not separate from, or different to, what pupils have explored at KS3. It is a coming together of everything they have done in their conceptual curriculum.

For example, think about the underlying concepts that we might want a pupil to be armed with before they study *Jane Eyre*. They need to know already that the text is a construct; they need to *expect* that its organisation creates certain meanings and seek out those meanings; pupils should know that Jane Eyre is characterised, she has been carefully crafted in order that the writer might say something about the experiences of women in the past. They need to know which bit of 'the past' is most relevant (i.e. the early Victorian era) and already have some knowledge of what it was like. And so on and so on. This is what KS3 study ought to be for.

What about Key Stage 2?

In terms of rolling this back through primary, there are far better experts to comment on primary phase teaching but we offer some thoughts here just to give you some ideas to talk about. A main part of the way we've thought about KS3 is to think about the underlying concepts that will prepare pupils for KS4. In order to lay the groundwork for the KS3 curriculum, from our perspective, primary might focus on:

- literacy (obviously!) including phonemic awareness, morphology, syntax and orthographical patterns;
- texts that help pupils build the kind of real-world knowledge that help them comprehend other texts;

- ways of grouping texts and encouraging pupils to make connections (e.g. according to genre, mood, historical period or authorial intention, etc.);
- studying authors to help pupils see that texts are constructs that represent something about real life;
- making explicit connections between texts and real life;
- a mixture of slow writing (to develop accuracy) and free writing to develop thinking and fluency;
- explicitly teaching that writing is an expression of thinking – they are not separate
- an emphasis on *organising* thought rather than organising the essay itself. An essay is ultimately just a product and one that will never even be produced if the underlying thinking isn't coherent, detailed and effective.

Possible limitations of a concept-led curriculum and our response to these potential problems

It reduces English to a list of concepts rather than a rich discussion about human experience

This would be a disaster! It isn't an either/or situation. A concept-led curriculum is intended to give pupils the vocabulary and understanding to talk about texts at a high level but not solely, or even primarily, so that they can pass examinations. Pupils can also use that language and that knowledge to find new and deeper appreciation of the written word. We can guide pupils to listen to and pursue their instincts and gut reactions all the way to sophisticated analyses of the texts that we hope have moved and inspired them.

It's too challenging

It feels challenging because concepts are so abstract and teaching the abstract is more difficult. But pupils are able to think at an abstract level wherever we break down and exemplify those ideas with more concrete examples. It is our shared capacity to model, explain and exemplify that might be at fault sometimes, not our pupils' capacity to think and explore.

It is too heavily focused on literature

Our subject is vast. Literary texts, and in particular the study of longer texts, provide us with a useful scaffold to both map the direction of travel but also tame the many strands of our complex subject. We can meaningfully 'attach' poetry and non-fiction texts to literary study, in a way that is authentic and not derivative, if we focus on *conceptual* connections between the different aspects of our subject. Doing some language work on an article about prisons just because we're reading a literary text that happens to be set in a prison might end up being rather inauthentic and we might struggle to get much out of it because the link feels somewhat flimsy (of course, we're not saying this is always the case). However, exploring the concept of setting in both a literary and language text might be very enriching. Both texts might refer to a prison setting, but how do the writers present those settings and how and why are they different? What rich story about the world and real human experience is each writer trying to convey through their presentation of the setting?

76 *Curating a curriculum*

It's too hard to assess

We talk more about this in the next chapter where we offer practical examples of assessing a concept-led curriculum in a way that captures, as authentically as possible, the real learning pupils are experiencing, as well as preparing them appropriately for eventual formal examinations.

Choosing texts

Ideally, departments will choose texts together and will thrash out the reasons for including or rejecting each text in depth. This is important not just to get to the final answer of which texts will be taught and when, but also because the conversations themselves are a mechanism through which we can explore how we see English as a subject, identifying priorities and crafting an authentic shared vision of what English should be. To help facilitate these conversations, we offer some suggestions for some of the questions departments might explore together:

- **What are we teaching and when?** (This means having an overview of what pupils have done at primary school. There might be little point in teaching *Holes* in Year 8 if they have already studied it in Year 5.)
- **How does this text fit with the need to both explore the canon and explore texts written by a diverse range of voices and experiences?** For further ideas on this, Bennie Kara's[2] book is extremely useful.
- **Is this text ambitious enough and how do we know that? What constitutes an 'ambitious' text?** We would tentatively suggest that an ambitious text is one that allows pupils to explore a subject concept through a range of sophisticated and nuanced examples. We would ask ourselves what opportunities the text presents for readers to create meaning.
- **Does the sequence of texts allow us to revisit concepts or make other connections to what has been learned previously?**
- **How do the text choices relate to GCSE set texts?**
- **Are we primarily teaching the text itself or are we using the text to teach broader concepts?** If the latter, when and how will we exemplify these?
- **Are we meeting the aim of the national curriculum to immerse pupils in a broad range of genres, both fiction and non-fiction?**
- **What is the text a great example of and what makes it such a useful example for pupils to see?** For example, it might be a great example of a particular genre because it represents it in a very 'typical' way, or because it subverts it. (Bear in mind that pupils need a strong sense of typical generic conventions before they can deal with examples that subvert those conventions.)
- **Are texts drawn from a broad enough range of historical periods? What constitutes a 'broad enough' range?** We would suggest that some immersion in key periods (Shakespearean, Victorian, etc.) is essential and that pupils should have an overall sense of literature as an unfolding story.
- **Do all staff have sufficient knowledge to teach all the texts, or time to develop that knowledge, and how might they be supported in that endeavour?**
- **How much influence should parental views have in the texts we choose?** (For example, if a parent (or a pupil) might object to a text on religious or cultural grounds.)
- **What would someone else say about your choices? What might the criticisms be?**

In summary

- We advocate a concept-led curriculum based on five deep concepts and a range of second-order concepts.
- The curriculum should serve as a progression model. Examples should become more complex and nuanced over time, concepts should be more intricately interwoven over time. Teachers should be able to give examples of where and how this happens.
- Choosing texts is something we might do later in the process rather than using texts as a starting point.

Teacher Insight

Liz Chillington, Head of English, Titus Salt School

Liz is a very experienced HOD and former AST working for the LEA. She was leading the redesign of the concept-led English curriculum in her school.

The process of identifying our foundation concepts formed the basis of really valuable professional development. Exploring what forms the core of an English secondary curriculum from Y7 to Y13 enables thoughtful discussion to take place about what should be taught when, how it might be exemplified and how it might be assessed. It also re-awakens subject expertise and allows a whole team of English colleagues to explore together, and as equals, what learners need to understand about the creation, interpretation and uses of texts.

This approach invites our team of teachers to unravel what it is to teach 'narrative' to Y7 in a way that our pupils will be adding to and developing their knowledge and understanding of narratology as they progress through KS3 and GCSE to A level and beyond. This shift is one that will continue to be the core focus of our faculty training.

So, we are in Year 1 of a curriculum design process – but it will be the last time we will need to do this in such depth. In future years, we will be reviewing the texts we use to exemplify the concepts; if our text coverage is diverse enough; if texts are challenging enough. Technologies will change, pedagogical ideas will change (or be recycled), examination specifications will (probably) change but for us this will just mean adjusting our delivery. We will not need to re-write the conceptual framework of our curriculum because those core ideas about the construction and uses of texts will not change.

Notes

1 Didau, D. (2021) *Making Meaning in English: The Role of Knowledge in the Curriculum*. Routledge: UK
2 Bennie, K. (2020). A Little Guide for Teachers: Diversity in Schools. Sage Publications Ltd: UK

6 How should the curriculum be assessed?

Assessment is a very large, complex topic – a book in itself – so here we present an overview that we hope will serve as a useful addition to conversations around assessment in English. In Chapter 3, we proposed that a curriculum underpinned by foundational concepts might address persistent problems in our subject. In this chapter, we will consider the implications for the way we might approach assessment.

In the past, assessment has driven curriculum. The relationship has become skewed. If we are to curate a more effective curriculum that might address persistent problems, we need to let it drive assessment rather than be constrained by it. **Curriculum needs to be the master, not the servant.**

Why is assessing English so tricky?

One of the problems in any subject is that no examination can test the whole of the knowledge domain that pupils have studied. It is simply too large and complex. Therefore, examinations are designed to combine strands of the whole domain of English into a series of essay tasks, tasks that only ever sample a tiny bit of everything a pupil knows. English contains vast amounts of knowledge. If literature is 'humanity talking to itself' then, in a sense, it contains the whole world. It contains all of life and all of our language. How could we possibly teach pupils all the history and culture and language they might need to understand in order to analyse any human thought ever written in our tongue? Perhaps this is why we have abandoned the attempt and focused on 'skills' we think will tame the subject. It's an attempt to impose order on something that feels unwieldy and we have allowed examinations to dictate the nature of that order.

And what makes English more complex than many other academic subjects is that knowledge in English is not just vast, it is also subjective. That means examiners aren't able to test against a pre-set list of things pupils ought to know because most of those things are open to interpretation. Take *Romeo and Juliet* – expert teachers can have opposing views on whether it is really a love story. All the examination can do is test a pupils' thinking in relation to a text, in order to get a sense of the domain knowledge that might have informed that thinking. Sometimes pupils are given full marks for an interpretation the examiner does not agree with. If the pupil has shown sufficiently thorough and complex thinking, they will be rewarded.

DOI: 10.4324/9781003033158-7

How should the curriculum be assessed? 79

This means, although English is a test of *thinking*, it is dependent on the creation of a product (*doing*). Where that thinking is 'successful' pupils are drawing on vast stores of conceptual knowledge stored in their long term memory. But how carefully do we consider, whenever we write or co-create a model for pupils, that we are always, for better or worse, modelling *thinking*. Do we realise that and do we tell our pupils? As teachers, we tend to be very focused on the fact that pupils will have to *do* something in the examination. They will have to produce a product, an essay. Perhaps sometimes we forget that this product will, for better or worse, be a natural consequence of the thinking the pupil has engaged in.

We might find ourselves focusing on a task – producing the (essay) product – rather than focusing on building the domain knowledge that lies beneath it. We do that at our cost, and it costs our pupils too. It means that when we teach, we explicitly prioritise teaching exam-style writing, moving too quickly to production (of an exam response) rather than exploring thought processes.

Figure 6.1 shows how an assessment tests a sample of a large and complex domain of knowledge. It also shows that helping pupils to develop their own personal 'big idea' in relation to a text can help them respond to any question they might encounter. By a 'big idea', we mean a central organising principle, unique to an individual pupil, that helps them make sense of the text as a whole. This significant, overarching meaning ought to be one that is present through every moment of the text, every character, every scene, as far as possible. It then becomes a secure base from which a pupil might pivot, tailoring their response to *any* essay question. These are pupils whose schema has developed to a point where it has become profound, well organised and highly flexible.

Unfortunately, if we don't build our curriculum conscientiously enough, that underpinning knowledge might not be profound, organised and flexible. We might miss out things that really need explicitly unpicking with pupils.

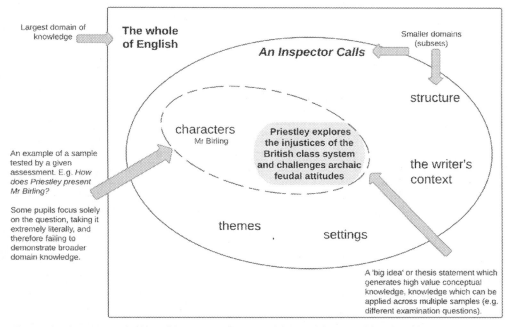

Figure 6.1 A representation of how an assessment is used to sample a domain

Let's think about what gets missed out or left behind. To do an original writing task, the domain knowledge a pupil might need consists of all sorts of concepts. Some of these might be:

- generic conventions
- structural choices create meaning
- grammar creates meaning
- themes are embedded within texts
- characterisation
- rhythm and pace
- setting
- symbolism.

They would also need to have:

- studied a wide range of examples;
- an understanding of the need to manage the emotional response of the audience and write with intention, and knowledge of how to achieve those aims;
- a sense of the requirements of the exam;
- a solid grasp of the conventions used in the forms or styles in which they might be asked to write.

That feels like a lot to explore with pupils but that's why Key Stage 3 is so important. It can seem daunting but once we put the focus back on exploring the domain of English more authentically – prioritising deep conceptual learning over short-term, surface features which temporarily boost performance – the examination will take care of itself. It is the underlying concepts that the exam is really testing, and these might now be more clearly and fully taught than ever before. This doesn't mean pupils should not practice writing essays and we will go on to say more about this below, but it does mean that we might need to rethink the balance.

Why is teaching essay writing tricky?

A primary concern is that we often tend to scaffold the *product* using writing frames, Point, Evidence, Explanation (PEE) or other such inventions. But we forget about what's really being tested; we forget about the underlying thinking that creates that product.

We might focus on the end product – the exam response – and think about how one might be 'built', approaching it in the same way that a carpenter might build a cabinet. We try to define and label the pieces of an essay and invent a process for combining them. *Start with a thesis statement, add some evidence, etc.*

But each 'piece' of the essay is very unlike the pieces of a cabinet. They are not solid or tangible. Each one is made of *language*. Language is *infinite*. Each piece of the product is therefore not really a piece at all, it's an endless list of slippery possibilities. We might not have adequately taught pupils how to select from this list, or even how to generate the list in the first place. Although we know it's complicated, we sometimes tackle complexity by just adding more elements to the PEE paragraph, perhaps adding 'C' for 'context' – the simple cabinet is given a bureau top. We still haven't enabled them to absorb what that piece of an essay really constitutes.

Let's approach this problem differently by focusing less on the product. Let's think of essay writing as a series of unfolding thoughts. What do expert essayists actually think about when they write? This is somewhat complex because experts don't particularly have to think about process at all – they have largely automatised it. However, they probably don't ask themselves *what will my 'point' be?* Or, *how shall I explain the 'evidence'?* Nor do they necessarily write in any specific order.

Even 'what, how, why', which has recently become a popular scaffold, might be problematic. It can sometimes work well as a method for discussing thinking in broad terms but perhaps not as a writing frame because it probably doesn't mimic expert thinking. If they ask themselves anything, rather than 'what, how, why' experts might ask themselves the below:

- *How does this connect with the thesis statement?*
- *Is there anything further I can explore here?*
- *What other examples might fit here?*
- *What idea is most significant?*
- *Is my explanation clear/detailed enough?*
- *Have I made sufficient textual references?*

Experts probably also focus more on **explanation and exemplification** than **justification and evidence.** We suggest this because, as experts, we're aware that others might have a different interpretation of a text, which might be just as valid as our own. We're therefore not trying to *win* an argument so much as we're trying to *present* an argument by elucidating our thought process. That isn't to say that winning isn't fun. It's just that a debate in English isn't necessarily winnable.

Whether experts really do think this way is certainly open to debate and we could well be wrong. However, it seems relevant to consider it when we think about the impact our language might have on how *pupils* approach the subject. It might be worth imagining the different products that are produced by these different underlying convictions about essays. If the focus is on *justifying* using *evidence*, do we inadvertently suggest that a quotation is enough? As long as we've 'proven' a link between our idea and the text, we might think the 'justify using evidence' box is already ticked. Pupils might see little need to explain in greater depth even if we tell them to do so.

Perhaps it is all of these underlying thoughts and insights that might be usefully shared with pupils. However we approach it, we might aim to model expert thinking as authentically and explicitly as possible. If we don't do this, the consequence might be that pupils can't write the essay because we haven't explicitly taught them how to *think* the essay. Cognitive load has been expended on an arbitrary production process (PEE?) that doesn't mimic expert thinking. Sequences have been learned that might actually need to be unlearned (a quotation or reference is not necessarily the second idea in an effective essay paragraph, for example). In addition, load has been taken away from the actual *thinking* processes required to create an authentic essay and spent instead on trying to conceptualise what is meant by 'a point' or what is meant by 'how' writers communicate. Some pupils spontaneously abandon PEE, impress the teacher and the teacher rewards them for it. Hence, they carry on. But lots of pupils cling to PEE and it is to their detriment.

Some of us might have wondered *how* to teach thinking, especially to knowledge-poor pupils. We often hear the argument that writing structures such as PEE work for 'low ability' pupils. But part of the reason those pupils remain knowledge-poor is probably because they have not had enough modelling and practice of thinking processes. What if some teachers have prioritised pupils' behaviour and social development to the extent that they've denied them rigorous academic teaching? Being nurturing and teaching rigorously are not mutually exclusive. We can do both. Those pupils who have the most to learn, the furthest to go, need the most rigorous teaching of all.

What about the English Language examinations?

The language paper is a different approach to testing a domain that strongly overlaps with literature, especially in its current iteration at General Certificate of Secondary Education (GCSE) level. We think that we have perhaps struggled to see this and have tended to teach the paper question by question, almost as if they have little connection to one another even when they are inviting responses to the same text. We are developing approaches to teaching the paper more holistically, a more detailed example of which is in Appendix A. Figure 6.2 is an example of a holistic approach to teaching the paper which encourages pupils to see the connections between the different reading questions on a GCSE English Language examination paper from the Assessment and Qualifications Alliance (AQA).

Teaching each examination question as if it is an entirely separate entity from all the others, and somewhat separate from KS3, does pupils a disservice because it denies them the thorough, holistic approach to understanding of a text that ought to inform and underpin every question about that text.

Moving away from practice questions feels like a big step for many senior leaders. But once we acknowledge the damage the current assessment focus does to learning, the step becomes very easy to take indeed. All most SLT really want is to understand what it is that we could do instead of endless past papers, and why it's a better approach.

What might assessment look like?

It's important, and somewhat scary, to acknowledge that we can never measure learning. We cannot peer into someone else's brain, even recent advances in brain imaging are not enough to tell me whether or not my pupil has learned anything from my lessons. It is only in a new context that we could really ascertain what someone has or has not learned. And any test of learning is always really a test of performance. Some sort of task must be performed. We have to hope that whatever task we set, it serves as a useful proxy for learning. This is obviously problematic when parents and headteachers want us to measure progress. We can only try to find the most useful proxies to measure learning and accept the limitations of trying to measure a human mind.

There are a couple of different approaches that might help us to do this. The first is the most similar to most current practice where assessment comes in the form of essay responses periodically carried out over the course of the academic year. Instead of a straightforward essay, which many pupils may not be ready for, we advocate a more mixed approach that snapshots understanding in multiple ways. Appendix B is an example of what an assessment might look like.

Recognising the connections: an approach to the English language paper?

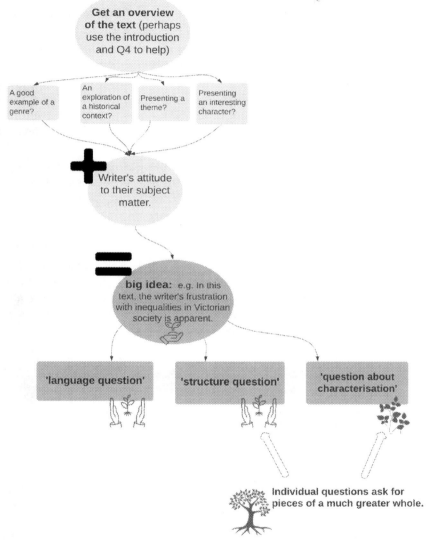

Figure 6.2 A draft of a holistic approach to the language paper. This encourages pupils to see the text as a whole, and each exam question as a particular lens through which to view that same, whole text. The same overall authorial intention runs through every aspect of the text.

The assessment consists of a mixture of tasks. The first is a series of short answer questions that focus on a foundation concept. There is also a section in which an important element of procedure is assessed, namely adding quotations to an extract.[1] There is an extended answer, although this would likely be a mini-essay rather than a full response. By *mini-essay*, we mean that it might explore one aspect of a bigger theme with just one or two examples. Rather than exploring masculinity in *A View from the Bridge*, pupils might focus on a spec character and

84 *How should the curriculum be assessed?*

a very short extract that might only be ten lines long, for example. This could easily be reduced further to the task of simply crafting an opening sentence. There is no particular need to measure everything in English with an essay.

Another approach might be to forego this kind of formal assessment in favour of an English portfolio. A range of approaches might be the best way forward rather than reducing our opportunities to one option – some sort of essay. The mixture of tasks aims to isolate particular aspects of performance so that between them, the tasks might better reveal gaps in understanding. If we accept that we can only ever measure performance, not learning itself, it's a case of trying to find the best proxy or proxies. The cognitive load involved in writing essays is so much greater than in many other tasks and might interfere with a pupil's ability to demonstrate the understanding they do have. It might look like connections haven't been made when that isn't really the case.

Pupil responses could be collated over time for inclusion in the portfolio. At an appropriate point (i.e. when pupils are ready), this could include longer essay responses and original writing. Until then, it would include the kind of quizzes and tasks we see in the example above, and diagrams like the ones below, which enable pupils to make connections but remove the extraneous load of having to write an actual essay.

Partial completion diagrams can be very useful but these need to be sufficiently exemplified and modelled over time to enable pupils to understand what an effective one would look like and how they might construct it. Figure 6.3 is a fairly simple Venn diagram mapping connections between Juliet and her father in Act 3, Scene 5 of *Romeo and Juliet*. We might tell pupils that the central part – what the two characters have in common in this scene – is perhaps the most interesting and most easily overlooked. Pupils could add to this as directed

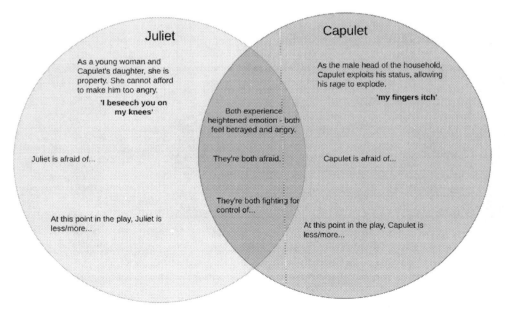

Figure 6.3 An example of a Venn Diagram comparing the characterisation of Juliet and her father

once they've seen an example or two. We could use questions rather than sentence openings to frame the thinking, and we would need to direct pupils in whether and how to use quotations. Venn diagrams can be limiting due to lack of space so this simple diagram can be built into something more complex – a comparative map or bubble diagram perhaps, over time.

Figure 6.4 is the beginning of a concept map which might end up looking like Figure 6.5 eventually. Pupils might add a little at a time, working with the teacher as appropriate. Any concept map has its limitations – we can't include everything – and they can be somewhat overwhelming. Having said that, they can be very useful as support for pupils during essay practice. Co-creating them with pupils also helps to emphasise something very important – English is about ideas and connections. These are not as mysterious as they might seem – we can record and map those connections.

There is some debate about whether concept maps are useful for retrieval but this study[2] by Karpicke and Blunt shows that concept maps, like most things, are useful *in certain circumstances*. They can serve as retrieval practice. However, we mostly advocate their use in helping pupils see how thinking can be organised in English. They are usually best when co-created with teachers, especially in the early stages of learning.

It might also be appropriate to add pupils' oral responses, either transcribed or audio recorded, with parental permission.

We have included, as Appendix B, an example of a Year 7 end-of-term assessment currently being trialled at a group of schools in West Norfolk. It invites pupils not only to carry out some extended response, though not a full essay, but also tries to capture basic conceptual and procedural knowledge, and some textual knowledge of the core text they have studied.

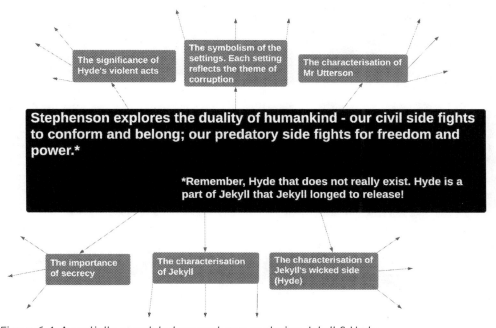

Figure 6.4 A partially completed concept map exploring Jekyll & Hyde

86 *How should the curriculum be assessed?*

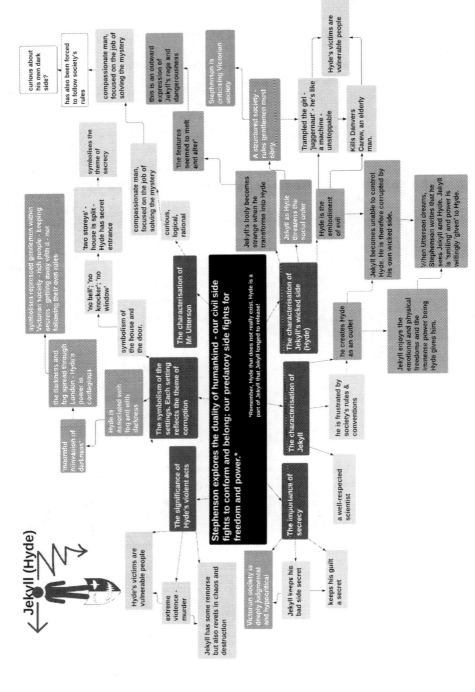

Figure 6.5 An almost-complete concept map exploring Jekyll & Hyde expanding on the one in Figure 6.4

In terms of doing the actual marking, comparative judgement might be an extremely useful tool. Daisy Christodoulou has conducted extensive research[3] into its accuracy and effectiveness. The teacher would rank pieces simply as top, middle, bottom and keep a record. Notes can be made to support whole class feedback as necessary. Whole class feedback foregoes writing in individual books in favour of actually re-teaching common errors to the entire class.

At regular intervals, a piece of work would be marked comparatively in the same way, but each member of the department would mark the entire year group. This sounds onerous but comparative judgement is actually very quick – decisions can usually be made in seconds and there is software available to help. The only difficult part is in scanning in the pupils' work so that it can be assessed. This is an administrative task but not a difficult one. There is no particular reason why pupil helpers couldn't scan in work, as long as they had some adult supervision, say in a reprographics room or a classroom where a teacher is already working. Teacher marking would decrease hugely, leaving more time to focus on researching, planning and collaborating.

In terms of ascribing levels or grades to such a portfolio, we would suggest that for much of a pupil's school career, this isn't really necessary. What we really want to know is, are they on track, ahead or not there yet? 'On track' might be determined relative to a given target grade perhaps. It is always possible to break things down further, using percentages for example, but what we really want to know is, *which teachers and/or pupils are **not** OK right now?* This is the information that is most useful and it's worth having a conversation with SLT about how best to approach assessment reporting in a way that is realistic and as accurate as possible, and not beholden to formal examination style approaches. Then we can dive in to trying to understand why they're not ok and how we might address it.

Assessment in English: What next?

In this chapter, we have pointed to one of the problems with our current assessment system, which is how it has come to drive curriculum, when it should be the other way around. If we are to curate a meaningful concept-led curriculum, we need to consider the ways we assess it, and this may mean questioning the purposes and intent with which we collect data about what pupils know, understand and can do.

One useful way to think about measuring learning is using curriculum-related expectations. David Didau has written in detail about this, arguing that:

> unlike age related expectations, (which is just something a child of a particular age is assumed to be able to do, regardless of what they've been taught) having **curriculum related expectations** helps us to specify, teach and assess the knowledge we expect children to acquire. It becomes reasonable to expect children to have met these expectations because they are – or should be – directly connected to what has been taught[4]

Making judgements about progress based on how much of a curriculum pupils have learned is a way to restore the balance between curriculum and assessment. If we are clear and specific about what we intend to teach, it should be clear how we can assess what pupils have learned. Most importantly, it provides us with meaningful data to inform teaching. If pupils have not made the progress we expect, we can begin to identify exactly what knowledge they are missing.

For many years we have worked within a system where formative assessment has been within the realms of our control but summative assessment has often dictated its intents

88 How should the curriculum be assessed?

and purposes. However, at the time of writing, the COVID-19 pandemic and the cancellation of formal examinations has necessitated a move towards centre-assessed grades. It may be that this way of determining pupils' final grades is a temporary situation; nevertheless, it has continued and accelerated a national conversation about how, when and why we assess pupils summatively. It is our hope that this conversation continues.

In summary

- Assessment should be curriculum driven rather than driving curriculum. We need to assess what pupils are actually learning, as best we can.
- There is a difference between learning and performance.
- An examination tests a small sample of a domain of knowledge.
- Learning can only ever be inferred. Any assessment is a proxy for measuring learning.
- Assessment should not over-rely on exam questions, especially at KS3.
- Essays are not the only way to measure learning. There are many alternatives that provide better proxies of what pupils might have learned.

Now that we know what we are teaching and how we might assess learning, in the next chapter, we will consider how we might draw on further research to consider how we might enact the curriculum in the classroom.

Teacher Insight

Lucy Clark, Head of English, Springwood High School

Lucy is a HOD who is developing strategies for assessing a new concept-led curriculum.

Working with Sam and Zoe on a conceptual curriculum prompted me to consider the rationale behind our assessment practice. What are we assessing? What is the purpose of the assessment? What will teachers learn from the students' performance?

In short, I realised that our assessment in English had historically been underpinned by testing our students' ability to produce GCSE style answers irrespective of whether they were in Year 7 or Year 11. This approach was driven by the requirement to report to senior leaders and parents termly or half-termly with a progress update, which constituted a predicted GCSE English grade. Like many schools and departments, we had fallen into the trap of applying a 'flight path' model of progression, vainly hoping that a student would progress by at least two sub-levels per year to reach their projected GCSE grade – as defined by their KS2 score – and that this trajectory of progression would be reflected in the assessment results. Of course, this model is highly flawed and did not allow us to assess students' learning in any meaningful way.

However, having worked closely with Zoe and Sam, we have been able to justify adopting an assessment model that breaks away from simply bringing GCSE assessment objectives down into KS3 and allows us to assess the acquisition and application of students' conceptual knowledge at optimum times. Our assessments are now curriculum-driven and have been carefully designed to offer a clear snapshot of the learning that has taken place, which can be used effectively in a formative sense whilst still fulfilling the requirement to populate reports with data in the form of an attained percentage; I feel now that this data is meaningful and tells us all something useful about the student.

Of course, our assessment approach is not simply based on formal tests during the designated assessment windows in our school's calendar; rather, the new curriculum that Zoe and Sam have designed with us promotes a range of assessment methods, all of which offer valid insight into students' learning: we have embraced hinge questions; retrieval practice; diagrams; the conversion of sentence fragments into analytical sentences; and many other strategies. These are all effective and efficient ways to assess learning ahead of the completion of more extended tasks; and, in turn, these extended tasks are now of a much higher quality.

Notes

1 This procedure still relies, like almost all procedures, on conceptual and content knowledge.
2 Blunt, Janell R., & Karpicke, Jeffrey D. (2014). Learning with retrieval-based concept mapping. *Journal of Educational Psychology, 106*(3), 849-858.
3 Christodoulou, Daisy, viewed on 10th February 2021, https://daisychristodoulou.com/comparative-judgment/
4 Didau, D. (2020). Curriculum related expectations: using the curriculum as a progression model. <https://learningspy.co.uk/assessment/curriculum-related-expectations/>. Accessed 1 February 2021.

7 Evidence-informed approaches to enacting the curriculum

Now that we have a sense of what we want to teach, we need to ensure that the pedagogical approaches we employ are faithful to, and align with, our curriculum intentions. If we are asking teachers to teach a concept-led curriculum, we need to see how we can draw together what we know about teaching abstract ideas and align it with other research-informed approaches to teaching and learning.

It isn't enough just to read research. Teachers need to make sense of it. To consider how we might build pupils' schemas, we might ask ourselves a series of questions and use relevant research to try to answer them. We are now thinking not so much about what the schema is comprised of but rather, how we might enable pupils to build them.

Here are some key ideas we've drawn on to inform our curriculum design. Of course, there is a wealth of research on all aspects of education. We cannot possibly cover them all. We focus on aspects of cognitive science research that might be relevant in helping pupils to build coherent schemas and are therefore particularly pertinent to the teaching of English.

The overall approach: how might we best deliver our expertise to pupils?

There are many choices to make about delivery itself, of course. For example, we might use presentation slides, we might not. We might have any number of different styles, unique to our own individual teacher persona. We would like to suggest that a particularly useful approach, largely because it helps pupils to see connections and know what is most important, is to live-draw word diagrams as we talk through important concepts. Most of us already make notes on the board or on a visualiser. Thinking a bit more carefully about spatial relationships, adding some arrows to show connections and so on, is a simple but effective way to make the thinking clear, and might be more valuable to pupils than many of us have realised. It also helps us direct pupils' attention to exactly what we want them to focus on. It's also conceptually clearer that an idea is unfolding, a thought process is taking place in front of pupils, one we are usually asking them to echo later on. We therefore strongly advocate diagramming as part of an overall approach. But what else might we consider?

DOI: 10.4324/9781003033158-8

Who are we teaching – novices vs experts

In building rich complex knowledge, we need to acknowledge that novices and experts learn differently. An expert has a sophisticated schema and enough interconnected knowledge to be ready to practice applying their understanding in new situations. A novice, on the other hand, has not yet built much of a schema and therefore needs more guidance in terms of how the thinking processes are meant to unfold in relation to concepts and tasks, and working memory needs greater support. Of course, there is a continuum of expertise. A school pupil might reach a level of expertise but they are still relative novices compared to a university undergraduate. In general, we are better thinking of our pupils as novices throughout their school careers, even though many will reach a good level of sophistication for a 16-year-old. We might adapt our practice as pupils become more expert, moving some way along that continuum of expertise, but we are unlikely to address them as if they were university undergraduates.

If you're unconvinced about this, perhaps ask yourself how much your strongest pupil really knows. How much could they achieve with unseen material entirely independently with no further input from you, or any other teacher, or even a textbook? And could they do this consistently across all aspects of the study of English including creative and rhetorical writing? Are they consciously competent? Could they teach the class as well, or better, than you do across all these aspects?

Explicit instruction (not just lecturing!)

In Barak Rosenshine's seminal paper, *Principles of Instruction*,[1] Rosenshine combines research from three areas: cognitive science; the study of master teachers and what he calls 'cognitive supports'. These include strategies such as modelling and thinking aloud.

The research demonstrates that pupils need more teacher input and more careful modelling and guidance than has generally been provided in the past. We have assumed pupils should remember what we teach them without understanding the difficulty this presents. We have also tended to move too quickly to pupils doing their own independent work without providing enough modelling and support first.

A common misconception about direct instruction is that it encourages lecture-style teaching where pupils remain passive. That is absolutely not the case. Rather than lecturing, teachers are encouraged to use frequent questioning; lessons are still interactive. Rosenshine advocates introducing new material in small steps, asking questions and providing models as part of explicit instruction.

Once we have taught our pupils something, what can research tell us about how we can help to ensure they remember it?

Enquiry-based learning?

Much of the time, enquiry learning does not help school-age pupils learn because it doesn't work well for novices. There is some evidence that enquiry learning and flipped learning (where pupils study independently in advance of lessons) are of some benefit but much of this research focuses on students working at graduate level.[2] The knowledge-base of a graduate is so much broader and deeper than a school-age pupil, they are better able to accommodate new information with little or no mediation from a teacher. Where a flipped learning approach is adopted, it needs to be very well curated to succeed and there might be easier ways to achieve the same outcomes.

Although some schools are making enquiry-based learning work, in many more schools it seems to be predicated on the idea that we should encourage pupils to figure everything out for themselves. But teachers are not mere facilitators. Pupils need to draw on the teachers' expert knowledge. Otherwise those pupils have to reinvent the wheel every lesson and this denies them their right to receive thousands of years of human civilisation.

Our resistance to just passing on what we know, our reluctance to tell pupils what to think, comes from a good place. We, rightly, don't want to foist our opinions on young minds. We want them to be independent. Our mistake was in thinking that independence can be achieved via this hands-off approach. It can't. As Kirschner, Sweller and Clark[3] point out, the best way to get pupils to be independent is not actually to get them to work independently. At least, not right away. Guiding pupils, telling them what we know, does not require any abandonment of our principle of valuing their opinion or nurturing their independence. On the contrary, it is the route to enabling them to develop independent, nuanced opinions.

Differentiation?

We are focusing this discussion on pupils who are taught within mainstream classes because this is within our area of expertise. Pupils presenting with severe of complex needs might need greater adaptation than that which is described here, including, if appropriate, an alternative curriculum with a specific level of challenge that meets pupils needs and prepares them for any further stages of learning.

If children really can get cleverer, which we think they can (hopefully, we will demonstrate this below), does differentiation really help, does it hold pupils back, does the answer lie in *how* we do the differentiating?

We're going to go out on a bit of a limb and suggest that the vast majority of differentiation is probably not helping. That's because, if the first wave, classroom teaching is good enough, it will support the majority of pupils who are in danger of falling behind, either because of their personal social circumstances meaning they have significant learning gaps, or because they present with a Special Educational Need or Disability (SEND).

We often seem to misguidedly treat the situation as if vast differences exist between how pupils *learn*. We might feel a need to provide pupils with a range of different tasks. But we are not all that different from one another at the most fundamental level: we all develop mental models, taking what we know and then adding to it.

The outdated theory of learning styles, which suggests that we each have a particular style of learning – either visual, auditory or kinaesthetic – that suits us best, has been debunked.[4] We all have preferences for how we learn but that doesn't influence whether learning actually occurs and we can be poor judges of whether we are actually learning or not.

There is no disputing the fact that if we look at prior attainment, some pupils will have done better than others. Maybe they have been doing so for a long time. It can look like an

Evidence-informed approaches to enacting the curriculum 93

objective 'truth' that one student is 'cleverer' than another. But like so much of our instinct, this can be deceiving and the truth much more complex.

To explore this further, we'd like to try to answer this question: *why do some children underachieve in the first place?*

There are so many reasons. There are social reasons, there are medical reasons, family reasons. Sometimes teachers don't teach well enough. That's a particularly uncomfortable reason but it's true all the same.

In *Making Kids Cleverer*,[5] David Didau points out that medical conditions like glue ear can affect children's early learning experiences. Glue ear is not a learning difficulty in itself but, because it can interfere with the development of phonemic awareness, it may appear like one if we rush to the wrong conclusions. It matters because rushing to the wrong conclusions can condemn a child to the 'bottom set' and that in itself may ensure they never leave it.[6]

And there are other things than can affect a child's early education: developmental delay; poor executive function, which can make concentrating and paying attention very hard, and any number of other problems.

Firstly, these problems may resolve as the child grows so we ought not assume they will be there forever. Secondly, even where problems persist, the way that any one human being learns is essentially the same way as every other human being. We have existing knowledge and we attach new knowledge to what we know already, forming ever greater and more complex schemas as we go. This is what leads to critical thinking and creativity.

At least, we will all learn this way if we're allowed to, if we're ever exposed to the greater complexity we need for deeper learning. Not all of our so-called 'weaker' pupils ever get this chance. Our labelling misleads us into thinking less of people. We may jump to conclusions based on their social class and the way they talk. We use terms like, 'less able'. But they might be capable, if we let them, of developing great knowledge and insight. We just have to teach it to them and be patient. But we must do so mindful of where we want pupils to get to and how we can best support them to rise to meet the demands of the curriculum.

Two ways whole class teaching can meet the needs of all pupils

Everyone has gaps and they all need filling...

Pupils with disadvantage and pupils presenting with SEND are two cohorts that might need to have gaps filled. But no pupil comes to school without gaps. Our experiences are far too varied. Whole class teaching ought to be mindful of this at all times, cycling back to prior learning and building on it as a matter of routine. Checking for understanding, as best we can, is an important part of this and extra help can, of course, be put in as soon as possible when a pupil does struggle. It's worth remembering that pupil might not have any particular disadvantage and might not present with SEND – anyone can struggle.

Teachers should already be working to resolve the most common problems

Although every pupil is unique and pupils might have a wide range of individual needs, in regard to teaching and learning, there are two potential issues underlying the majority of pupils' difficulties. Teachers should already be working to address this with the whole class. They are:

- Pupils don't remember
  Whole class retrieval practice, vocabulary practice and elaboration tasks that allow for extension and consolidation should already be in place for the whole class. Some pupils might need even more than most. Again, that can be managed through extra support. But much of the time, first wave teaching will support all pupils to remember their learning.
- Pupils struggle to organise the incoming and/or outgoing knowledge. Thoughts, both their own and other people's, feel loose and disorganised. Knowing what matters most and identifying sequences and hierarchies are therefore problematic.
  Strategies such as word diagramming, comparison tables and so on, can be used with the whole class and will support pupils in seeing how knowledge is organised. All pupils can benefit from this so it doesn't need to be reserved for one particular cohort. Pupils can also be asked to identify the most important concept and orally explain connections. If this is carefully managed so that is done with some precision, it can benefit all pupils.

As part of exploring the importance of organising and remembering learning, it is helpful to think about a theory of memory that can be of practical use in planning learning.

Cognitive load theory in English

Cognitive load theory, first developed by John Sweller[7] in the late 1980s, is based on the notion that working memory has limited capacity. Working memory is the conscious, 'thinking' part of memory. It carries out information processing using input from the environment and from long-term memory. Figure 7.1 is Caviglioi's representation of this process.

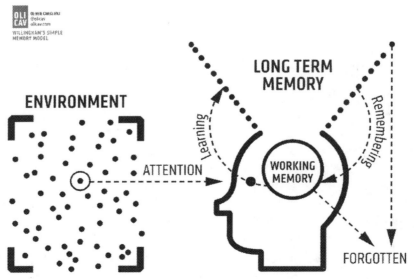

Figure 7.1 A version of Willingham's Simple Memory Model from the website of Oliver Caviglioli (olicav.com)

Evidence-informed approaches to enacting the curriculum   95

Cognitive load theory suggests that working memory can only hold a finite amount of information before it becomes overloaded and can no longer process effectively. This implies that if we try to do too much at once, we might overload working memory and any schema we are trying to develop will likely fail to materialise. The details of exactly how much we can hold are not really relevant here. We take the broad principle that there comes a point when we are giving pupils too much to think about simultaneously.

To help pupils to learn, we need to focus their attention on exactly what is most relevant. As psychologist Daniel Willingham says, 'we remember what we think about'. And we need to support their working memories with external prompts (examples, models, etc.) to free up the processing capacity needed to complete a task. A couple of simple principles are helpful. Figure 7.2 helps us to think a bit more about this concept.

- **If the information we are conveying to students is complex**, they will need more working memory capacity to process the knowledge. This means we might need to:
    a   keep any associated tasks fairly simple – in English that often means avoiding essay writing until pupils have acquired enough knowledge and practice to make it a meaningful process; a simpler task is preferable as they begin to explore complex new ideas, and
    b   increase the amount of support available from the environment. In English, this might mean leaving relevant notes, a diagram or annotated model visible to pupils.

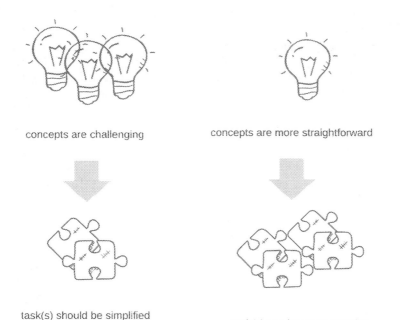

Figure 7.2 A representation of the relationship between conceptual complexity and task complexity as expressed in cognitive load theory

- **If the information we are conveying is simpler,** or there is far greater pre-existing knowledge to draw on, we can afford to make the associated tasks more complex (see Figure 7.2). This means we might be able to:
    a   include more elements in the sequence of tasks (more steps). In our subject this might mean we invite pupils to annotate the text according to a particular focus, finish a partial completion diagram and write a short response in quick succession and with little guidance, and
    b   increase the complexity of the practice, perhaps by combining elements, as happens when pupils write a full essay response or answer a language question, for example.

There is one important note here – we are not necessarily trying to *minimise* cognitive load: students should be learning complex ideas. Rather, we are trying to *prevent* cognitive *overload*. If we make things too easy, we might be avoiding the rich complexity we want pupils to access.

Why traditional differentiation is problematic

We can't do this through traditional differentiation. 'All/most/some' or 'must/should/could' might be two of the worst catchphrases ever to make it into the world of education. This approach misunderstands the problem we're trying to address. They cause teachers to waste time, and it is a waste of time, coming up with different tasks for students, or different levels of task, which simply serve to ensure the pupils we are most worried about get the least opportunity to grow.

Differentiated questioning is just as problematic. It places a cap on what pupils will be able to do before they've even tried. Breaking up a complex question into parts so that we build up understanding slowly is a good thing and can work for all pupils, but assuming certain children can't handle the tough end of the question spectrum is fundamentally flawed.

And, finally, if we're going to hand out sentence starters, we need to ensure pupils intentionally practice with them (more on practice below) until they are internalised and can be used creatively and independently. Having to provide the same starters over and over again because the tool has not been internalised by our pupils is proof our approach is not working.

Can all pupils really access the same concepts? Really? (Spoiler: YES.)

Our 'struggling' pupils need opportunities to learn and remember the most valuable **knowledge**. If there are significant gaps, we might not have time to teach them everything. But that's why we have to be intelligent about what knowledge we select. We advocate a focus on the most high value knowledge.

These pupils might need knowledge to be somewhat more *condensed*, but they do not need it to be *simplified*. That's an important distinction. For example, as things currently stand in many schools up and down the country, in teaching *Animal Farm* to a 'nurture' group, a teacher might be tempted to forego abstraction and complexity and focus more on teaching characters and their, fairly straightforward behaviours. Activities might remain heavily focused on knowing who is who and having a sense of the main characters' traits and relationships with other characters. Pupils might, for example, think a lot about how the character, Napoleon, is a 'bully'.

But is this time well spent? Is this the most important, or interesting, thing to know about this text? What about the concept of oppression itself? We would argue that this approach is unnecessarily oversimplified and denies pupils the opportunity to explore conceptual knowledge. Of course, pupils do need to know which character is which, but this often becomes clearer anyway if we attach the knowledge to a clear central thread, something about oppression would be appropriate with this text. We can give most of the attention to oppression and other themes, just as we would with other pupils.

However, it is also true that 'bottom set' pupils might struggle to make the kinds of gains that we would see in a 'top set' so what do we do?

Firstly, don't assume these pupils can't make huge gains. They can.

Secondly, notice pupils' *thinking* as well as their *production*. Developing pupils' confidence and articulacy, particularly in writing, will take time, but these pupils can often grasp tricky concepts just as quickly as anyone else. And it's the thinking that is most important.

When Zoe taught *Animal Farm* to a nurture group, she began by exploring the concept of oppression, drawing on real-world examples, and helping pupils practice using this word in its various forms (*oppress, oppressing, oppressive, oppression*). Discussions around the book focused on this central organising principle. Discussions around characters were focused on how they were experiencing the act of oppression, whether they were the oppressor or the oppressed, or perhaps neither. When class members expressed their thoughts, they were asked to recast phrases like, 'Napoleon is bullying them' to make use of key vocabulary (in this case using something like, *Napoleon's actions are oppressive because...* NB Oppression wasn't the only thematic concept explored but it is rather key in this particular text!). Exemplification (quotations, etc.) were selected according to how well they helped us recognise the facets of oppression as it occurs within the story. Sentence practice and short responses focused on building conceptual explanations. Everything was carefully modelled.

The resulting assessments at the end of the term were, for some pupils, three grades higher than they had ever achieved before, and every pupil improved by at least one grade. 'Nurture' pupils can handle it. Pupils who might have been held back for some time relish the opportunity to bask in having deeper, more interesting material to play with. Things that are tough to wrestle with are always interesting, especially if we add in the passion of a great teacher. As long as we're mindful to organise thinking and discussion carefully and we provide short, focused and modelled tasks, these pupils can make huge gains in relatively short time.

It is worth mentioning here that practice is key to building automaticity in domains such as phonics, spelling and the use of specific sentence constructions. More complex domains, such as writing essays, also require practice and feedback. Pupils simply don't get enough of this as we race through the curriculum at break-neck speed. And our specificity in breaking down our own mental models for pupils – thinking out loud about what we're writing and why, elucidating our genuine, messy but manageable thought processes, is often vague and poorly planned.

For example, a knowledge of vocabulary and sentence structures, which are known so intimately that they spring into consciousness with little effort, is what allows great writers to create wonderful expressions and new meanings. Our pupils deserve access to this world and we can give them that through carefully building knowledge and generating practice.

What about the pupils who are achieving? Is this going to be too easy?

The good news is that **everyone**, whether they are 'underachieving' or not, benefits from lots of knowledge and lots of practice explaining and exploring it. If we want our pupils, all of them, to build sophisticated schemas, we need to give them the opportunity to practice, to return to things, to seek out the detail and make deep connections.

And **all** pupils need their teachers to be aware of cognitive load. We want pupils to have enough desirable difficulty to ensure learning happens, but want to stop at the point that working memory may become overwhelmed. It should be hard enough but not too hard. Judgements like that are not easy to make but it does get easier with experience. We should pay careful attention to the relative value or the knowledge we're sharing.

In fact, what we really need is to think of those pupils who appear 'weaker' as the barometer for whether our teaching as a whole is working effectively. If they're not learning then probably *nobody* in the class or the year group is learning as well as they could.

The suggestions we have for supporting those pupils who might struggle are the same things we would use with all pupils. They're the things we already discussed. This is not an exhaustive list but: a focus on the highest value knowledge; central organising principles; retrieval practice and lots of it; dual coding and diagrams; explicit exemplification of abstract ideas; opportunities to imagine and predict; modelling parts of high-quality examples and building up over time; lots of opportunities to practice thinking.

Remembering

Retrieval practice

In the 1880s, Hermann Ebbinghaus[8] performed a series of experiments, which led to the development of his 'forgetting curve'. He used himself as a test subject, recording his own ability to repeat a list of made up syllables. Figure 7.3 helps us to understand just how quickly we might forget what we are taught.

He demonstrated that careful retrieval practice of learned information enables us to better remember that which would otherwise have been lost. More recent research suggests

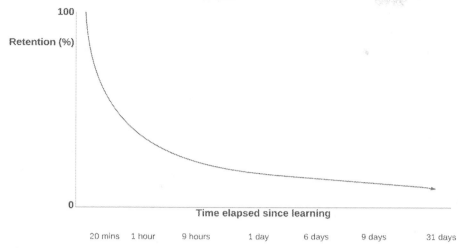

Figure 7.3 Ebbinghaus's Forgetting Curve

that when a memory first begins to form, it is 'laid down' in our long-term memory and held in working memory simultaneously.[9] While it may remain in long-term memory – it is still 'there' – our ability to retrieve the memory will usually quickly fade once we are no longer consciously thinking about the material. It is this ability to actually retrieve the knowledge, in other words, to consciously reconstitute the newly formed memory, that we need to develop.

Ebbinghaus's study has its limitations. His experiments were based around teaching himself nonsense syllables that were devoid of meaning. It is easy to see that this does not generate a full and accurate representation of how memorisation and forgetting work in the real world, where meaning is usually sacrosanct. However, the idea that we naturally forget things and that we should try to interrupt this process and revisit important ideas seems very applicable to real life. The most useful idea that comes out of this study and others that have built upon it since is probably the idea that we need to be *actively engaged* in remembering, attend to it deliberately and do it ourselves rather than hoping we'll absorb things by osmosis or by relying on re-reading, or listening passively to a recap.

Retrieval is not the same as recap

There is a real difference between these two things, although they do, of course, overlap. Both are intending to draw out students' prior learning so that they can activate knowledge and build connections to new knowledge. However, retrieval practice is a specific, evidence-based *type* of recap which is more effective than other methods.[10]

'Recapping' seems to be a blanket term for a number of approaches teachers might undertake. Such approaches may not even involve pupils directly – short on time, a teacher may simply summarise pointers from a previous lesson without necessarily involving students. Where they are involved, it may not be all of them, and once an individual has contributed the teacher may not return to them, which means that pupil might no longer be engaging in the conversation. A recap might come in the form of a video, which goes over prior learning and from which pupils may take notes. But is this a good way to learn? It does not involve retrieval; it is the equivalent of re-reading and highlighting, neither of which is very effective.[11]

In fact, the term 're-cap' comes from both old French and Latin and while it is a bit complicated, it basically means 'to summarise' and to 'restate by heads or chapters'. *Recapping* only requires headings and chapters and is, therefore, primarily about summarising (a thank you to Mary Myatt[12] here for teaching us the importance of etymology!) But a summary is not enough. In order for information to make that precious and difficult journey into long-term memory, pupils need to over-learn. They need to repeat the *detail*, not just the headings in order to build the complex, integrated schemas that make up deep learning.[13]

Retrieval practice means something very different to just recapping. This is more than just 'semantics' – there is a real difference in the learning intention if we talk about practicing, which requires a lot of repetition, to be able to retrieve specific information. *Re* means 'again' and *trouver* means 'to find'. So, retrieval practice basically means, 'to repeatedly find the same information again and again until it sticks'. It tends to come in the form of knowledge quizzing and free recall, where pupils come to the information 'cold' and have to consciously, effortfully retrieve it from memory.

If done well, this approach allows learning to be deeply incorporated by all pupils so that they build cohesive knowledge and can use that as a springboard to independence, critical thinking and creativity.

For retrieval practice to be effective, retrieval has to be successful. In other words, creating an opportunity for retrieval to take place is not enough; it has to actually happen and it has to happen within each individual pupil. For this reason, prompts are useful and encouraged, particularly with very new information. For example, this might involve giving students the first letter of an answer to help them achieve successful retrieval of a keyword.

It's useful practice to do retrieval at the start of the lesson, rather than the end. As well as facilitating storage in memory, it can be used to activate pre-existing schemas ready to incorporate the new knowledge being presented in the lesson. However, retrieval practice is not a 'tag on'. It should be used continually throughout each lesson to help pupils make connections between prior and new learning.

Retrieval should also, as far as possible, involve elaboration. Elaborating on an idea helps to create connections and 'wrap' the new learning in a web of related knowledge.

In English, an example of useful retrieval practice in a lesson about the characterisation of Mr Birling in *An Inspector Calls* might see pupils retrieving what they can remember about how the characterisation of Scrooge is tied to the theme of social injustice in *A Christmas Carol*. This might be done as a partial completion diagram. In this way, pupils remember a previous text they haven't seen for a while *and* prepare for the new learning, which is to explore how the characterisation of Mr Birling also says something about social injustice within a class system. Pupils can be asked to elaborate on how the two characters, and the two writers, are similar, but also why there are subtle differences between them.

Modelling and practice

The other side of developing schemas, besides acquiring complex knowledge, is practice. Practice means *applying* the learning within some sort of task. We can carefully select exactly what we want pupils to practice and ensure there is sufficient guidance for them to do it successfully.

Effective Modelling

Effective practice relies on effective modelling. For many years, Ofsted discouraged teachers from talking too much. We were to facilitate rather than teach and the onus was on pupils working everything out for themselves in what was usually a particularly poor manifestation of enquiry learning. However, in practice, this not only means that teachers struggle to pass on their expert knowledge, it also gives us little or no time to model our thinking and writing for pupils. But pupils need a sense of how to think, how to approach things before they can become truly independent. This generally doesn't happen by osmosis. We need to show them.

Those of us that have tried to model for pupils have often fallen into the trap of trying to model the building of a product – a piece of writing. But we really need to model thought processes. One of the thorny issues here is that we have to strike a balance. Showing pupils *how* to think inevitably involves telling them a certain amount of *what* to think. If I'm to show them how we might explore a poem, I have to use examples from the poem and comment on how I think they contribute to meaning. That means I am inevitably telling pupils *what* to think as well as *how* and it means that their own interpretation might really just be my own, an interpretation that they co-opt. Clearly, we want independence. But to get there, we have to be prepared to live with the fact that we're sometimes influencing what pupils think as well as how. It cannot be avoided. To do so would mean that many pupils would not have had sufficient modelling to ever be able to do the thinking on their own and that would deny them the beauty of our subject.

Modelling thinking isn't easy. We often try to sanitise true thinking, which is messy, into a streamlined perfect version of thinking, an accurate thought chain with no false starts or wrong turns. Pupils need to see that uninterrupted, accurate thought chain to know what a good one looks like, but they also need to realistically see thinking happen, and in English that tends to involve those false starts and wrong turns as we navigate a text. We might use mind-mapping, sketching and visual metaphors to help break down what is happening inside our own heads. It's the story not just of a text itself, but of our own interaction with it.

Figures 7.4, 7.5 and 7.6 show the kind of thing we might live-draw for pupils, having prepared it in advance, to illustrate effective thinking in English. Drawing out the whole thing might take too long so we could use a pre-prepared skeleton that we then add to. It can also be useful to do a version of this which incorporates some false starts for a more realistic example of thinking something through. Figure 7.4 overuses icons and probably

102 *Evidence-informed approaches to enacting the curriculum*

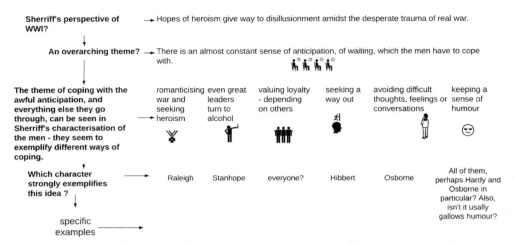

Figure 7.4 An example of live diagramming based on Journey's End by R.C. Sherriff

just amounts to visual clutter. The simple visual metaphor of the pyramids in Figure 7.5 is better. It provides a familiar visual metaphor for the concept of hierarchy. In Figure 7.6, we see an attempt to match symbols with aspects of thinking, symbols which we could potentially reuse in order to keep the emphasis on thought process rather than product. Pupils would keep a copy of the model to refer to. The model could be improved but this was a tricky situation where a teacher was required to teach language paper practice to a Year 8 class. This is something we'd advise against. It's an approach that sees English

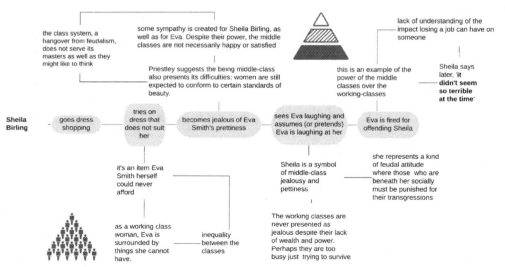

Figure 7.5 A map of an episode in An Inspector Calls where Sheila 'confesses' that she had Eva fired from her job in a clothes shop

Harry Kirby

Starting to compare non-fiction texts

A worked example about the first text, which we created together:

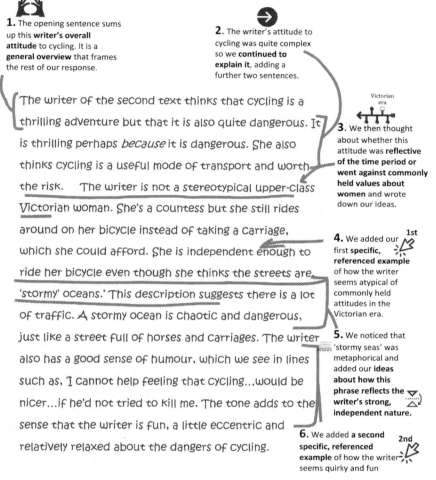

Figure 7.6 A worked example (language analysis of an article about cycling) where the thought process has been mapped

as skills-based rather than a body of complex conceptual knowledge that we can draw upon to analyse texts.

Practice

Practice should lead to improvement. There's no point asking a pupil who isn't very good at writing essays to just keep on writing whole essays; they will continue to be of poor quality. They are essentially practising failure. It would be like asking them to run a marathon when they haven't done any training. Instead, we can break down the practice into useful parts. Essays start with a sentence. Constructing a thesis statement is something of an art form. But other sentences and fragments, such as introducing a quotation, need practising too.

Research by Soderstrom et al[14] has revealed a need to change the way we approach pupil practice over time. When learning something new, pupils need a block of time to repeatedly practice. Once they are improving, we can probably move to interleaved practice. In English, that might mean spending some time just thinking about crafting thesis statements. Then we might spend similar time on embedding quotations. At some point, we begin to interleave these, meaning that we incorporate both within the same lesson. It might also mean having pupils write about one character, several times, then another, and then eventually combining those into a longer single paragraph that might be comparative.

Managing practice – How can we move from guided practice to independent practice in English?

What do we mean by guided practice?

In a guided activity, the vast majority of the time is spent with the teacher modelling a series of worked examples. It is usually important that the first couple of times involve no interruptions or cold calling. Pupils can begin to contribute to the modelling process when we think they're ready. At the end of the modelling process, there should be a version of a similar task that pupils can then have a go at. The teacher can assist them throughout.

What do we mean by independent practice?

When pupils work independently, once the teacher is sure they understand the task, the teacher should then step back as much as possible. Pupils must have a chance to practice without intervention or interruption. Having said this, it is often necessary to support working memory while pupils work, perhaps by having a model visible. In this scenario, the pupil is still responsible for all of the thinking in terms of how they use and apply the model they can see.

Using intermediate steps

It is usually appropriate to introduce a transition step between guided and independent practice. This might involve pupils working independently of the teacher but with a partner or in a small group. It will often involve pupils working independently but with models, notes and/or diagrams visible to support them as they practice their thinking and/or their reading, writing, speaking and listening.

Bear in mind that once pupils understand the procedure and can remember how to do it, they will still need sufficient knowledge of any particular text (whether the teacher

Evidence-informed approaches to enacting the curriculum 105

1. Useful phrases for essay introductions:

A Christmas Carol
uses the festival of Christmas
vehicle to explore/question
attitudes of the Victorian middle class
change and redemption
confronted with scenes of
emotional resonance
chips away at Scrooge's steely veneer
compelled to transform
more compassionate
character sketches
somewhat romanticises the poor and downtrodden
advocates for better treatment of the vulnerable

An Inspector Calls
social injustice
British class system
challenges feudal attitudes
even the nouveau-riche
failed to destabilise
the upper middle classes
maintain status quo
fail to recognise
vulnerability of the working classes
award themselves moral authority
divide the poor into deserving and undeserving
upper middle classes also suffer
suffocated by
a layer of society obsessed with reputation

Macbeth
the nature of duplicity
supernatural forces manipulate
succumb to dark desires
self-delusion and the deception of others
false narratives are conjured
commitment to fate
the ramifications **of**
betraying **not only** the king **but** God himself
warning against insurrection
characters operate with hidden motives
close relationships are fractured and destroyed

Jekyll & Hyde
the duality of human psychology
Victorian society
consequences **of**
restrictive social mores
obsession with reputation
freedom versus conformity
secretive lives
so-called gentlemen
repressed emotion

Supporting Essay Writing Practice

2. Generic phrases to develop the rest of the essay:

To introduce examples of the writer's intentions:

When x [explain briefly what happens in the story]

the writer
intends to show us...
explores the idea/theme of...
characterises x as someone who...
creates a world in which...
uses the setting / character / relationship / symbol of x **to**
establishes a relationship which...
suggests...
implies...

To begin to explain the writer's intended impact:

creates a sense of...
allows us to see that...
encourages us to see that...
reflects the writer's attitude towards...
mirrors our society in that...
significant moment because...
meaningful moment because...
important moment because...

To develop the argument with further examples:

the idea is **also** reflected later/earlier when...
we also see this in...the setting / structure / language
another character that reflects this idea is x because

To conclude the essay

The writer
has crafted
immerses us in
a tale in which
we might learn to better appreciate/understand/value

Figure 7.7 A document that might be used to support practice

provides that or they can work it out independently) to be able to annotate it and select quotations. Although it does incorporate procedures like the one above, English is a knowledge-based subject.

Figure 7.7 is an example of a document that might be used to support literature essay writing practice. It includes some generic phrases but also offers suggestions for introducing key ideas within GCSE (General Certificate of Secondary Education) texts.

3. Early attempts might use just one fragment

Fragment: the duality of human psychology

Examples:
1. Stephenson explores **the duality of human psychology.**
2. **The duality of human psychology** is a major theme in Stephenson's novel.
3. Stephenson is interested in **the duality of human psychology.**

4. Later attempts will combine two fragments:

Fragment 1: duality of human psychology
Fragment 2: Victorian society

1. Stephenson explores the **duality of human psychology** and criticises aspects of **Victorian society.**
2. Stephenson explores the **duality of human psychology** and challenges aspects of **Victorian society.**
3. Stephenson challenges aspects of **Victorian Society** in this story about the **duality of human psychology.**

5. Later attempts will combine three fragments:

Fragment 1: duality of human psychology
Fragment 2: Victorian society
Fragment 3: restrictive social mores

1. Stephenson explores the **duality of human psychology** and wrestles with **the restrictive social mores** of **Victorian society.**
2. Stephenson's novel explores the **duality of human psychology**, challenging aspects of **Victorian society** and bemoaning its **restrictive social mores.**
3. Stephenson explores the **duality of human psychology** and critiques the **restrictive social mores** of **Victorian society.**

6. Later Attempts – a full introduction might look like:

Refers to the *Introduces major* *Could begin a response to any question*

Jekyll & Hyde
Stephenson uses the novel to explore the duality of human psychology and to criticise aspects of Victorian society. In a tale of freedom versus conformity, he shows us the consequences of restrictive social mores and an obsession with reputation. Exposing the secretive lives of so-called middle-class gentlemen, Stephenson reveals the repressed emotion lurking within mankind's innately evil spirit.

No quotations or

Figure 7.7 (Continued)

Now that we have some research principles on which to base our teaching, how do we begin to use this in our classroom practice to address persistent problems? How do we build discipline schemas that are well-organised, flexible and durable? The answer is that we need to plan for it and in simple terms, our general approach might be something like Figure 7.8, bearing in mind that there is much we can feed into this simple skeleton.

Evidence-informed approaches to enacting the curriculum

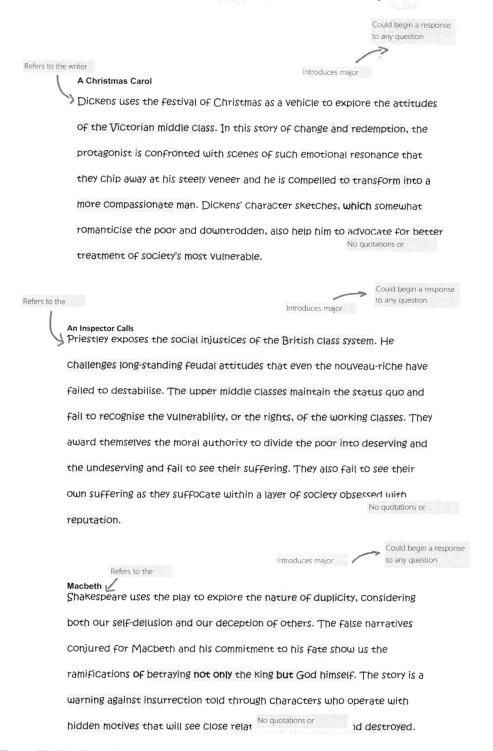

A Christmas Carol

Dickens uses the festival of Christmas as a vehicle to explore the attitudes of the Victorian middle class. In this story of change and redemption, the protagonist is confronted with scenes of such emotional resonance that they chip away at his steely veneer and he is compelled to transform into a more compassionate man. Dickens' character sketches, which somewhat romanticise the poor and downtrodden, also help him to advocate for better treatment of society's most vulnerable.

An Inspector Calls

Priestley exposes the social injustices of the British class system. He challenges long-standing feudal attitudes that even the nouveau-riche have failed to destabilise. The upper middle classes maintain the status quo and fail to recognise the vulnerability, or the rights, of the working classes. They award themselves the moral authority to divide the poor into deserving and the undeserving and fail to see their suffering. They also fail to see their own suffering as they suffocate within a layer of society obsessed with reputation.

Macbeth

Shakespeare uses the play to explore the nature of duplicity, considering both our self-delusion and our deception of others. The false narratives conjured for Macbeth and his commitment to his fate show us the ramifications of betraying not only the king but God himself. The story is a warning against insurrection told through characters who operate with hidden motives that will see close relat[...]d destroyed.

Figure 7.7 (Continued)

108 *Evidence-informed approaches to enacting the curriculum*

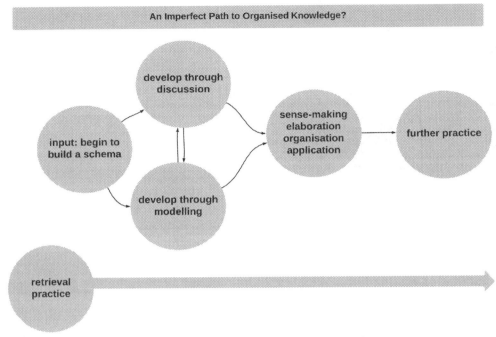

Figure 7.8 A representation of the main aspects of teaching English

Planning the lesson

We are now ready to consider actual classroom delivery. We're going to imagine that we're teaching an introductory lesson about the concept of *structure* in relation to text. Figure 7.9 provides some further details and associated images that we would use in this lesson.

Making initial choices

An individual teacher will have some initial choices to make. If we don't put the teacher in the driving seat, they can't learn and, probably, their pupils won't either. Making everyone follow someone else's presentation slides runs the risk of deskilling and disincentivising teachers. Many teachers are creative and want autonomy and that should be actively encouraged. In Chapter 10, we discuss how senior leaders might make judgements about teacher autonomy and levels of teacher guidance and support.

So, each individual teacher will need to decide how to deliver their lesson.

The start of the lesson: beginning to narrate the thread

To begin a lesson like this, we're going to want to give pupils the thread. A short sentence summarising what we'll learn is useful but this is *not* a traditional learning objective. Instead, it's a sentence that captures the thought we want pupils to own. Bear with us to see what we mean by that. It could also be written as an enquiry question but, depending on how the

Evidence-informed approaches to enacting the curriculum 109

Structure Unit 1
Title: What is structure?
Overview & Resources:
Key Knowledge for teachers to consider

When we think about structure, we think about how the organisation of ideas creates connections and patterns that contribute to meaning. In other words, how things are put together affects how we *understand* them. The meanings we make might be emotional, instinctive, visuo-spatial (as in enjambment being used to suggest an uncontrollable emotion, for example) and difficult to articulate in words. We might not consciously be aware that the process is even happening.

These are three separate images which actually have nothing to do with each other. However, because they all contain a pot, we can construct meaning. We can make a story out of them. In this order, the pictures suggest that the adult and child found a broken pot and worked together to mend it.

But, in this order, the exact same images are more suggestive of the idea that an adult and child actually made the pot. The pot was then smashed and, later, put back together.

Meaning is also influenced by the elements that are included. For example, because there is a child included, we might make the assumption that the child broke the pot because household accidents often happen when children play.

If we repeat the first image later in the sequence, we might read it differently the second time, even though it's the same picture. For example, they made the pot, broke it, and remade it together as well.

And, if we do it this way, the first image might not suggest a broken pot, it might suggest an ornate pattern. We might think that what happens next is that an adult gives the pot to the child, who then breaks it.

Figure 7.9 A rough outline script that might serve as a basis for a lesson introducing the concept of structure.

110 *Evidence-informed approaches to enacting the curriculum*

So, the elements included and the sequence of events influence how we make meaning.

Writers think carefully about sequencing. Imagine a writer wants us to feel sorry for a character, even though they've done something pretty bad. Here is a young girl who has bullied another pupil in her class. Which sequence makes us feel the most sympathetic to Sasha? Think first about what elements are included.

1	Sasha calls Sam names	
2	Sasha is bullied herself, by an older child	Sasha calls Sam names

Think about the sequence of events too. Which makes us feel more sympathetic to Sasha?

1	Sasha is bullied herself, by an older child	Sasha calls Sam names
2	Sasha calls Sam names	Sasha is bullied herself, by an older child

Figure 7.9 (Continued)

question is phrased, the most important ideas that we want pupils to focus on might become lost in something rather huge or rather vague. If it is phrased as a question, how will pupils know which part(s) of the answer are most useful or significant?

Compare these:

LO: to be able to define structure and give an example.

vs

Writers choose and organise their ideas.

Vs

How do writers choose and organise ideas?

The first sentence is a vague, woolly idea of something we have a sense our pupils need to know. It's poorly defined and won't help pupils remember anything; it's too long and it also introduces a word that they currently have no concept of (structure) so the word might feel meaningless or confusing at this point.

Evidence-informed approaches to enacting the curriculum 111

The second sentence is the actual abstract thought we want our pupils to own. The sentence is short enough to be processed fairly easily, and it only uses words that pupils are likely to have a sense of already. The teacher can keep referring to this sentence throughout the lesson. They can get pupils to repeat it, etc. It's memorable.

The third sentence is phrased as a question that has so many different possible answers, some more common than others, that it becomes rather too vast to comprehend, especially at this early stage of learning.

Planning to activate prior knowledge using retrieval practice

Then we will want to seamlessly flow into finding out what pupils might already know about structure. This is partly to activate that knowledge and prepare pupils for the new knowledge they will receive in the lesson. But we also want to draw out any possible misconceptions, such as that structure is really just a synonym for the word, 'layout'. Or confusions that arise from having heard the word in a different context, such as the *structure* of a building. We might do this through:

- Q&A
- a free recall activity where everyone simply writes down anything they know about structure.

Whatever we do, it shouldn't feel separate to the rest of the lesson. While lessons do inevitably have 'parts', dictating a specific formula is probably always too restrictive. And it might be dangerous to have teachers focusing on *parts* of lessons rather than seeing the lesson as an opportunity to immerse pupils in a cohesive learning experience. Lessons should feel whole, they should feel fluid. The fewer disruptions and transitions the better because those shifts can interfere with pupils' cognitive load and make learning harder.

The input phase: exploring the concept, as promised

We can keep narrating the thread. This is what we said we would teach today. The most obvious way to complete the input section of the lesson is to simply keep to the examples and explanations and deliver the piece as is – we could potentially even use it as a script. However, while scripting how we might explain a specific concept can be very useful, scripting an entire lesson *might* result in a lack of spontaneity that makes teaching less responsive than it should be. We might, therefore, use the initial explanation of structure. We want pupils to be thinking about what elements are included in each version of the stories in our example above, and how they are sequenced so that we can show them that such things matter – choosing and sequencing content influences the meanings we conjure. And if we think the explanation of structure is overly sophisticated for this point in the learning, which it probably is, we can simplify and focus the language just like we did with the learning objective.

Assume nothing!

We might need to remind pupils what we're talking about when we refer to *meaning* too. We tend to describe that by saying that writers have ways of helping us to understand things about characters, feelings and situations, and how they relate to real life. By '*meaning*' we are thinking of anything and everything we can learn from or about a text. If they haven't studied this at all, we might need to go back and do that first before tackling structure. Or it might be enough to just give a series of examples, e.g. *we understand that Scrooge is a miserly character who has redeemed himself by the end of the novella – Dickens has created that meaning for us.*

Modelling, exemplification and dual coding

It's important to remember that, in English, teachers are constantly **modelling thinking**. It might be done well or done poorly but it is almost constantly going on one way or another. In our subject, almost every time a teacher speaks, they are modelling the type of thinking in relation to texts that they would like pupils to be able to echo. Not *what* to think but *how*. Initially, we have to tell pupils what *we* think in order for them to see how we think, how we reached our conclusion. Thinking independently comes later. It's important we realise this or we ask pupils to be independent long before we've shown them how.

In this particular lesson, we would be inclined to keep the idea of having two versions of the exemplification process, one which is image-based and one which is written in words. Where a concept is expressed both visually and verbally, we are beginning to use dual coding, which might make learning more effective. We could create more examples if we are concerned there won't be enough here for pupils to grasp the ideas. Pupils who might struggle will tend to need more examples, straightforward ones, perhaps presented in relatively quick succession. This might provide a greater chance to see the abstract concept lying underneath the examples, although it will still need to be explicitly pointed out.

Checking understanding (as best we can)

As we move on in the learning, we will want to get a sense of whether the ideas are 'landing' or not. There are many ways to carry out a check for understanding and they must all be used with caution. It is impossible to truly measure what someone has learned. We are always measuring proxies for learning, e.g. how pupils perform in a test; how well they can answer a question in class, etc. The method offered as an example in this particular unit is one where pupils are invited to **finish a sentence**: *how a text is put together influences….* We might alter this so it becomes a **centre fragment** for pupils to work with: *…a text is put together influences…* Or, we might not use a fragment or starter at all. We might offer pupils a **multiple choice question with three options** for how the sentence *might* be finished, followed by a justification for why they selected their chosen option. In practical terms, pupils might complete the task by writing on a mini-whiteboard or in their books. Or we might invite them to **discuss it with a partner** and then listen to responses. All of these have their advantages and disadvantages. The point is, as teachers, we have plenty of individual scope.

Practice

The practice elements can also be changed, or added to, to make them more appropriate and/or responsive to the needs of a particular class.

After a few lessons introducing the concept, we would move to a longer text which has particularly good examples of the concept within it. Pre-reading this text – simply reading through the text with little or no time spent on analysis – enables all pupils to receive the full story and develop their own narrative schema around the text before they begin any in-depth analysis. It is an opportunity to develop a love of reading for pleasure. Pupils can then return to interesting and relevant moments to see how the writer created the text they have (hopefully) enjoyed.

The plenary will happen next lesson

This is in line with what is understood about retrieval practice – there is little point retrieving what we have just learned. Better to wait until next lesson, allowing pupils to start to forget.

During the lesson – overall tips

Perhaps the most important thing once the lesson is up and running is to manage attention and minimise distractions. This doesn't just mean addressing pupils' behaviour. It probably means:

- focusing on the main concept;
- signposting how each lesson element is meant to help pupils learn that concept;
- live modelling/drawing where possible;
- warmly confronting any misconceptions that come up.

Minimising distractions might also mean asking fewer but better questions, or at least ensuring that the questions encourage a greater depth of thinking rather than scatter-gunning questions that don't facilitate developed responses. It might mean exploring less of the vocabulary or reducing the length or complexity of an extract.

Those suggestions might seem counter-intuitive but we've recently observed a number of lessons where almost every other sentence spoken by the teacher was a question and a lot of those questions were repeated. It might seem engaging to be so interactive but so much interaction creates a lot of attentional shift. Pupils who struggle to concentrate might find this rather disorienting and exhausting because different people and ideas are competing and the brain does not have an inexhaustive capacity to process inputs from the environment. A calmer atmosphere where more attention is focused on the teacher for longer periods is often really rewarding for both staff and pupils. We suggest that, contrary to some ideas in circulation, pupils *like* listening to their teachers, especially when teachers talk about things they are passionate about. Why wouldn't they?

After the lesson

Be responsive. Teaching is not about ploughing on regardless just so that we cover what we think we have to cover. Coverage means nothing if pupils aren't actually understanding or retaining the understanding we're trying to pass on. If our teaching hasn't landed, we have a responsibility to go back in and try again, perhaps collaborating with someone or seeking advice before we do.

In summary

- Research can inform lesson delivery and make it more effective.
- We need to think about the most useful aspects of research for our subject and make sense of how we might meaningfully apply them.
- We need to think about how we will help pupils to make sense of, articulate and remember their learning.

We now need to think about how we might implement all of this in practice. There will need to be an effective programme in place to support this process. We explore this in the next chapter.

Teacher Insight

Charlotte Cowles, 2nd in English, Smithdon High School

Charlotte is an experienced English teacher who also has responsibility for developing reading in her school.

My relationship with teaching has been a complicated one. I qualified in my 20s and, after achieving Qualified Teacher Status, only lasted until the following February. Seven or eight years later, I was back teaching again and, that time, managed about four years before deciding it really wasn't for me. Necessity however dictated that I stayed in the profession, but it wasn't a happy time for me. I had no faith in what I was doing in the classroom.

Enter the knowledge-rich, conceptual curriculum, an approach which places the onus back on the teachers as professionals. The approach instantly made sense, from the introduction of a concept, modelling of the thought processes and great discussion through to an 'I do, we do, you do' approach to practice, building them up to exploring their own understanding. For me, this is teaching. We share, explore and secure knowledge. I model often short but highly ambitious responses and then, over time, help them develop their own processes. Because I am back to sharing my passion and love for English, I can see improved engagement in my students. Not only that but also because the process is logical and supported, my students are able to see improvements, which makes them more invested. Finally, because teaching makes sense again and planning and delivery is less cumbersome, I actually love and enjoy what I do on a daily basis.

Notes

1. Rosenshine, Barak, *Principles of Instruction*, American Federation of Teachers, viewed on 10th February 2021, https://www.aft.org/sites/default/files/periodicals/Rosenshine.pdf
2. Brewer, R., & Movahedazarhouligh, S. (2018). Successful stories and conflicts: A literature review on the effectiveness of flipped learning in higher education. *Journal of Computer Assisted Learning, 34*(1),1–8. https://doi.org/10.1111/jcal.12250
3. Kirschner, P. A., Sweller, J., & Clark, R. E. (2006). Why minimal guidance during instruction does not work: An analysis of the failure of constructivist, discovery, problem-based, experiential, and inquiry-based teaching. *Educational Psychologist, 41*(2), 75–86. https://doi.org/10.1207/s15326985ep4102_1

4 Kirschner, Paul (2016). Stop propagating the learning styles myth. *Computers & Education*, 106, 166-171, 10.1016/j.compedu.2016.12.006
5 Didau, D. (2019). *Making kids cleverer: A manifesto for closing the advantage gap.* Crown House Publishing, UK.
6 Mazenod, Anna, Francis, Becky, Archer, Louise, Hodgen, Jeremy, Taylor, Becky, Tereshchenko, Antonina, & Pepper, David (2019). Nurturing learning or encouraging dependency? Teacher constructions of students in lower attainment groups in English secondary schools. *Cambridge Journal of Education*, 49(1), 53-68. DOI: 10.1080/0305764X.2018.1441372
7 Sweller, J. (1988). Cognitive load during problem solving: Effects on learning. *Cognitive Science*, 12, 257-285.
8 Ebbinghaus, H. (2013). Memory: A contribution to experimental psychology. *Annals of Neurosciences*, 20(4), 155-156. https://doi.org/10.5214/ans.0972.7531.200408
9 Bjork, R.A., & Bjork, E. L. (1992). A new theory of disuse and an old theory of stimulus fluctuation. In A. Healy, S. Kosslyn, & R. Shiffrin (Eds.), *From learning processes to cognitive processes: Essays in honor of William K. Estes.* Erlbaum: Hillsdale, NJ.
10 Rosenshine, Barak, *Principles of instruction*, American Federation of Teachers, viewed on 10th February 2021, https://www.aft.org/sites/default/files/periodicals/Rosenshine.pdf
11 Brown, P. C., Roediger, H. L. III, & McDaniel, M. A. (2014). *Make it stick: The science of successful learning.* Belknap Press of Harvard University Press: Cambridge, MA.
12 Myatt, M., (2018). *Curriculum: from gallimaufry to coherence.* 1st ed. John Catt Educational Ltd: Woodbridge, UK.
13 ibid
14 Soderstrom, N. C., Kerr, T. K., & Bjork, R. A. (2016). The critical importance of retrieval - and spacing- for learning. *Psychological Science*, 27(2), 223-230. doi:10.1177/0956797615617778

8 How should we implement change?

In previous chapters we considered the research that might help us address persistent problems in English and argued that a concept-led curriculum might be the most effective way to do this. We suggested many schools might re-evaluate their provision, especially now that there is a new Ofsted focus on curriculum. One of the mistakes we have sometimes made in the past is to think of the design of a new curriculum as an end goal in itself – perhaps assuming that uploading long- and medium-term plans onto a shared drive was sufficient for teachers to be able to deliver it – and that our judgement of its effectiveness would be determined by pupils' results at the end of the year. We have tended to treat curriculum as a product or a one-off event.

Rather, the production of a newly designed curriculum plan is just the first stage in an ongoing process of implementation. Before we can expect teachers to be able to deliver it effectively in their classrooms, we need to assess their readiness and then plan for any training and support which may be required. We also need to acknowledge that our carefully designed curriculum plan will change the moment it is passed into the hands of teachers – and so it should, because the teachers themselves will need to *enact* the curriculum. They are the ones who will breathe life into it within their classrooms, making it relevant and meaningful for the pupils in front of them. A challenge for subject leaders is to ensure the balance between respecting the autonomy and creativity of teachers, while maintaining fidelity to the most important principles and content of their plan.

The readiness of teachers to deliver, and the training and support that will be required, are things which need to be considered before a new curriculum is rolled out, but these are the things we have tended to neglect. There have been understandable reasons for this. It often feels that there is little time in education for considered reflection, and instead we are under pressure to show instant impact. But while rushing things might lead to quick wins, it rarely leads to sustainable improvement.

If we are to break the cycle of constant change with little improvement, we need to spend more time planning to implement change.

What does the evidence tell us about effective implementation?

In their review of the research in *Putting Evidence to Work: A School's Guide to Implementation*,[1] the Education Endowment Foundation (EEF) makes six recommendations:

1 Treat implementation as a process, not an event; plan and execute in stages.
2 Create a leadership environment and school climate that is conducive to good implementation.

3   Define the problem you want to solve and identify appropriate programmes or practices to implement.
4   Create a clear implementation plan, judge the readiness of the school to deliver that plan, then prepare staff and resources.
5   Support staff, monitor progress, solve problems and adapt strategies as the approach is used for the first time.
6   Plan for sustaining and scaling an intervention from the outset and continually acknowledge and nurture its use.

Implementation is presented in Figure 8.1 as a cyclical process, incorporating four stages: Explore, Prepare, Deliver and Sustain. Over the following chapters, we will exemplify how this process may unfold within an English department.

The process of implementation of a new initiative might be of greater consequence than the quality of the initiative itself: we may have designed the most rigorous, detailed, research-informed English curriculum, but the measure of its success will be *how* we put it into practice.

Before the new curriculum we have carefully designed makes its way into our classrooms to be delivered to pupils, before its implementation begins, sufficient time needs to have been spent on the preceding stages, which the EEF determine to be 'explore' and 'prepare'. Essentially, the first stage is to identify the problem we are trying to solve and explore as

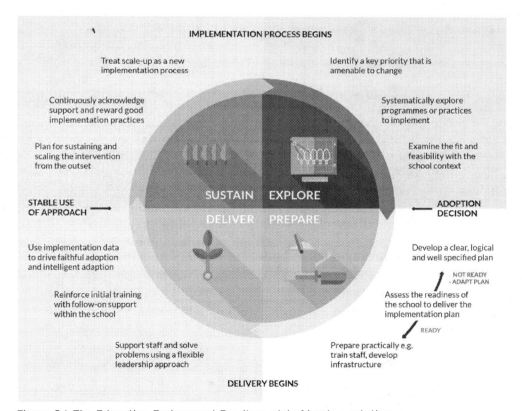

Figure 8.1 The Education Endowment Fund's model of implementation

many potential solutions as possible, considering which are most feasible within the context of our own school and/or across a whole trust. In relation to implementing a new curriculum, the 'problem' relates to the curriculum intent: what are we aiming to achieve, and why? Why this curriculum, in this school? How will it close the gaps we currently have? How do we envisage it being delivered, and why is this likely to be the best way? A pre-mortem might be helpful here. Pose the question, 'if this initiative were to fail, what would have gone wrong, and why?'. The answers will help to determine if this initiative is likely to be the right one.

The second stage, 'prepare', is a metaphorical pressing of the pause button to give ourselves time to reflect. We can consider whether the implementation plan is well-thought out and detailed enough to have a high chance of success, and how ready the department and teachers are to deliver the plan with fidelity.

In the past, curriculum design has often been seen as the responsibility of the Head of Department (HoD) or someone to whom they delegated the task. Rarely has it been a collaborative endeavour. Once the curriculum outline was handed over, it was usually up to teachers to put flesh on the bones by themselves, which is the kind of solo planning that characterises the experience of many teachers. An assumption is made that all teachers can translate an outline into effective lessons but before we ask them to, we need to pause and assess their readiness.

Once the delivery stage of an implementation begins, keeping a close eye on the fidelity with which plans become a reality is crucial, as is the provision of support, training and problem-solving as required. It might seem that all of this is incredibly time-consuming for an already very busy English department with many plates to spin, but let's consider what happens when we attempt to implement new ideas and initiatives without following each of these stages.

What happens when implementation fails: the cycle of planned failure

In *A Cambridge Approach to Improving Education*, Frank Achtenhagen's *Cycle of Planned Failure*[2] is used to exemplify the consequences of a poorly explored problem leading to the implementation of an ill-fitting solution and the perpetuation of the cycle of failure. The example given in the report is the replacement of coursework with controlled assessments. Many teachers will immediately recognise the context, where a system of assessment with tight rules and regulations was brought in to replace one which was considered unreliable. It was perhaps predictable that controlled assessment would not solve the problems created by the previous system, because the problem it was designed to address – unreliability of coursework data – had not been fully explored: the same issues of teacher accountability within a performativity culture – a culture where exam results dominate how teachers' effectiveness is measured – remained.

Let's consider a further example within the context of an English department. Imagine the scenario below. We chose this because we think many teachers will have experienced something like this in their own school.

- Year 11 mock exam results are analysed, and a significant number of pupils are at least two grades from their end of year target. In order to decide what actions to implement to improve pupils' performance, department leaders crunch the data.
- Question level analysis reveals that many pupils have underperformed on English Language Paper 1, Question 3,[3] with over half achieving four or fewer marks out of the

available eight, and for a large number this has prevented them from achieving in the next highest band.
- A department meeting is held, and strategies to improve performance on Question 3 are discussed; exemplar answers are analysed; teachers who examine this paper share their knowledge and expertise. Staff decide that all pupils will be taught to answer this question in a more uniform way, using a writing scaffold, which should help them to address the higher grade criteria.
- In the coming weeks, teachers deliver this approach to pupils.
- Following the next round of mock exams, the data is analysed again. A number of pupils have improved their performance on Question 3, but marks are inconsistent: while some pupils have gone up, others have stayed the same, and some have actually gone down. Overall, performance on Question 3 has improved, but marks for Question 4 have now decreased slightly.
- In the next department meeting, teachers will discuss what actions to implement to address underperformance on Question 4.

While the implementation of actions to address the problem appear to have had some impact – some pupils have improved their marks on Question 3 – it is unclear why some marks have decreased, and whether the improvements which have occurred are sustainable. Furthermore, a new problem has been created, in that some pupils are now underachieving on a different question, and the reasons are also unclear. Achtenhagen's *Cycle of Planned Failure*, Figure 8.2, can help us to unpick this scenario.

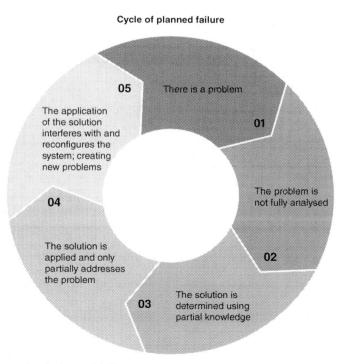

Figure 8.2 The cycle of planned failure

We think there continues to be a problem because the teachers did not accurately diagnose what was causing the underachievement. The real issue is not that pupils don't have an effective model for answering question 3. What is really going on is that they simply don't know enough about the concept of structure. This is a curricular deficit – a knowledge deficit; it has not arisen due to difficulties in acquiring the 'skill' of answering an exam question.

Why does this misunderstanding occur? Rather than having a rigorous curriculum into which exam practice fits and where we have predicted potential barriers, we tend to do exam practice without thinking of it as a function of curriculum. We treat it as something that happens *after* we've taught the curriculum. Because of this, as we'll try to demonstrate, we often misdiagnose what is really a curricular deficit as a lack of understanding of an exam question.

Let's look more carefully at how we inadvertently 'planned' to fail by not properly diagnosing the right underlying cause of pupils' difficulties.

1   **There is a problem**
    Pupils' performance on Paper 1 Question 3 is poor.

2   **The problem is not fully analysed**
    It is important to remember, as we discussed in Chapter 6, that any assessment is the testing of a sample from a larger domain. It would be impossible to assess the whole discipline of English so any assessment, formative or summative, is a sample. It provides a proxy for each pupil's wider learning. In English examinations, pupils apply their knowledge to a question and create a product – a written answer to that question. If we analyse the marks achieved by pupils, what we are really analysing is their ability to create that product. Based on their performance, we make inferences about their understanding of English, a whole discipline. Our inferences are useful to a point but they only help us to gauge a level of thinking about a particular task on a particular day.

    However, the product – the pupils' written response – is not in itself a very good diagnostic tool: it is a measure of performance – albeit, in the final examinations, a high-stakes one. It is a summative measure but not a particularly good formative one, in that it cannot tell us a great deal about the underlying gaps in knowledge and understanding that have caused the poor performance.

    A better way to analyse the underperformance is to look beyond the product itself to the thinking process employed in its creation, and to do that we need to consider what the examination question is really trying to assess. In this example, the question requires the pupil to explore the writer's use of structure in a previously unseen extract. We've argued that *structure* is a foundational concept in English. We also assert that for pupils to develop a disciplinary schema in the subject, the underlying concepts which form the discipline need to be broken down, explicitly taught and exemplified. To determine the underlying causes of the problem here, we need to dig deeper and ask:

    - *Do pupils understand the concept of structure? How do they explain it* **to themselves***? If we asked them to explain it to us, what might they say?*
    - *Where pupils are beginning to understand, what gaps might they still have in how they conceptualise structure? Have they seen a sufficient, and sufficiently broad, range of examples?*

- *What connections are they not yet making between structure and other foundational concepts? For example, in this exam question they often need to be able to see how structure connects with characterisation, or grammar and meaning?*

By analysing gaps in conceptual understanding, we can look to solutions which *genuinely* address what pupils need to learn to improve their performance. If we only look at their performance, any solutions are likely to be superficial, because we are dealing with the problem rather than its underlying causes.

3 The solution is determined using partial knowledge

Deciding to teach a writing scaffold assumes that pupils are not achieving well on the structure question because they don't know how to construct an answer that meets the requirements of the mark scheme. It may well be that this is true for some pupils, but even where that is the case, further practice of whole answers is unlikely to be the best way forward.

As we argued in Chapter 2, we don't get better at a 'skill' by practising the skill itself: as Daisy Christodoulou states in *Making Good Progress*,[4] runners don't train for a marathon by running marathons. What we might consider to be 'skills' in English are the result of the application of huge amounts of knowledge, including procedural knowledge but going far beyond it too. Practising the *component parts* which make up the 'skill' of answering Question 3, such as writing analytical sentence fragments using literary terminology, is far more likely to improve performance on the exam question than practising whole answers over and over again.

A further issue that ought to have been explored is the limitations of writing scaffolds. Most scaffolds in English are designed by looking at successful exam answers and extrapolating the things pupils did to achieve them, or by looking at the highest band criteria and trying to encapsulate high attainment. A common scaffold used for the structure question is 'At the beginning.../In the middle,.../By the end...'. This is designed to encourage pupils to cover all parts of the extract and to lead them to follow patterns throughout the text. However, the problem with any scaffold used to support essay writing is that it structures *writing* not the actual thinking processes behind it.

To be able to write, pupils need something to write *about*. Simply providing a writing frame may superficially improve writing but it will be superficial because sentence starters rarely promote thinking and can actually become a barrier to it. Such structures are not going to deepen a pupil's conceptual understanding of how a writer uses structure to create meaning. Instead, they need explicit teaching and exemplification of the concept itself – they need to know, for example, that structural choices, such as motifs, create patterns that contribute to meaning, and that other choices, such as foreshadowing and juxtaposition, also create meaningful connections.

Therefore, the solution to the problem proposed here – to try to improve exam performance through introducing a uniform approach to answering the exam question – is likely to fail, because it has been determined with partial knowledge of the problem. The real problem is that the majority of pupils do not have sufficient understanding of the concept of structure.

4. The solution is applied and only partially addresses the problem

One of the difficulties created by using exam performance as a diagnostic tool is in trying to isolate the factors which have improved performance. In this scenario, some marks have undoubtedly gone up – but it's not entirely clear which interventions have worked. Some pupils may have felt that having a clear writing scaffold was useful, because they lacked enough procedural knowledge of the exam paper requirements beforehand, and the scaffold has given them a format to structure their response that is more effective than the one they had before. Thus, the problem *appears* to have been partially addressed. **However, there is no way of knowing if it was the writing scaffold, or one or more of a number of other variables which led to their improvement.**

It is likely that something other than a writing frame has made the difference. For instance, teachers and pupils may now consider this question to be higher stakes and are giving it more attention than they had done previously. With a renewed focus on Question 3, teachers will likely have put a great deal of effort into the clarity of their explanations; perhaps they have used very careful modelling, or much clearer examples in their teaching. Maybe pupils have been shown more models of high attainment, or received more formative feedback in the lessons following the last mocks. Any or all of these factors could have contributed to higher marks for pupils who did perform better the second time around.

It also isn't clear yet whether the improvements are sustainable. To ensure that pupils who have improved continue to do so, and to support other pupils to make similar progress, we need to be able to identify the active ingredient(s) for improvement so we can replicate it. But in trying to extrapolate the specific intervention that worked, we need to be mindful of our tendency towards confirmation bias. It's tempting to believe that the things we put huge amounts of time and effort into are the things that worked. We might assume that, in this case, the writing scaffold led to the improvement, but it could have been the clarity of teachers' explanations, the additional modelling and thinking aloud – metacognition, in other words, instead of scaffolding.

Why does it matter which intervention worked, so long as the marks went up? In ascribing success to an intervention that only *appears* to work, we miss the true nature of the problem. The real problem here is a lack of modelling. Our failure to realise that, and address it, will mean that the problem perpetuates. And if, as in this example, the second set of mock examinations reveals a different picture – some pupils have improved but others have remained the same or got worse – we can be led to repeating the same mistakes. We can end up misdiagnosing the problem again – this time, the issue is underperformance in Question 4 – and applying a similarly sticking plaster solution. Only by addressing the underlying causes of these problems can we find solutions which fully address them. For example, pupils might need more quizzing on the concept of structure and/or more practice writing analytical sentences about it.

5   **The application of the solution interferes with and reconfigures the system, creating new problems**

Teachers may believe that the new writing scaffold has helped pupils with improved marks to succeed, and pupils may believe it themselves, and want to stick with it. But for pupils who were doing well before, a new approach may have caused confusion. If it becomes a department expectation that every teacher uses the new system, for some pupils this will mean changing the way they respond to this question type, even if what they were doing before was yielding results.

Likewise, some teachers may change their practice to incorporate the new method, perhaps in ways that are less effective for some pupils. Pupils may feel confused, and teachers frustrated, especially if they feel they have been forced to change what they saw as effective practice to do something that seems instinctively wrong. Even though some pupils have increased their marks in this series of mock exams, some have seen a decrease in marks on Question 4, and this creates a whole new set of problems. In response, we might stick with the writing scaffold and spend even more time re-teaching and practising it. Or, we might abandon question 3 and turn our attention to Question 4, given that it is worth significantly more marks. Either way, we are back at the beginning of the cycle.

The perpetuation of the cycle of failure in this scenario originates from a misdiagnosis of the problem. Summative assessment was used to make formative judgements: it was assumed that pupils who had performed poorly on a question had done so because they did not know how to construct an exam answer. The solution was therefore deemed to be the teaching of an exam strategy, using a writing scaffold, and more practise with it. But we are back to building the cabinet again: we are too focused on piecing together at product rather than developing the thinking process which lies behind it.

Underlying this surface-level solution is a deeper, persistent problem in English. We know that pupils often struggle to construct exam responses and that the structure question can seem particularly tricky, but let's consider again what we know from the evidence that might lead us to more than a partial solution.

Effective implementation: applying the evidence

As we have previously seen, any effective implementation is preceded by significant time spent identifying and exploring the problem it is designed to address. In the example we are considering, the cycle of planned failure could have been avoided by a more thorough examination of the issue and its context. Let's consider how evidence-based approaches could assist in this scenario.

Understanding the gaps: thinking about schema-building

In Chapter 2, we looked at how learning happens through the development of schemas. Cognitive science can help us to see why pupils commonly struggle with the structure question and assist us in clarifying the underlying causes of the problem. Pupils lack knowledge and understanding of the concept of structure: they don't see that writers are making conscious choices, and they haven't seen enough models or engaged in enough practice to have developed their schema. The real problem isn't necessarily an inability to articulate their ideas in the form of an exam answer, but a lack of organised, flexible knowledge they need to think with in the first place.

We need to consider gaps in teachers' schema here, too. It might be that some teachers don't yet have a grasp of the concept that is articulable – they may have an instinctive sense, perhaps, but don't find it easy to explain. This is a component of expertise-induced blindness: we systematically overestimate what others know and underestimate what we know ourselves. Likely, many teachers have been trained in a performativity and assessment-driven

124 *How should we implement change?*

system which has not prioritised subject-specific training. In examining the problem, we also need to consider what gaps in knowledge teachers may have which need to be filled – what do they know about assessment and performance, for example? Some teachers have gaps in their knowledge about the most effective ways to teach complex concepts in ways which develop pupils' discipline schema.

In order to facilitate this, leaders need to identify the current training needs of each department member and assess their current schemas around curriculum design and delivery. Shulman[5] states that effective teachers have three types of knowledge:

- content (their subject knowledge),
- pedagogical (knowledge of effective teaching strategies and approaches),
- pedagogical content (knowledge of how to effectively teach their subject to pupils).

This framework helps us to define the mental models we need to build in our teachers for them to be able to deliver our curriculum plan with fidelity by identifying any gaps in their current schema.

Figure 8.3 is a document we might share and discuss with teachers to explore the sorts of knowledge we might expect teachers and pupils to work through.

Having identified the knowledge gaps, we can begin to formulate a plan to address them. We are ready to begin the 'prepare' phase.

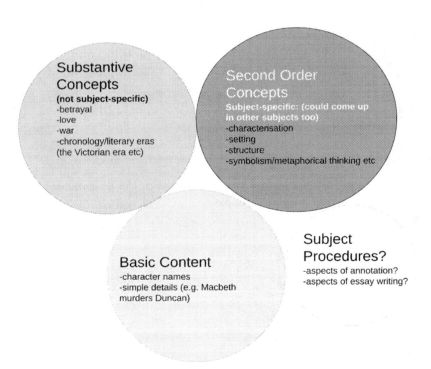

Figure 8.3 A representation we might share with teachers of the types of knowledge we can have in English

Developing a plan: 'tight but loose'

In the previous example, the implemented solutions were ill-fitting because they didn't address the root problem. In essence, teachers were being trained to teach exam technique but were not being encouraged to address gaps in underlying knowledge.

A plan to address this problem therefore needs to have at its core the active ingredients for successful implementation. The value of identifying the most important things to help us intervene successfully, is that it allows us to spend less time on the things which contribute the least to the success of the plan. Dylan Wiliam[6] refers to this as being 'tight but loose'.

In the scenario above, teachers' attention needs to be drawn to pupils' lack of conceptual knowledge. This might require some additional teacher training to help them identify the underlying conceptual knowledge and a series of useful examples. Their own schemas, therefore, might need developing in order that they might help pupils.

So, a successful approach to implementing something new is to work out what the problem really is and then work out what support teachers might need in order to address it. This is where we need to be tight – we need a tight focus on practical ways to move teachers on. We might be loose on the specific approaches and examples a particular teacher uses to approach the exam question in future, as long as we think they have the conceptual knowledge which underpins effective concept-led teaching.

All of this might seem time-consuming but as we see here, a misdiagnosis of the root problem led to the perpetuation of the cycle of failure. All the time was wasted anyway.

Planning to evaluate

It might seem counter-intuitive to think about evaluating something before we even deliver it – often evaluating is something we do after the event, or not at all. Or, most likely, we look to pupils' mock examination results. The problem with this is that by the time we receive exam results, it is too late to make any adaptations to the plan: results will always be what Wiliam refers to as a 'lagging indicator' of success. And so many things can impact results – so how can we know that what we're doing is working? We need to do think about how we'll measure the success of an intervention during the 'prepare' stage – as part of a clear, specific plan. We need to consider how we will check the progress of our intervention along the way and what tools we will use. Two useful pieces of research can assist us with this.

Leading and lagging indicators

We have briefly mentioned a lagging indicator – summative assessment results will always be 'lagging' behind other potential indicators because they arrive months, if not years, after a new curriculum is implemented. But Wiliam also suggests that 'leading indicators' can help us to assess the likely success of an implementation by identifying the things we should be looking for along the way. We don't have to wait for the results. This way, we have time to intervene and make changes to the plan, rather than waiting until it is too late to make a difference. Some examples of leading indicators we might look for in the early stages of implementing a new curriculum are:

- Clear goals are *shared* by teachers (for example, everyone is keen to embed retrieval practice).
- Observance of teachers adopting pedagogical strategies, preferably by subject specialists who are research-informed. Observation can go badly, particularly when it happens out of subject or by someone whose understanding of pedagogy is not secure.
- Discussions and meetings are more focused on teaching and learning.
- Staff spontaneously talk about concepts as well as texts.
- Resources produced by teachers show familiarity with cognitive science.

Planning to measure teacher professional development: the Guskey framework

Preparing for curriculum delivery should include the design of a curriculum for teacher learning which develops their expertise. Measuring the success of a subject curriculum also, then, needs to include evaluating the learning and expertise of teachers.

It is important to reiterate, here, that it is the *professional development* we are evaluating here – not the performance of the teacher. Teachers' classroom practice is a proxy for making inferences about the impact of training we have delivered. By observing teaching, we aim to draw some conclusions about gaps teachers may have in their mental models. Rather than checking a box against their performance management standards, we use this approach to gain useful information that refines and improves the training we give them.

The Guskey framework[7] is a helpful planning mechanism for thinking about how we might evaluate the quality of teacher professional development. We've found this model useful because it goes beyond the idea of results, staff surveys and lesson observations to measure teacher learning. Instead, it offers a way to think about *planning* training by thinking about what we want pupils to understand and be able to do. Guskey states that 'professional learning that increases educator effectiveness and results for all students uses a variety of sources and types of student, educator, and system data to plan, assess, and evaluate professional learning'. Five levels of useful data are identified:

1 Participants' reactions
2 Participants' learning
3 Organisational support
4 Participants' use of new knowledge and skills
5 Pupil learning

This framework helps us to see that, just as we do with pupil learning, we need to plan for teachers' learning by identifying the outcomes we hope to achieve and planning backwards.

We can apply the same framework to overhauling an entire curriculum, which might look something like this:

How should we implement change? 127

A suggested approach to planning curriculum implementation: key points

1 **Explore**
   - Define your vision by identifying the desired outcomes, e.g. closing the gap for disadvantaged pupils.
   - Identify persistent problems to be addressed, both their symptoms and underlying causes.
   - Consider the fit and feasibility of the implementation in your school context and the likely scope for success. For example, what is the climate for learning in the school? What is the level of experience and expertise among staff? Would external support be useful?

2 **Prepare**
   - Develop a clear, specific plan for implementation and identify the active ingredients for success.
   - Assess the readiness of your team. What training mechanisms will you employ? Which are best suited to the outcomes you are aiming for – training days, coaching, co-creation of resources, or a combination of these? Who is equipped to lead it? How equipped is everybody else?

3 **Plan to Deliver**
   - How will staff be supported in delivery? For example, what resources might need to be created? Who will drive the strategy and what is the process? Who is presenting the ideas to teachers and how will they establish their credibility and build rapport? How will training be reinforced?
   - Plan how you will collect implementation data to ensure fidelity to the active ingredients and any adaptations which need to be made.

4 **Plan to Sustain**
   - Plan to sustain and scale up from the outset. Consider piloting something with one school or department and what the next steps would be for scaling up. Be realistic about what is achievable. Moving too quickly is likely to create problems.
   - Identify leading and lagging indicators of success. Pupils' examples will always lag behind other indicators of success. Leading indicators might include changes in teachers' behaviour and attitude with increased use of pedagogical strategies. We discuss more about how to measure the impact of a curriculum in Chapter 9.

In summary

- Implementation is a process, not an event.
- It should be rigorously planned for and continually reviewed.
- Any new initiative should address defined problems or needs within a school or department. It is important that problems are explored carefully enough that the correct underlying cause is identified.
- The implementation of a curriculum needs to consider the readiness of teachers to deliver it and should plan to address training needs.

In the next chapter, we will consider how we might support teachers to enact our curriculum plans.

Case study: Olly Mackett, Director of English

Olly Mackett leads English across a Trust of four secondary schools. We began working with Olly and his teams in 2018 to support them in developing and implementing a new knowledge-rich, concept-led curriculum. So far, it has been rolled out across Key Stage 3, with work ongoing at Key Stage 4.

I am incredibly lucky to work across four secondary schools with passionate and dedicated teams. We are on a fluid and continuing journey together to improve our curriculum in English.

Standing in front of an entire Trust of English teachers can be very daunting. Everybody has his or her own perception of what the English curriculum should look like, and which books should or should not be taught. English teachers, rightfully so, deeply care about which texts will be involved. But before you reach this stage, a number of things need to happen first to ensure success and buy-in from staff.

When we embarked on this journey, the first thing we needed to do was to assess our current English curriculum across the schools. Broadly, they were aligned at KS4 but were incredibly different at KS3. This was part of a wider Trust process in assessing the whole curriculum. Also, with one of our schools being involved in testing the new OfSTED framework, we had some insight into the deep dive process which helped guide our own assessments.

We started as a core team of HoDs working with Zoe and Sam, deciding how our curriculum would be sequenced. These conversations were fantastic! We discussed how foundation concepts could be sequenced, but then questioned how you might foreground them successfully while not neglecting others. In partnership, over time, we were able to have a really clear idea what the long-term overview of our KS3 curriculum would be, how it built from KS2 and led to KS4 and beyond.

Then, the discussions surrounding what texts best exemplified our concepts began. We asked for suggestions of extracts from our teams but we sat down as HoDs to make the final decisions on the longer texts we were using to exemplify the concepts. The staff must question these decisions. Why that particular text and not this one, for example? Why this extract? This was a really important way to achieve 'buy-in' from teams as their leaders were heavily involved in this process. Concessions had to be made but we came to an agreement where the HoDs agreed on the texts.

We continued to work closely with Zoe and Sam as they 'fleshed-out' our long-term curriculum into carefully sequenced, detailed knowledge by having an open dialogue throughout about what would work and what might need changing to fit our individual contexts. We reached a point where we had a very detailed, very carefully sequenced curriculum on paper. But a curriculum isn't paper. The curriculum is the teacher.

For the delivery of the English curriculum to be successful across the Trust, we would need our staff to make changes to their practice and continue to develop it. One way we approached this was through coaching of staff in each of the schools. In each team, two staff members were carefully selected to receive individual, tailored coaching relative to their knowledge and understanding of the delivery of this new curriculum. Even a teacher who has been teaching a number of years might still be a novice in particular aspects. Coaching has been incredibly beneficial for staff and they have then been better able to support their colleagues in their respective schools.

Currently, we are at a point where our curriculum needs evaluating. We need to not be afraid to ask questions along the way. Why is this working really well? Why is this not working? We now have the benefit of a clear action plan in place, so we can continue embedding our English curriculum and assessment across our subject, and our students can achieve the very best outcomes.

Notes

1 Education Endowment Foundation (2019). *Putting evidence to work – a school's guide to implementation*, viewed on 10th February 2021, <https://educationendowmentfoundation.org.uk/tools/guidance-reports/a-schools-guide-to-implementation/>
2 Cambridge Assessment (December, 2017). *A Cambridge approach to improving education*, viewed on 11th December 2020, <https://www.cambridgeassessment.org.uk/Images/cambridge-approach-to-improving-education.pdf>
3 AQA GCSE English Language Paper 1, Question 3. This question is always: 'How has the writer structured the text to interest you as a reader.'
4 Christodoulou, D. (2017). *Making good progress?: the future of assessment for learning*. Oxford University Press: Oxford.
5 Shulman, L. (February, 1986). Those who understand: Knowledge growth in teaching. *Educational Researcher, 15*(2), 4-14.
6 Wiliam, D. (2016) *Leadership for teacher learning: Creating a culture where all teachers improve so that all students succeed*. Learning Sciences International:, West Palm Beach, FL.
7 Guskey, T. R., Roy, P., & von Frank, V. (2014). *Reach the highest standard in professional learning: Data*. Corwin: Thousand Oaks, CA.

9 Resource design – supporting teachers to enact the curriculum

We now have our vision of a curriculum so in the 'prepare to deliver' phase, we need to translate our intent into working documents that teachers can use, and we need to consider the readiness of our staff to deliver the curriculum. In Chapter 3, we argued that curriculum is a manifestation of an expert schema. We can't assume all teachers share these mental models. English teachers come from such a wide variety of backgrounds – some have literature degrees, others may have studied journalism, etc. – and it's such a vast subject that it is impossible for any of us to be experts in all of it. We need to build mental models. We need to secure a level of conscious competence so that teachers don't just know what to do, they know how and *why*.

The process might be broken down into three key steps:

1 Subject leaders create long-term plans to show and teach staff how a disciplinary schema might be developed across the course of study.
2 From this, medium-term plans are designed. These help to create parity in terms of the diet each pupil receives. It can also be used to arm teachers with the knowledge of conceptual and cognitive science approaches which best align with English teaching, if these are embedded in the design.
3 Teachers are supported to interpret medium-term plans into a learning pathway for their pupils. This allows some autonomy and gives breathing space for responsive teaching without things becoming too far removed from the original curriculum design and intention.

We would argue that an 'off-the-peg' curriculum is not generally the best approach, although they can improve upon whatever existed prior to their introduction. However, we tentatively suggest that at the very least, they require a careful process of refinement to suit the teachers and the school context. There needs to be genuine understanding of why elements have been included in an externally designed curriculum, and why they have been sequenced in a particular way, in order for staff to buy in to the approach and deliver it authentically. If teachers aren't involved and a curriculum approach is simply thrust upon them, they will be far less able to deliver it in a way that has fidelity to the original concept and, often, they might be somewhat less willing to try.

Embedding a new curriculum is a long game and leadership teams can expect no quick fixes. But that doesn't have to be a problem. Curriculum design and resource creation are training opportunities and as many staff should be involved as possible for as long as possible. It doesn't mean all staff will necessarily have equal input or that all staff will be involved in every level of planning. That would be impractical and perhaps undesirable. Experienced teachers with both very good subject knowledge and good pedagogical content knowledge ought to be leading the way. It might be that a small number of teachers need to be trained up first, perhaps by external experts, before the rest of the teaching staff are involved.

Let's look at the three planning stages we identified above in a bit more detail.

What does effective planning look like?

Effective long-term planning has to be more than just the notes a Head of Department (HoD) might have in their head jumbled into some sort of order, perhaps scattered into lots of boxes on a large piece of paper. It has to be coherent and detailed enough for teachers, new and experienced, to understand each element and the connections between those elements well enough that they could then explain it to someone else. We include an example in Chapter 3 but there is no one way to lay this out. As long as staff can see the thinking behind the elements included and are able to interrogate the sequencing, it doesn't matter what it looks like.

Once we've developed a long-term plan or curriculum overview, whatever it looks like, success will depend upon faithful implementation. This means involving staff as much as possible in the next stages of development. The long-term plan needs to become some sort of meaningful medium-term plan. And those plans need to balance creating some parity so that all pupils have similar experiences with ensuring what is designed leaves space for teachers to be autonomous, to enact the curriculum in a way that suits them and their pupils.

The process of designing those medium-term plans should also consider any persistent problems that need addressing, including common misconceptions that pupils might have about the learning. Finally, it needs to draw upon the research we began to explore in Chapter 2 and be effective in building towards an expert schema in our subject.

Revisiting the research – Do staff know the underlying science?

Research offers us a sort of list of ingredients that we might need to include in our teaching. The structure is essentially: a retrieval and input phase, and then a 'model, practice, feedback' phase. That doesn't mean that lessons must always contain all these elements. There will be times when it's appropriate to spend the whole lesson on one element, or two elements. Flexibility allows teaching to be responsive. However, each learning cycle – however many lessons it might take – will probably have:

- An element of retrieval practice to help pupils remember their learning.
- An input phase where we share our expert knowledge with pupils. This knowledge needs to be meaningful, clear and organised. In our subject, it's useful to always remember that the 'marathon' we are always training for is the ability for pupils to think through an entire essay on their own. In other words, they need to be able to use a text to explore an

abstract concept using examples from that text. We might ask ourselves, how does this learning need to be sequenced to help pupils? They need to:
- Understand the abstract concept(s).
- Understand the examples that illustrate the abstract concept(s).
- See connections between abstract concepts. For example, how genre and theme are connected to each other and to a writer's overall intention.

But to achieve this they also need to:
- Understand what is the most important thing to know about this concept or this text.
- Understand how knowledge is connected – how do the examples connect to the abstract idea?

- Some dual coding during this phase might be useful so that abstract concepts are explained using visual metaphors where possible, and word diagrams can be used to map thinking.
- Explaining things off the top of our heads is difficult so, to avoid misconceptions, some scripting of key explanations.
- Some modelling of the thinking processes (even if the task is writing an essay, it's the thinking processes we are modelling; after all, writing is a *thinking* process).
- Opportunities to practice the thinking (which may or may not involve a writing task).
- Some sort of feedback.
- Checking for understanding, as best we can. This will always be a proxy, not an exact science. And it won't mean that pupils will remember everything we've taught them without us having to revisit.
- Opportunities for pupils to make predictions and imagine scenarios. We want to provide time for reflection and time to experiment.
- An awareness of the need to manage pupils' attention and manage cognitive load.
- We advocate teaching mixed ability but where pupils are in sets, all of the above applies. We also need for the 'bottom' sets to be:
    - Trusted to achieve.
    - Taught abstract concepts with a laser focus.
    - Be explicitly made aware of how the knowledge they are learning is organised. What is the hierarchy? How do the pieces connect? Low structure builders might struggle to see this without explicit teaching.
    - Asked potentially fewer, but better chosen, questions to maintain attention on what really matters and avoid too many distracting interjections.
    - Shown more, not fewer, examples of the main concept we're teaching, starting simpler and rapidly increasing in complexity
    - Taught well-chosen, core vocabulary using a lot of repetition and practice so that they understand the relevant accompanying syntax and can actually use the words they're learning.
    - Given lots of repetition and retrieval practice to counter any deficits in working memory.
    - Given short, focused practice tasks based on **high quality** models. As a side note, 'bottom' sets are often given very poor models in the misguided belief this will make it easier for them. It won't. They're essentially practising the wrong thinking. For example, to start with, we might only ask pupils to practice explaining a writer's overall intention in relatively simple terms:

o   ... *is exploring what it's like to...*
   But we teach this construction repeatedly and expect pupils to use it. The point is that it is sophisticated enough to appear in a high-quality essay. Later we can teach them to add a little more explanation, then to add an example, then to add and *explain* their example, etc. An essay is comprised of a thesis statement and some worked examples of the theory we're trying to espouse. This is the marathon we are training for.

One of the barriers that we might have to achieving all this with our pupils is that teachers might not all be in a position to deliver this straight away. We need to model it for them, just as we model learning for pupils.

One way to do this that we have experimented with is to design teacher booklets that act as models of lessons that include all of the above. The booklet becomes both a medium-term plan and a model for short-term planning too. Where we've done this, we've tried to do so with a keen eye on ensuring that the teachers have space to adapt what they've been given, but they at least have detailed guidance, including models of thinking. Teachers can struggle to be metacognitive so we need to help them.

How do we break down the long-term plan into medium-term plans? Teacher booklets *might* be the answer

Teacher booklets might be a very useful way of dealing with some persistent problems, problems such as teacher subject knowledge (lack thereof), lack of parity, teachers not knowing enough about research-informed pedagogy. This is a very different approach to the kind of lists of 'things to teach' we often see in medium-term plans where detail is often lacking and individuals might feel very much left to their own devices.

Teacher booklets can also help maintain teacher autonomy while at the same time ensuring that pupils all have access to the same high-quality knowledge and practice. The teacher knowledge booklets broadly illustrate what teachers should cover and also include some loose elements to include in delivering it to ensure that relevant approaches from cognitive science, such as retrieval practice, are embedded. But there is space to be adaptable and responsive. It's an attempt to present a 'tight but loose' approach of the kind Dylan Wiliam advocates.[1]

In creating booklets for teachers, we have adopted some principles of design to help steer us towards an effective resource that can be used year on year. A booklet like this might be more or less prescriptive depending on the needs of the department. Any booklet needs a central organising principle and some active ingredients.

Nine principles of design

1   Teachers and teacher educators will **emphasise thinking rather than doing**; pupils will be encouraged to remember, connect and articulate their learning.
2   The knowledge of all the English teachers in the department should be pooled in order to find the **highest value knowledge** and the best examples of what we want to teach.
3   The aim is to **build pupils' disciplinary schema**, via the concepts selected, with an eye on how the domain will be sampled in a high-stakes exam. This means drawing on curricular knowledge in terms of exam specification and where pupils need to get to by end

of GCSE (General Certificate of Secondary Education) but it does not mean teaching to the exam. To do this, consider the aspects of English that the exam assesses. For example, teach the concept of structure rather than focusing on teaching Language Paper 1, Question 3. That means exploring the structure of a series of poems and other texts to identify common approaches without requiring pupils to do an exam question. We could explore a series of works that all use a cyclical structure, for example. Doing exam questions in KS3 takes the focus away from thinking about structure and its relationship with meaning, and beginning to articulate ideas about it through discussion, writing careful sentences or doing partial completion diagrams, and puts that focus squarely on creating a product – an essay response – which pupils are not really ready to pull together.

4. The booklets **must be adaptable by the teacher. The teacher enacts the curriculum** and their teaching needs to be responsive to their pupils. (It just helps to have a very solid exemplification document on which all practitioners base their classroom practice.)

5. Resources **should be informed by research and should map out the intention to develop schema** and explicitly refer to retrieval practice, explicit modelling, examples of deliberate practice and high quality, carefully selected examples of dual coding, etc. Teachers will still switch to using their own versions of this but they might not know how to if no models are provided.

6. In general, there should not be a separate resource for 'bottom set' pupils. Where 'bottom sets' exist, teachers can be trained to adapt an existing resource so that the highest value knowledge is condensed and repeatedly exemplified. These pupils need focus, repetition and exemplification and lots of practice with **the same concepts everyone else is learning about**. These will be of benefit to all pupils, but especially those who might struggle most. For example, if we were teaching 'Animal Farm', we might front up the idea of oppression, teach it explicitly and frame every lesson around it so that pupils could see characters and events as manifestations of that theme. Each character is discussed in terms of the most important themes rather than trying to explore everything about them. In our experience, pupils will remember characters and plot more easily this way anyway, because everything they learn is firmly and explicitly attached to the same thematic concept.

7. The resource will flag up the best opportunities to **reflect back to prior knowledge earlier in the course or pre-empt knowledge coming later** in the course.

8. The resource will predict **common misconceptions** or oversimplifications pupils present in relation to the learning so that teachers can take action to prevent this. For example, many pupils oversimplify the characterisation of Lady Macbeth, seeing her as evil, and/or seeing her as wholly responsible for Macbeth's behaviour. We can prepare staff for this possibility.

9. The booklet will provide **detailed examples of modelling and deliberate practice**. For example, we might have scripted tasks and offer examples of sentence practice.

How do we *start* a booklet so that all staff understand the central organising principle?

Whether a booklet is to be based around a particular GCSE text, or around a particular second-order concept, it needs to be framed in some way, and we suggest creating pages at the beginning that help teachers understand the big idea.

Figures 9.1 and 9.2 show examples of pages from teacher knowledge booklets exploring a key GCSE text, which illustrate how we might plan to explore a 'big idea' with a department.

Figure 9.1 focuses on 'attaching' a thematic concept to the foundational concept of characterisation. Figure 9.2 is an example of how we might think through essay planning, and the intention here is to show how an overarching idea manifests within themes and characters, etc. Both pages can be used directly with pupils.

To support the idea of building knowledge around a second-order concept, let's take a look at Figures 9.3 and 9.4, taken from the opening of a booklet about structure. It is quite a prescriptive guide but is useful in getting staff on the same page. They could co-construct these essential introductions. Such detail is also useful where staff are very inexperienced

expose (v.)
early 15c., "to leave without shelter or defense," from Old French *esposer*, "lay open, set forth, speak one's mind, explain" (13c.), from Latin *exponere* "set forth, lay open, exhibit, reveal, publish" Meaning "to exhibit openly" is from 1620s; that of "to unmask" is from 1690s. Related: *Exposed; exposes; exposing*.

Priestley uses his play, *An Inspector Calls*, to expose the injustice of the class system

injustice (n.)
late 14c., from Old French *injustice* "unfairness, injustice" (14c.), from Latin *iniustus* "unjust, wrongful, unreasonable, improper, oppressive," from *in-* "not" + *iustus* "just"

class system
"to divide into classes, place in ranks or divisions"
"to organise the universe into parts"

Each character contributes something to Priestley's big idea

Eva Smith
Although we never actually see Eva, she is a very important character. She represents the suffering of the working classes who have to live in an oppressive and unjust class system. But she also represents their energy and strength. Her downfall reminds us that self-sufficiency fails at some point, if you're poor.

The Inspector is not real. He is a mythologised character who functions somewhat like a Greek chorus in the sense that he helps us make sense of events and frames our reactions to characters. He reminds us of Priestley's most important idea: "We are all members of one body. We are responsible for each other." But he might also suggest that attaining it is probably impossible. Just like his own mysterious existence, he represents a mythological, a world of peace and equality, a world that can never really come true. It is an ideal we can only imagine, like the Inspector himself.

Mr Birling represents the failure of the nouveau riche to destablise the feudal attitudes of the upper classes He is a self-made industrialist who could have challenged their hold on things and made really changes for the poor. But instead, he buys into feudal ideals of status; he longs for his knighthood. He represents those who saw the workers simply as a means to make money. He also reveals their arrogance and naivety. Priestley humiliates Birling by showing how little he truly knows, such was his disappointment in men like this.

Mrs Birling represents the upper middle class (almost aristocratic) old world view of society. She is the embodiment of the feudal attitudes Priestley rages against. She sees herself as a moral authority and divides the poor into deserving and undeserving. She believes that good manners are a way of showing that wealth and status are well-deserved. Priestley humiliates her as a poor mother for not realising her son, Eric, is Eva's father.

Sheila Birling represents the younger generation, who have the opportunity to reflect on how things are and make changes in the world. She also symbolises the increasing independence of women of her status in this era. Unfortunately, her failure to decisively separate from Gerald despite his infidelity suggests that even this great hope has limitations. We are reminded how difficult it is for even the best of us to change, so ingrained are the feudal attitudes that permeate our society.

Eric Birling represents the younger generation and the sense of the same unlikely hope of change we see in Sheila. He also exposes the continuing patriarchy, where men easily exploit women, even if they do regret it later on. And he is shows the lack of closeness and intimacy in upper middle class families. His frustration with his parents is a constant source of fury. He is indulged and indulgent but not truly happy.

Gerald Croft is the son of Sir and Lady Croft. He represents the indulgent nature of the upper classes and their resistence to change over time. Although he is of the younger generation, he cannot see the world ever changing in the way that Sheila and Eric might. And he representes the ever-present threat of those feudal attitudes perpetuating down the generations. He, and those like him, are a significant barrier to change. Although he seems to feel some embarrassment about the betrayal of his wife and his exploitation of Eva, he may well see his awful behaviour as a natural consequence of privilege. It's just the way the world is. After all, lots of 'gentlemen' had mistresses.

Edna, the maid serves as a constant reminder of the hierarchy. She allows us to watch Mrs Birling interact with the working classes - mainly by using them to show off her own good manners and benevolence. Edna also represents a different kind of working class mentality to Eva. She seems to passively accept her lot in life, which makes her acceptable in Mrs Birling's eyes.

Figure 9.1 A sample page from a teacher knowledge booklet exploring characterisation in terms of a thematic concept

136 *Resource design*

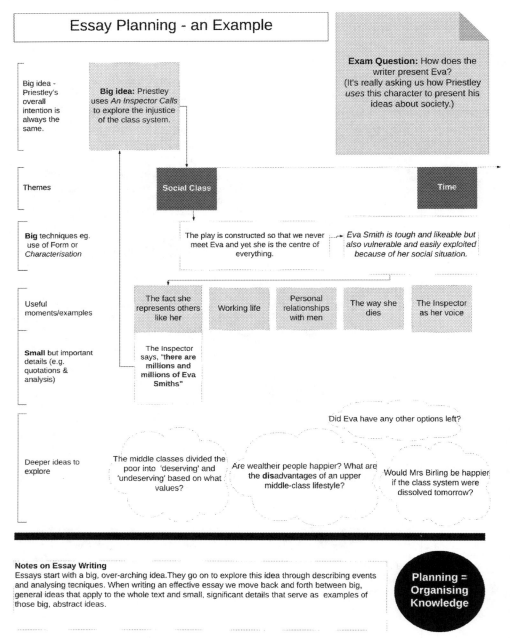

Figure 9.2 A sample page from a teacher knowledge booklet which attempts to map essay planning

or where they haven't really taught concepts before and might need further exemplification. Anyone who is learning anything, whether they are already a qualified teacher or not, needs explicit modelling and exemplification in order to learn.

If we were exploring symbolism, we might give the teachers some useful notes about what they might say about this concept (Figure 9.5).

The whole 'script' would not necessarily be read or shown to pupils.

When we think about structure, we think about how the organisation of ideas creates connections and patterns that contribute to meaning. In other words, how things are put together affects how we *understand* them. The meanings we make might be emotional, instinctive, visuo-spatial (as in enjambment being used to suggest an uncontrollable emotion, for example) and difficult to articulate in words. We might not consciously be aware that the process is even happening.

These are three separate images which actually have nothing to do with each other. However, because they all contain a pot, we can construct meaning. We can make a story out of them. In this order, the pictures suggest that the adult and child found a broken pot and worked together to mend it.

But, in this order, the exact same images are more suggestive of the idea that an adult and child actually made the pot. The pot was then smashed and, later, put back together.

Meaning is also influenced by the elements that are included. For example, because there is a child included, we might make the assumption that the child broke the pot because household accidents often happen when children play.

If we repeat the first image later in the sequence, we might read it differently the second time, even though it's the same picture. Eg they made the pot, broke it, and remade it together as well.

And, if we do it this way, the first image might not suggest a broken pot, it might suggest an ornate pattern. We might think that what happens next is that an adult gives the pot to the child, who then breaks it.

So, the elements included and the sequence of events affect how we make meaning.

Figure 9.3 Introducing the concept of structure to pupils

138 Resource design

Writers think carefully about sequencing. Imagine a writer wants us to feel sorry for a character, even though they've done something pretty bad. Here is a young girl who has bullied another pupil in her class. Which sequence makes us feel the most sympathetic to Sasha? Think first about what elements are included.

1. Sasha calls Sam names

2. Sasha is bullied herself, by an older child | Sasha calls Sam names

Think about the sequence of events too. Which makes us feel more sympathetic to Sasha?

1. Sasha is bullied herself, by an older child | Sasha calls Sam names

2. Sasha calls Sam names | Sasha is bullied herself, by an older child

Figure 9.4 Introducing the concept of structure to pupils

Symbolism: connotation, imagery and metaphor

Aim – To use a range of examples to help students understand that **writers create symbols to explore themes that are important to them. (Or even just** *writers use symbols to express ideas*)

Explaining **symbolism** to pupils:
- This concept is really broad and should be taught authentically as such. Literary symbols are an extension of a kind of thinking we do anyway. Our language and culture are full of symbols, some of them dating back to a time before most people could read. We might think of banners and emblems used in battle, or the signs we see on pubs. Popular idioms such as 'it's raining cats and dogs' are also interesting to explore. That said, literature has evolved to contain many **shared symbols** – things that people who read a lot can easily recognise and interpret. This is just the same as someone who practices solving crosswords becoming able to see patterns in the phrasing of the questions that help them to see solutions. We are not born knowing that light can symbolise truth and realisation. Some of us learn to recognise patterns through osmosis if we read a lot. Some never will, regardless of how much they read. Teaching must be explicit and we can't expect all pupils to guess and guess correctly every time.
- Symbols might be expressed through language choices (these are usually image-based but might not be – for example, a writer might be said to use phonetic spelling to symbolise a character's class), through structural choices (for example, using a cyclical structure to suggest the characters are trapped in some way, that history is destined to repeat etc), through characterisation (a character might be a particular trope used to symbolise a certain idea) through setting (like the farm in *Animal Farm*) or anything else.
- **The writer's attitude towards their subject matter** is extremely important knowledge to explore in the academic study of English. Their use of symbols relates to the themes they want to explore.
- Non-fiction writers also use language symbolically.
- The language here can be tricky. We often use these words fairly interchangeably (rightly or wrongly!) which may lead to confusion. Consider how you might use and explain the following:
    - metaphorical
    - figurative
    - symbolic
    - has connotations of…
    - represents…
    - imagery of…

Figure 9.5 A page from a teacher booklet exploring the concept of symbolism

> **Exemplifying the concept of *symbolism* within *Lord of the Flies*:**
>
> A 'big idea' for this text might be: *Golding explores humanity's need for societal structures (democracy etc) to control its innate savagery.* Or just, *Golding explores humankind's innate savagery.**
>
> Symbols we might explore (not an exhaustive list):
> - **the conch** (democracy, civilisation, societal structures imposed on individuals?)
> - **the beast** (externalising the fear of the beast within – humankind's innate selfishness and savagery; the brutality of the survival instinct?)
> - **the Lord of the Flies**; **the sow's head** (the name is the literal translation of Beelzebub, a demonic creature sometimes thought to be the devil himself. It might be the beast made manifest; it might be said to trigger the beasts within the boys)
> - **the signal fire** (its being allowed to go out might symbolise the abandoning of the hope of rescue; their acceptance that they are cut off from civilised existence and will inevitably descend into greater savagery?)
> - **Piggy's glasses** (rational thinking? intellect?)
> - **the pig being killed** (the death of compassion?)
> - **characters as symbols** expressing values and/or states of mind:
>   - Ralph as order, leadership, civility?
>   - Piggy as rational argument, logic, reason?
>   - Jack as unbridled savagery and lust for power?
>   - Simon as humankind's innate goodness?
>   - Roger as humankind at its most extreme: intense bloodlust?
>
> *A 'big idea' is a starting point to help pupils build their understanding by attaching new knowledge to a common thread. It is **not** an end point. Pupils' knowledge will become more flexible over time, allowing them to write their own *individual* thesis statements.

Figure 9.6 A page from a teacher booklet. This one exemplifies a second-order concept (symbolism) in relation to a key text (Lord of the Flies by William Golding)

We can also share how it might be exemplified within a key text (Figures 9.6 and 9.7) and how we might introduce the idea to pupils (Figures 9.8 and 9.9).

We also offer an example of how we might start to organise and present some of the knowledge we want our pupils to acquire (Figure 9.10). Teachers could use these to curate their own lessons.

> | | When tracking symbols, we can think about the relationships between those symbols. Connections and meanings are established that say something about our needs as a society and how certain ideas and behaviours interrelate and depend upon one another. |
> |---|---|
> | **Key moments for exploring humanity's need for societal structures to control its innate savagery in *The Lord of the Flies*** | • Track across the text to see what becomes of the conch from its introduction to its eventual destruction. Piggy and the conch are destroyed at the same time, which might suggest that rational thinking and democracy go hand in hand. |
> | | • Track across the text to see what becomes of the signal fire. This starts off as a great symbol of hope but that hope appears to be abandoned as the boys' civilisation crumbles. Without the appropriate social structures of democracy and rule-making, pragmatic decision-making and prioritisation of tasks and resources start to falter. |
> | | • Explore the use of animals as symbols. An actual pig is killed. Later, Piggy is killed, perhaps marking the boys' descent into animalistic, beast-like behaviour.* Is this our innate state in the absence of law and order and those institutions that might otherwise facilitate civilised discourse? |
> | | *Many pupils (thankfully) have a very different attitude to animals than were traditionally held in the past. This can mean they find it very difficult to understand the idea of an 'animalistic' nature as a bad thing. They just don't have that negative view of animals, even wild ones, so it can take some explaining. |

Figure 9.7 A page from a teacher booklet. Continuing to explore a second-order concept (symbolism) in relation to a key text (Lord of the Flies by William Golding)

> **Symbolism Unit 1 - Introducing the concept of symbolism to pupils**
>
> **Core Knowledge:**
>
> - **Symbols reflect the themes an author is exploring**
> - Non-fiction writers also use **symbols**. They use the same themes as fiction writers.
> - Symbols are a type of *language*. Symbols have shared meanings that are not just spontaneously invented (though they were at one point in the past.) Pupils can *learn* the language of literary symbols and it is much easier than learning a foreign language.
> - Most symbols are images the writer describes using words. This is probably because human minds are so good at 'reading' pictures and spatial relationships. Many common visual metaphors are already established by the time we're three years old. For example, someone fills our 'sippy cup' and we realise that up = more. (The level rises as the volume increases.) We keep that metaphor for the rest of our lives which is why graphs suggesting something is increasing look something like this, with the line going diagonally left to right and upwards:
>
> - and pyramid diagrams have the **more** (most) important concepts at the top:
>
>   monarch / lords / knights / serfs
>
> It isn't just spatial relationships (up, left, right, next to, etc). Our language and our thoughts are full of images too. [There are some suggested examples below but use whatever you like. **You'll need to draw them as well as write them. That's because some pupils (approx. 2%) cannot generate mental images spontaneously at all. They won't necessarily recognise this language as image-based unless they see an actual picture.** (Aphantasia is not an illness, disability or problem and it has nothing to do with learning styles - these don't exist anyway - or intelligence. It's just a variation in how people process thoughts.)]
>
> ❏ symbols for the boys' and girls' toilets—fairly universal but would not be understood by primitive tribal cultures.
> ❏ a 'no entry' sign -fairly universal because most countries have adopted the same system of symbolic language but some countries, including Kenya and sometimes Ireland (Ireland uses both) use this alternative:
> ❏ it's raining cats and dogs. – cultural; it doesn't work in other languages
> ❏ I have a 'dead' leg – cultural; it doesn't usually work in other languages but non-native speakers might work out the meaning because it's based on simple exaggeration.

Figure 9.8 An example of a suggested introductory learning unit (not necessarily equivalent to one lesson) in the teacher booklet. The teacher would curate this in their own way

> **How might we move on to talking about storytelling?**
> Explore the next slide with pupils. It suggests some common symbols and possible meanings. It provides a 'way in' for pupils who won't learn by osmosis.
>
> Film clips and trailers are useful for teaching mise-en-scene. This knowledge can then be transferred to written texts. E.g. The trailer for 'Woman in Black' – explore the symbolism of the objects, the weather, the setting etc.
>
> Colour symbolism – white, red, green symbolising nature, as in *Sir Gawain and the Green Knight* – is also quite easy for pupils to pick up.
>
> Some literary symbols can mean more than one thing. To work out what might be a valid interpretation, we have to look at how the writer is using the symbol. We think about the context surrounding the symbol and test the validity of our ideas against what we already know about the text, the characters and the overall authorial intention.
>
> **Check for Understanding**
>
> Which is NOT true?
> 1. A symbol is really anything that *represents* a concept
> 2. Writers use symbols to help them present and explore themes
> 3. When you look at a symbol, you can just always just invent your own meaning
>
> [3 incorrect. This is somewhat controversial but is trying to raise and address the misconception that we can essentially make up meanings without taking our literary heritage into account or thinking at all about *shared* meanings. It's about moving pupils away from the idea that any interpretation is *automatically* valid, and the misconception that there's no way to work out what *might* be a valid interpretation. We can. We do it using the context surrounding the symbol and by testing the validity of our ideas against what we already know about the text, the characters and the overall authorial intention.]
>
> **Guided Practice**
>
> Practice identifying and selecting symbols in relation to authorial (or, in the case of film clips, directorial) intention.
>
> Consider keeping explanations fairly short and focused at this point so that core connections are clear.
>
> Consider live diagramming your thoughts, using words and pictures, as you respond to a particular quotations etc, so that pupils can see how you make connections. You are giving them a road-map for how meanings are created.

Figure 9.9 Part two of our example of a suggested introductory learning unit (not necessarily equivalent to one lesson) in the teacher booklet. The teacher would curate this in their own way

Resource design 141

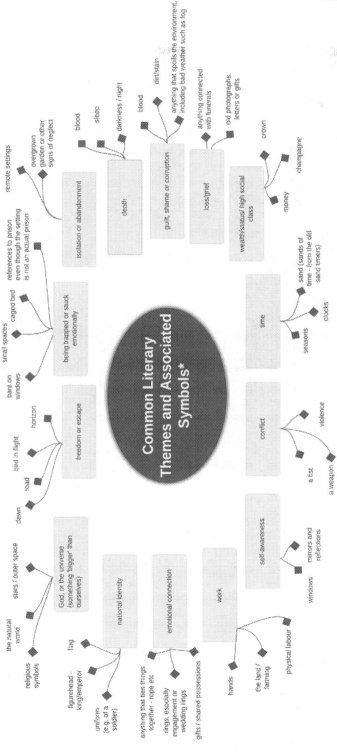

Figure 9.10 A further resource, included in the booklet, that teachers might use directly with pupils to help them organise their knowledge and better understand the discipline

What might the rest of this booklet look like?

Where appropriate, the entire booklet might be just as detailed as this. This often doesn't work in practice though. Teachers might depend a bit too much on it, or feel too restricted by it for lessons to be authentic, responsive and effective.

A better approach might be to include elements that teachers might find tricky. For example, there might be scripted explanations of concepts like *structure* that the whole department can work on and agree together and include in the medium-term plan. Perhaps even some scripting of the examples. How would we explain the cyclical ending in *An Inspector Calls*? What would the best explanation look like? How would we tie it to the central organising principle we are using to build pupils' knowledge of the play? Let's try to do that:

Priestley wrote the text to expose and challenge the injustices of an entrenched class system with its roots in feudalism. We might suggest that the cyclical structure contributes to this meaning by suggesting that we are trapped in a society destined to repeat these mistakes. Perhaps that is why Sheila never quite walks away from Gerald. Perhaps the characterisation of the inspector as a mythologised figure is further evidence of the impossibility of the world he promotes – it is as unreal as the inspector himself. British society is stuck and will never change.

When teachers have to do it themselves, we realise how hard it is! And it is always best approached together as a team. It raises everyone's game and creates better parity of experience for pupils.

The medium-term plan might also include lots of examples of both texts and associated model responses, where appropriate, for teachers to draw upon. Links to the main concept should be made explicit so that teachers can find the thread and lessons can come together around a central organising principle. Again, this can be used as a training opportunity. Staff might annotate a text together for links to a key concept. Many teachers annotate far too much, some not enough. It would be an opportunity to show staff how much annotation is appropriate, how to keep it focused, what form it might take and how we might show pupils the purpose of such annotation by linking it to thinking and to essay writing.

Where staff might already be more confident and in need of less guidance, we might produce a simplified booklet. It might start off with a similarly detailed introduction to a concept, but then branch off into a less prescriptive pattern that allows teachers to curate more of the learning independently, making it easier for teachers to respond to pupils' needs. It might be half as long, for example. However, we would need to consider whether there is sufficient detail for all staff to teach to the same high standard, including those who might lack experience with the specific material. It is probably better to have too much than too little.

Potential barriers to using teacher booklets

The teacher enacts the curriculum. They have to live and breathe it and understand it well enough to deliver the learning to their pupils. But teachers sometimes wrongly see booklets or long-term plans as 'the curriculum', sticking to them word for word, rather robotically. A plan or booklet is a support mechanism to create parity and speed up planning, to guide our thinking and agree a shared body of knowledge. If planning documents become a strait-jacket, that would be a lethal mutation, by which we mean it would no longer reflect the original intention.

Teachers often worry about keeping up with other teachers and covering everything. They worry about future assessments and how they will prepare their pupils for those assessments. It is hard to be sure how much we can drift away from a booklet like this before being accused of having abandoned it altogether. Clear guidance and examples are essential, and teachers should be encouraged to ask questions openly.

Another difficulty is that many teachers, unused to working this way, take time to understand how to drill down to what is conceptually most relevant. Some teachers simply might not notice, unless it was modelled for them, that the structure lesson in the first example above can be boiled down to two ideas: (1) *sequencing contributes to meaning* and (2) *what's included overall matters – each element is there because it contributes to meaning.*

If teachers don't realise this, then whatever they do in their lesson, it is unlikely to have fidelity with the original intention of teaching this concept. Pupils won't understand if the teacher doesn't understand. It is therefore important to make it clear to staff what the intended learning outcomes are rather than assuming they will know or that their understanding is the same as our own.

Finally, teachers might believe that having curated a curriculum, that is the end of the process. But no curriculum will ever be perfected or even finished. We need to continually revisit it and think about what is and isn't working and how we might improve upon our offering.

Knowledge organisers

We might choose to include an associated **knowledge organiser** which pools the highest value knowledge and illustrates core connections in a clear, easy to access format. Knowledge organisers can be an effective way for teachers to present important content to pupils and a useful resource pupils can use for self-testing.

However, there is a danger that what we produce is more lethal mutation than effective knowledge organiser. This tends to happen when the focus is so much on the knowledge itself that the *organisation* of that knowledge, which is just as essential, is somewhat arbitrary. The organisation of the knowledge should be well thought through so that it supports pupils to make appropriate connections and develop a disciplinary schema.

There is also the thorny issue of what knowledge should go into the organiser and why, and how we avoid pupils and parents wrongly believing this is all there is to know. Pupils need to be explicitly taught how to use a knowledge organiser to self-test and given class time to practice in order for them to succeed with this tool.

Figure 9.11 depicts an example of how we have tried to encourage staff and pupils to see thought processes in English so that they might be encouraged to use the organiser to self-test and make connections.

Some suggestions for how we might guide pupils to use a knowledge organiser are:

- Short tests or quizzes on the content (there is a lot of research to show that low stakes testing, where children know that the result has no consequence, is far more effective than simply reading the material).

144 Resource design

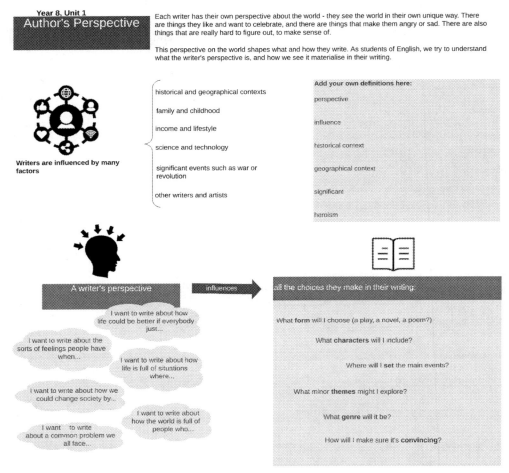

Figure 9.11 An example of a knowledge organiser. The emphasis is on organising knowledge

- Use cues – give them sections of the knowledge organiser which have some of the words or diagrams missing. The completed sections act as cues which trigger memory of what has been taken out. Take the cues away gradually, as they get better at remembering.
- Ask them to recreate diagrams, maps or images – first by copying, eventually moving on to recalling entirely from memory.
- Get them to re-write parts of the knowledge organiser in their own words.
- Show them how to test themselves on the material. Give them a blank piece of paper and ask them to recreate as much of the organiser as they can. When they have done all they can, give them a different colour pen and ask them to finish it by using the original to add the information they couldn't recall. Over time, you can see how much stronger their memory is as there will be less added in the second colour.

Resource design 145

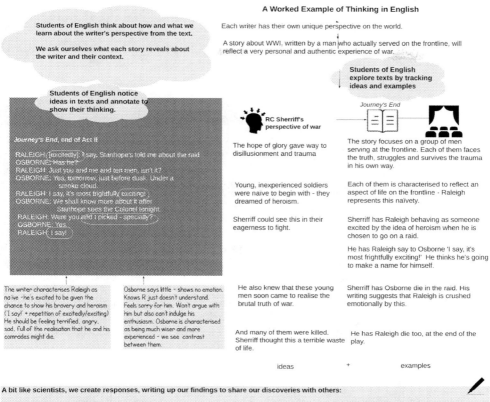

Figure 9.11 (Continued)

- Another important caveat is that the basic knowledge is not an end goal in itself. We want children to have a much deeper and wider understanding of the topic they are learning about, and for this to happen they need to broaden their knowledge beyond the organiser.
- Ask them some more challenging questions about the material.
- Ask them to write different sentences using the key vocabulary.
- Encourage them to look further into areas of the topic – reading books or magazines, or using the Internet.

In summary

- Resource creation is a training opportunity which can improve teacher knowledge and create a better learning experience for pupils.

146 Resource design

- Teacher booklets might be helpful as an approach to Continuing Professional Development (CPD) and as a curriculum planning tool. They can also reduce workload in the longer-term.
- Continually improving our curriculum resources is a fundamental part of the ongoing cycle of curriculum development.

We have designed the curriculum and useful resources. In the next chapter, we think about how we can measure the impact of everything that has been implemented.

Teacher Insight

Jamie Warner-Lynn, Deputy Headteacher at Springwood High School

Jamie was tasked with supporting the English departments across the multi-academy trust to help develop a more research-informed culture.

We have four secondary schools working together within our Trust. Inevitably, teachers had a range of experience and different expertise from which to draw upon in their teaching. Some were experts in literature, others were stronger on language. Many teachers had not yet had an opportunity to learn from research or cognitive science, and it was important to us that any new approaches we introduced should be evidence-informed. We felt it was really important to pool the extensive knowledge we had already within our schools so we could learn from each other. But we also invited external experts to train everyone up to the same high standard in terms of pedagogical and subject knowledge because we had a gap in terms of understanding current research and its implications specifically within English teaching. The booklets that were co-created have been a really big part of creating parity and developing subject knowledge without taking away autonomy or creativity.

Note

1 Thompson, Marnie, & Wiliam, Dylan (2008). *Tight but loose: A conceptual framework for scaling up school reforms*. Educational Testing Service, viewed November 2020, <https://www.researchgate.net/publication/258423197_Tight_but_loose_A_conceptual_framework_for_scaling_up_school_reforms>

10 How can we measure impact?

In this book, we have proposed that a concept-led, evidence-informed English curriculum, carefully implemented, might address some of the persistent problems faced by pupils and teachers in the subject. We have laid out a model for what such a curriculum might look like in a long-term plan at Key Stage 3, suggested how it could be built upon at Key Stage 4, and shown how it could be assessed. In the previous chapters, we also considered how it might best be delivered in the classroom. As a vital part of the continual process of improvement, we can now consider the impact of everything we have tried to implement.

What do we mean by 'impact'?

In order to ascertain the impact of a curriculum, we need to have clarity about what exactly we are measuring. There is no one definition of 'impact'. The clear overarching aim of any curriculum implementation is to improve pupils' outcomes, but we need to break this down further still. We obviously want pupils to gain good qualifications but this isn't the only desirable outcome. We also need to consider whether our wider curriculum aims are being met. What those defined aims are will depend on several things: the context of the school, its ethos and values, and the curriculum vision defined by the department. If, for example, one of the defined aims is to prepare pupils adequately for the next stage of their education, impact might be measured in terms of the number of pupils who enter further study. If one of the aims is to develop a lifelong love of reading, we might survey the extent to which pupils consider themselves readers by the end of Year 11. Once we have clarity about what we want to achieve through our curriculum, the more able we are to define exactly how we intend to measure its success.

Another consideration is what counts as 'success', and again we need to break this down further. Do we mean success for specific cohorts of pupils, and what does this look like? Having defined end points for each stage of the curriculum is helpful here. In Chapter 6, we argued that when we assess pupils' learning of the curriculum, we need to align our assessments to what has been taught at each stage. By using the curriculum as the progression model, we are able to measure the extent to which pupils have acquired knowledge and can apply it with a greater degree of accuracy than when we assess them using examination mark schemes.

DOI: 10.4324/9781003033158-11

We suggest three questions we might ask ourselves when we look to measure curriculum impact:

- Is learning taking place?
- Are pupils developing rich schema and conceptual understanding?
- Are our wider curriculum aims being achieved?

By defining impact in this way, we are more likely to be able to connect outcomes back to our curriculum and know when and how to make further changes. Before we explore these ideas further, we will first consider *why* measuring impact can be so problematic.

Why is measuring impact tricky?

The curriculum is not the paper document

We can't assume a curriculum will be impactful just because it's designed effectively. Long- and medium-term plans and lesson resources are useful indicators of a well-thought out curriculum, but they don't tell us what is happening in the classroom, which is where the real impact is made. We need to look at how it is being enacted by teachers.

Learning is invisible

This brings us to another problem with ascertaining impact. When we look for evidence that a curriculum is being taught effectively, we are really looking for evidence that pupils are learning, but we can't see learning. There is no way to download the contents of pupils' brains and discover what they have thought about, understood or transferred to long-term memory, and certainly not during a ten-minute learning walk, which is a notoriously unreliable way of measuring either teacher effectiveness or pupils' learning. Instead, we need to rely on proxies for learning and draw inferences from them.

Reliability and validity

When we make inferences about learning we need to remember that they are just that – things we have inferred, not things which are necessarily factually true. We will need to consider the extent to which inferences are reliable by questioning their likely consistency – for example, by asking, would another observer of a lesson arrive at the same judgement? The higher the likelihood of consistency, the more reliable the judgement probably is. We also need to question the validity of our inferences, which is the extent to which they are accurate conclusions to draw from a given set of circumstances, and free from bias, and this is particularly tricky.

Cognitive biases

As human beings we are innately susceptible to cognitive biases and we need to be consciously aware of them as they can undermine the validity of our inferences. When trying to measure the impact of a curriculum we are prone to falling prey to these in particular:

- *Confirmation bias*: we tend to seek out, favour and recall information that supports our previous biases. If we are already convinced of the likely success of an approach, we will look for evidence which backs up what we already think.

- *Accountability bias*: we are more likely to be biased in favour of something when we are accountable for the outcome. If we've designed the curriculum ourselves, we will obviously sway towards a positive view of it, especially if its success brings reward.
- *Sunk cost bias*: when we have invested significant time and resources in something we want it to be successful because we cannot recoup the cost involved in the work we've done. For this reason, we tend to look for supporting evidence that what we've done is working. This is especially true in education because schools are extremely busy places and the workload of teachers is so high – time is a very valuable commodity that we never seem to have enough of.

Monitoring vs evaluating

We need to take care when ascribing the impact of a curriculum of the difference between monitoring and evaluating. As the Education Endowment Foundation (EEF) point out, the two are not the same.[1] Monitoring pupils' progress is more straightforward: we are checking if they have met targets or milestones, and they either have or they haven't – there is no need for fine-grained, nuanced judgement of the effectiveness of a process. Evaluating, on the other hand, is an act which leads to a judgement about how effective something is, for the purposes of deciding whether it has achieved our defined purposes, whether it is worth continuing with, and how we might make adaptations.

If, for example, we had put in place an intervention to improve writing in Year 7, we would want to monitor the overall results at the end of the intervention, but that alone wouldn't give us a full picture. It might be that the overall intervention was successful, but how do we know which particular strategies or approaches made the difference? It might be that other factors also contributed to the success – for example, were teachers of other subjects focusing on writing at the same time? Were reward systems in place for writing which encouraged pupils to expend more time and effort on the quality of their writing? Only by evaluating *how* something happened and interrogating *why* it was or wasn't effective can we arrive at a more valid judgement about its impact and determine whether the intervention is worth continuing with.

Correlation and causation

When we interrogate an approach, we need to exercise caution in judging what exactly has worked and what has been less effective. Sometimes we rush into assuming direct cause and effect, partly because of our tendency to fall prey to cognitive biases and partly because we also tend to look for clear patterns. It may be that we find causation – where one event is the direct result of the occurrence of another – but in reality, things are often more nuanced. It is probably more likely that there is correlation between the approach we have implemented and the overall outcome – that is, the two are linked, but the approach was either not a direct cause of the outcome, or was one of several contributing factors.

To go back to the Year 7 writing intervention example above, we might be tempted to look at overall improvements in the quality of the work pupils are producing and immediately ascribe impact to the intervention we put in place by assuming direct impact. It might be that this is true, but it could also be true that there was a correlation between the two, and that other things, such as reward systems, also had a correlation to the final outcomes. If we rush to judge that A directly caused B, we might continue with approaches that had less impact than others.

How do we know it's working? (And what do we do if it isn't?)

Given the inherently problematic nature of ascribing impact to a curriculum, how then can leaders make judgements about whether or not approaches are working? There is no one 'right' way to measure curriculum impact. It can be especially tricky for senior leaders who are not specialists in the subjects they are responsible for to make sound judgements, and we talk further about this in the following chapter. There are, however, some useful guiding principles and questions which can assist us.

Earlier, we pointed to the importance of having clarity about the vision for the curriculum you plan to implement, and of setting clear aims. Only when we have this clarity around what we wish to achieve can we consider how best to measure our success.

We suggested three questions we might ask ourselves when looking to make judgements about the success of a curriculum, and we return to these now.

Is learning taking place?

If learning is a permanent change in long-term memory, it is not something we are going to be able to 'see', but we can look for indicators that it is happening. We might look for evidence that pupils are building new knowledge gradually from prior knowledge, that they are making explicit connections, and that they are able to retrieve more knowledge over time. This will be evident in lessons, from the quality of talk and written work, and in the formative and summative inferences we draw from assessment. The quality of curriculum planning in a department is a strong indicator of whether learning is likely to be happening in meaningful ways in the classroom, and in Chapter 9, we proposed some design principles which could also be used to measure likely success.

Are pupils developing rich schema and conceptual understanding?

We have proposed that concepts sit at the heart of a rich disciplinary schema in English and therefore efforts to measure the extent to which pupils are developing such schema must focus on the depth of their developing conceptual understanding. We have already explored how we might assess this in Chapter 6. For a senior leader who does not have subject expertise, curriculum planning again offers helpful indicators of the likelihood of this aim being achieved. As we have said previously, the curriculum plan is the manifestation of the schema we want pupils to build. We might look for how concepts are defined and sequenced, when and how they are revisited, and explicit connections being made between them. We would want to see misconceptions being preempted and retrieval practice embedded to strengthen retrieval and storage strength. Again, we would hope to see evidence of pupils' developing schema through the quality of their talk and written work.

Are our wider curriculum aims being achieved?

How we measure the success of our wider aims will obviously depend on what they are, but the more specific we are in what we intend, the more likely we are to be able to ascertain success. The aim of 'parity for pupils', for example, is quite broad and would benefit from being broken down further.

Alongside these three questions, we would also suggest the following as further considerations:

Be aware of the limitations of judging 'learning'

Learning can only ever be inferred through proxies, and some proxies are probably more useful than others. Lesson observations are problematic, especially if they are episodic, but there are obvious benefits to conducting them as part of a broader evaluation. The most important thing is that we are mindful that what we are observing is a snapshot and that we avoid being too prescriptive. Lesson observation pro-formas which prescribe specific strategies can lead us to focus on what teachers are doing rather than what pupils are learning. A classroom review which points us to interrogate the underlying principles of effective teaching and learning will likely lead to more meaningful inferences.

What a classroom review looks like will depend on what constitutes excellence in each department, but a starting point might be to draw on what we know about how learning happens. For example, an observer would want to notice whether pupils are led to make explicit connections between stored and new knowledge, whether the teacher provides opportunities for guided and independent practice, and whether formative assessment strategies are used to identify and respond to misconceptions.

Triangulate evidence

No one piece of evidence is going to provide us with enough data to evaluate impact. Lesson observations by themselves provide us with very limited and mostly unreliable evidence, but if we triangulate our findings with other meaningful data, conversations with teachers and pupils, anonymous teacher surveys and a review of lesson resources and text choices, we have a much richer pool of information from which to make inferences. We might also benefit from comparing our own provision with that of other schools, and with subject associations.

Gathering all of the information we have, we then need to return to our vision and aims, and to our guiding questions. Based on the fact that pupils need to build schema over time, that learning is a permanent change in long-term memory, is our interpretation about curriculum impact likely to be a valid one? By keeping a close eye on what we set out to achieve, and by being mindful of the limitations of measuring learning, we can make better decisions about what might be adapted or refined.

The most important thing to keep in mind is that 'impact' is part of the continuing cycle of an implementation. If our evaluation of impact suggests that things aren't working, we will need to make adjustments: we begin the cycle of implementation again. The purpose of evaluating impact is to determine what to do next, either to review and refine the approach or to sustain the high standards achieved. We explore this further in the next chapter.

In summary

- Measuring impact is not an event, it is a process that should be woven into everything, right from the beginning. Having clarity in your aims and measures of success is essential.
- Measuring impact is tricky. Base your curriculum design on clear, evidence-based principles and evaluate likely impact against them.
- In evaluating impact, we should draw on multiple sources and consciously work to mitigate against bias to make our judgements more valid and reliable.

In the next chapter, we'll explore how we can sustain and continue to build upon the improvements we've made.

Note

1 Education Endowment Foundation (2021). Assessing and Monitoring Pupil Progress, https://educationendowmentfoundation.org.uk/tools/assessing-and-monitoring-pupil-progress/measuring-impact/. Accessed on 24/05/2021.

11 Sustaining high standards

One of the problems with sustaining any new approaches in schools is that we have been, and continue to go through, so many changes. Schools are uniquely complex places. Any teacher, leader or support staff with more than a few years' experience in schools will recognise the cyclical nature of change in education – indeed, for many, the current focus on curriculum is a revisiting of debates and policies they have seen before.

And of course, the biggest barrier to the deep work of curriculum in schools is time. Already it feels there are simply not enough hours in the school day to plan, teach, assess and carry out the many other daily tasks of a teacher, nor for leaders with so much responsibility and accountability in so many areas of running a school. The vast amount of operational work involved in school leadership has often led to an over-focus on processes. Furthermore, external accountability has sometimes led us to invest the limited time we have in immediate fixes for short-term gains, or to try to change too many things at once. We work in a sector where other contextual factors – national problems with teacher recruitment and retention, or, at the time of writing, a global pandemic – add difficulty and complexity to our work.

We believe there are particular issues within the subject of English which make curriculum work more problematic for teachers and leaders. We have already pointed to the lack of a codified body of knowledge in English, as well as how its conceptual nature makes it especially tricky to teach and assess. The debate around exactly what pupils should learn, and what specifically they should be retaining, has reignited long-held arguments about the tension between the discipline and the subject.

It can be difficult in this context to have clear sight of the priorities. What are the most important things to focus on? Which changes are highest leverage right now? Sometimes, what feels like the priority now isn't always the thing that will make the biggest impact long-term. Often, we don't have enough clarity about the nature of the problem we are trying to solve. And what exactly are we trying to change when we introduce a new curriculum? It isn't processes, it's people. And that is much harder. It necessitates bringing about changes in thinking, behaviours and habits. Anyone who has ever tried to implement a new year's resolution will tell you how difficult it is to adopt new ways of doing things – there's a reason that gyms are packed with well-intentioned fitness-seekers in January only to be half-empty by March. Real change is preceded by an uncomfortable phase where we have to admit that it is necessary – that we need to learn something. It can be difficult for teachers to reimagine the world, especially if they have always taught in the same way, and perhaps in a way that seems to have worked. As we move through the uncomfortable stage, we often need support to keep us on track, to remind us of the vision for which we're working, to show us the progress we're making. It's why some of those fitness-seekers employ personal trainers.

You can have a brilliant curriculum and you can even implement it well, but without the pillars to support it, it will fail. We have already pointed to the significant research which tells us that expert teaching is the biggest driver in improving pupils' outcomes, so improving teachers should be the aim of everything we do in schools. Ultimately, we need to make curriculum, and developing curriculum expertise, the priority. We need to strip back everything which doesn't directly contribute to this aim, and free teachers from unnecessary tasks to allow them the time and headspace to plan and deliver a quality curriculum. To do this, it is likely that we will need to let go of other things which are also important and have impact. But, as Dylan Wiliam says:

> The only way we can improve schools, therefore, is to stop people doing good things - to give them time to do even better things. This is the uncomfortable reality behind the trite phrase "work smarter, not harder", and it is why change in schools is so hard.[1]

Leading the curriculum in English

The role of Head of Department (HoD) in English is particularly complex. Leaders are required to be experts in the subject, in pedagogy, in assessment and data, to manage both up and down, to be operational and strategic. The priority has often been on securing results and explaining data.

For any new curriculum to stand the test of time, it must be research-informed, rigorous and robust; it has to be carefully designed and implemented with fidelity. Teachers need to be supported so they are equipped to deliver it. And we must acknowledge the, often uncomfortable, reality that this work is never finished: we must always be engaged in the process of reviewing and refining.

But to support English teachers in delivering a new curriculum, to guide them to change their thinking and behaviours, leaders need expertise. They need to understand the root causes of persistent problems and have knowledge of how curriculum design and implementation can address them. This implies that department heads really need to focus on being curriculum curators and teacher educators. They might not always have viewed themselves as such.

How can we develop curriculum expertise in English?

So, leaders of English need to see themselves as teacher educators. If we are to ensure parity of experience for our pupils, we need greater parity of expertise across a department. This requires teachers to have access to high-quality, evidence-informed, subject-specific training, and to be supported to implement their learning in their classrooms. There are a number of tools we can use to do this.

Subject-specific training

One of the most frustrating things we experienced during our time in the classroom was the amount of training we attended which had no direct relevance to teaching English. There is a place for generic approaches to teaching and learning. But without opportunities for teachers to make sense of and apply new ideas within their own subject, it is unlikely to have much impact on their practice or on pupil outcomes.

We also need to consider how department time can be used to deliver subject-specific training. A substantial amount of departmental meeting time is often taken up by the operational aspects of a school. All of these things need to happen, of course, but when collating and analysing data on pupils' progress consumes more of teachers' time than developing their knowledge of how to achieve that progress, we would suggest that the balance has tipped in the wrong direction. The primary purpose of departmental meeting time should be for teachers to develop their subject and pedagogical knowledge. And not just their knowledge of the subject content, but of evidence-based approaches to teaching and learning. Crucially, teachers must be given opportunities to make sense of research, and to practice its application within their subject.

In planning training for teachers, we can return to what we know about how we learn. As Harry Fletcher-Wood states: 'as experienced teachers, teacher educators already have effective approaches to learning they can transfer to teacher learning. Teacher learning is just learning: plan accordingly'.[2] Teachers who are developing expertise in areas where they are more novice benefit from explicit instruction, modelling, practice and feedback in the same way that pupils do. Good training incorporates all of these aspects.

On its own, though, even subject-specific department training sessions won't be enough. The EEF recommends that leaders 'reinforce initial training with expert follow-on support' and use 'highly skilled coaches' to sustain high standards.[3] We might like to think that training days are enough but they really aren't. There is far too much for a teacher to think about for them to truly absorb a new curriculum through just the odd training day, particularly in a subject like English. And this is especially true if the training is whole-school and not subject specific. Teachers need to be guided in contexualising the generic.

Figure 11.1 is an attempt to map the learning cycle for both teachers and pupils. Like pupils, teachers need support to navigate this process.

Coaching

The most powerful way of supporting teachers to implement new ideas is probably to coach them. It is important for teachers to revisit and embed their learning, and coaching can be an effective means of doing that. At regular intervals, someone who has a better handle on the new curriculum, the pedagogical approach, or whatever it is you're introducing, sits down and offers support to a teacher who is still learning about it. Perhaps they video a bit of a lesson and discuss that, perhaps they co-plan something together. What matters is that an expert voice speaks with authority to someone who may be a very established teacher but also happens to be new to a particular idea or process. Other forms of buddying or pairing up teachers are useful too but they're never as effective as having a coach who has significant expertise and can guide others to reach the same level of understanding and skill.

Components of a Pupil Learning Cycle

CONNECTING
- **identify knowledge hierachies and/or central organising principles**
- **elaboration tasks** to embed new learning within existing schema
- **connect abstract ideas to a range of concrete examples**
- **non-examples** reinforce understanding of true connections by exposing those that are invalid
- **oracy** think aloud, rehearse, recast and refine
- **increasingly varied opportunities to practice making connections**

REMEMBERING
- **activate prior knowledge** so that new knowledge can attach on to it
- **retrieval practice**, particularly of key concepts and connections - used throughout the learning cycle
- **interleaving** so that no learning is left behind
- **elaboration tasks** to embed new learning within existing schema
- **oracy** think aloud, rehearse, recast and refine
- **increasingly varied opportunities to practice** to embed learning

SENSE-MAKING
- **have private headspace and thinking time** learning happens outside as well as inside the classroom
- **reinforce knowledge hierachies and/or central organising principles**
- **connect abstract ideas** to a range of concrete examples
- **discuss detail** and unpick nuance
- **challenge perceptions** explore the outliers - uncommon examples or ideas which still have some validity
- **non-examples** reinforce understanding of true connections by exposing those that are invalid
- **apply learning** in new contexts
- **oracy** think aloud, rehearse, recast and refine
- **respond** to feedback
- **increasingly varied opportunities to practice**

ARTICULATING
- **elaboration tasks** to embed new learning within existing schema
- **explore and emulate** high quality **models** co-create models with the expert teacher
- **vocabulary and associated syntax** to develop nuance and precision over time
- **sentence fragments and sentence combining as core strategies** to develop thinking and, by association, writing
- **oracy** think aloud, rehearse, recast and refine
- **increasingly varied opportunities to practice** to embed learning

Figure 11.1 Components of teacher and pupil learning cycles

One misconception about coaching is that only the weakest or least experienced teachers need it. But it's a mistake to assume that experience always equals expertise, or that expert teachers don't benefit from coaching too, especially when implementing a new curriculum.

New approaches to curriculum, or teaching in general, involve thinking about abstract concepts. These are all abstract:

- Working memory
- Cognitive load theory
- Interleaving
- Sequencing
- Progression

Components of a Teacher Learning Cycle

CONNECTING
- **identify knowledge hierachies and/or central organising principles**
- **collaborative tasks** to embed new learning within existing schema
- **identify explicit examples of abstract concepts**
- **non-examples** reinforce understanding of true connections by exposing those that are invalid
- **explain connections** with precision
- **increasingly varied opportunities to practice making connections** to embed learning
- **observe skilled practitioners**

REMEMBERING
- **activate prior knowledge** so that new knowledge can attach on to it
- **retrieval practice**, particularly of key concepts and connections -used throughout the learning cycle
- **interleaving** so that no learning is left behind
- **increasingly varied opportunities to practice** to embed learning

CPD sessions
Dept Meetings
TLCs
Coaching
Personal reflection

SENSE-MAKING
- **have private headspace and thinking time** learning happens outside as well as inside the classroom
- **engage with research**
- **reinforce knowledge ierachies and/or central organising principles**
- **explain how and why explicit examples reflect abstract concepts**
- **discuss detail** and unpick nuance
- **challenge perceptions** explore the outliers - uncommon examples or ideas which still have some validity
- **non-examples** reinforce understanding of true connections by exposing those that are invalid
- **apply learning** in new contexts
- **opportunities to practice** to embed learning
- **observe skilled practitioners**
- **consider learning and materials from the perspective of a novice teacher**
- **consider learning and materials from the perspective of a pupil perspective, including different cohorts (yr groups, SEND etc)**
- **consider learning and materials from the perspective of a parent**

ARTICULATING
- **elaboration tasks** to embed new learning within existing schema
- **explore and emulate** high quality **models** of planning and delivery
- **co-create** models with expert colleagues
- **script explanations or parts of explanations**
- **explain connections** with precision
- **increasingly varied opportunities to practice** to embed learning

Figure 11.1 (Continued)

There are subject-specific concepts to think differently about too: in Chapter 5, we identified foundational concepts which we suggest underpin a disciplinary schema in English. All of these will need careful unpicking, modelling and exemplification for teachers who are new to thinking about English in this way. Until we pin all of these abstract concepts down through subject-specific, concrete examples that make them meaningful to teachers, they remain hard to visualise and hard to grasp. This is why English teachers should be coached by experts within their own subject, who can help them to make sense of its complexities.

For many teachers this will be a very different experience of feedback than they are used to. Most feedback in schools is tied to performance and accountability systems, rather than developing expertise in teaching subjects. Often, lesson observations are episodic, whereas coaching is part of a continuing cycle of professional development. And coaching is matched to teacher need, not a one-size-fits-all approach.

Implementing coaching successfully across a department takes careful consideration and planning. The components of coaching we identify below will need careful adaptation depending on the expertise of the teacher being coached. It may be less appropriate, for example, to direct an action step for a more experienced teacher, who may benefit from co-constructing their own focus towards a goal they have identified themselves. It may be that some teachers initially benefit from more directive coaching but need to move more quickly to a less directive approach as their expertise grows.

It takes time to become a really skilled coach who can adapt their practice to meet teacher need. An expert coach has a high level of conscious competence: they can break down their expertise into granular components and plan a sequence of learning for a novice to support them in building mental models. They can also enable more expert teachers to become more consciously competent. As such, training and continuous professional development for coaches should be a key part of any coaching program and embedded in a culture of wider learning in a school.

There are many models of coaching and we cannot hope to explore them in enough detail here, but in relation to our defined core purpose, which is to support a more novice teacher to deeply understand and effectively deliver a new curriculum, we would suggest the following as essential components:

Identify a problem and set a goal

By observing the teacher in action, the coach can support them to gain what Jim Knight[4], refers to as a clear picture of the reality in their classroom. A coaching conversation can then focus on what problem or challenge the teacher is facing, and the change they would like to see. In *The Impact Cycle*, Knight emphasises the importance of a teacher being emotionally invested in achieving a goal. By asking the question, 'what would it mean to you if you could achieve that goal?', teachers are more likely to be motivated to engage in coaching and be willing to invest their time. Having clarity and shared understanding around the identified goal also allows the coach to focus the sessions on what is of most importance to the teacher and most likely to make a difference to pupils' learning.

Expert insight and a model of better

In order to support the teacher to move towards meeting their goal, an expert coach will draw on their own existing knowledge, and the relevant research base, to provide insights. They will consider the teacher's existing knowledge and the context they are working in.

In the same way that we would always provide pupils with a model before we ask them to apply their learning, teachers who are developing their practice benefit from the same. In planning to share a model of better, a coach should consider the best way to exemplify the ideas to be discussed, including any visual metaphors or analogies that might enable the teacher to see more abstract concepts, and any misconceptions that are likely to arise.

The coach should exemplify their model better, either by performing it themselves, or by sharing a product or artefact. This might mean demonstrating a technique, such as a countdown to bring pupils' attention back to the teacher after a group discussion, or talking through a model of dual coding which exemplifies how the research might be applied in the classroom. Modelling by an expert coach makes it far more likely that the teacher will be able to take the action step on board and apply it with fidelity.

Clear, manageable action steps

The coach should identify one clear, manageable action step for the teacher to implement in their classroom. For many leaders and teachers, this will feel very different to the traditional model of observing a practitioner two or three times a year and providing them with a long list of broad targets. But there is a significant body of evidence to suggest that this form of instructional coaching, where a more novice teacher is guided by someone with greater expertise, works precisely because the action steps are so small.[5] It is the difference between giving a teacher a target like:

> Improve your questioning techniques

and one with a much more specific focus, such as:

> After you have explained the new concept to pupils, check their understanding using targeted questioning. Choose a strategic sample of pupils to give you a more accurate proxy for understanding.

Over time, granular action steps accumulate to have a very powerful effect on a teachers' practice: Paul Bambrick-Santoyo suggests that by receiving frequent observations and feedback 'a teacher gets as much development in one year as most get in twenty'.[6] A skilled coach will have a clear vision for the teacher's development over time, in line with the identified goals, and will sequence the action steps towards that goal.

Practice and feedback

The coach should provide the more novice teacher with an opportunity to put their action step into practice and give them some feedback. Practising the components of effective teaching isn't something we are used to in our profession, but a skilled coach will create a culture for practice and normalise it. Opportunities to practice away from the busy classroom make it more likely that a teacher will be able to enact their action step once they 'go live' in front of pupils.

Teacher learning communities

Another way to develop departmental expertise is by the establishment of teacher learning communities (TLCs) of the kind described by Dylan Wiliam.[7] They are quite straightforward to set up and run. Teachers are given some reading in advance, which is usually research-based, or perhaps subject knowledge-based, they arrive at a TLC meeting ready to discuss the reading and make decisions about how to act upon it. An individual action step is agreed for each member of the group. This pushes staff to put research into practice and actually apply their learning. Staff can then be warmly held to account next time for the actions they said they would take. Usually, TLC sessions occur every two to three weeks. This is what helps change habits: the drip, drip, drip over time which allows new ideas to become embedded because teachers are constantly reengaging and having to act on what they're learning. It also provides staff with a useful forum in which to ask questions and perhaps share resources.

Whatever training strands (TLCs, coaching, departmental sessions and so on) a department chooses to adopt, an important consideration is the coherency between them. By focusing these different strands on the same aims, we streamline our provision to ensure the greatest impact on teacher education and, therefore, on pupil learning and outcomes.

How can senior leaders support English departments?

One of the most challenging aspects of senior leadership is knowing how to effectively hold department leaders to account in a subject that is not your specialism. This is particularly tricky in English, because of the lack of codified agreement of what English is. As a subject rich in abstractions, it is open to subjectivity and individual choice, and perhaps more susceptible to fads and fashions. How, then, can senior leaders and governors ascertain the quality of an English curriculum and its delivery?

Figure 11.2 is an attempt to capture what, in an ideal world, different stakeholders would know and understand about English.

We offer this as a tool which might be used by school leaders to interrogate an English curriculum. It could be that questions are derived from it to ask of department leaders. For example, how has knowledge of key concepts been sequenced and why are they in that order? How would you break this down for pupils? Can I see a copy of a written exposition so I can see how you're explaining that to pupils? How do the texts you have chosen exemplify this concept?

Creating a culture for teacher learning

Creating a culture for professional learning and collaboration is essential to the continued success of a newly implemented curriculum, but department leaders cannot create it in a void. Clarity of vision and a commitment to teacher education must come from the top.

This needs to take place in a supportive environment based upon trust. Punitive systems serve no one. A demoralised staff will underperform. There has been a culture of fear in many schools where accountability itself has become more important than the actual teaching and learning. Honest, open relationships lead to more accurate understanding of what is and isn't working, to the benefit of all.

Another important aspect of a culture conducive to learning is focus. Too often in schools, leaders try to change too many things at once. This might sometimes lead to quick wins, but it rarely leads to sustainable improvement. For real change to happen, we need to focus on doing less, better. And to get buy-in from staff, they need to see that the reasons for change are genuine, and that if they commit to making changes, they will be supported, not judged. As Mary Myatt says:

> Thoughtful leaders working to create the conditions for high challenge and low threat know that, in order to make a difference, they have to focus on fewer things in greater depth.[8]

This means communicating a vision for change with absolute clarity and following it up with support. If teachers are to meaningfully focus on developing their expertise, they need the time to do it: training, coaching, co-planning and professional learning communities are all effective teacher education tools but to effect real change they necessitate a time commitment. It might be that in order to make room for these things, other things have to go. The most important way senior leaders can support an English department is to ensure they can devote their time to planning and delivering a great curriculum, by stripping away anything that doesn't directly contribute to that aim.

Sustaining high standards 161

Figure 11.2 An attempt to capture the different levels and types of knowledge required by teacher educators, teachers, pupils and parents

Monitoring learning

Once curriculum planning is in place, we might consider how leaders can monitor learning. Often, this is done through data gathering based on summative assessments that might be carried out several times across the school year. Such attainment data often lags weeks behind when the actual learning itself was supposed to take place. Waiting weeks for work to be marked and data to be crunched means that by the time we're looking at it, it is out of date. Using such data to identify and resolve problems is therefore problematic. This might be another argument for a portfolio, rather than periodic assessments of a particular format.

162 Sustaining high standards

Figure 11.2 (Continued)

But we also need to think about lesson observations. Many is the time when we have carried out paired observations with members of a school's senior leadership team (SLT) who were not subject specialists. On one occasion, we watched a lesson in which year 9 pupils were being asked to construct similes. The Vice-Principal thought it was a good lesson and enjoyed watching the teacher move names up a progress ladder, rewarding them for being able to write similes.

However, in the eyes of a subject specialist, there were several problems with the lesson. Firstly, it didn't seem to fit within any particular scheme – it was very disconnected from anything else. Secondly, writing similes with no context or intention might be rather a waste of time. Questions we asked ourselves were – Why are we doing this? What mood are we trying to create? What theme or character might the simile pertain to? How is it symbolic? But the lesson did not address any of these deeper ideas.

Through no fault of his own, the non-specialist didn't really know what questions to ask or how to interrogate what they were seeing to know if, or how, the teaching was effective. Sometimes this problem results in leaders enthusiastically encouraging teaching approaches that are unsound.

We have included Figure 11.2 to help us to consider who needs to know what in order for effective English teaching to take place. On its own, it might not work as a diagnostic tool. Whoever wields it really needs to understand what the examples of these behaviours would look like in an English classroom. But a well-trained HoD might be able to use it to help themselves and senior leaders, or the department itself, to see and track the training needs of their staff.

Some examples of general questions a senior leader might ask are:

- Is there sufficient depth?
- Is the central organising principle, or thread, made clear?
- Are valid connections being made between this and previous learning?

These are useful. But to really answer these questions, they need some sense of what effective teaching and learning in English looks like. Having access to the medium-term plans and teacher booklets helps, as would a discussion with a strong teacher on what to look out for.

Effective implementation: lessons learnt

Having gone through the process of implementing a new curriculum several times, both in schools where we worked as teachers and leaders, and in schools where we have supported as external consultants, we have learned a few important lessons which we will share here.

Ofsted's three-layered approach to curriculum - Intent, Implementation, Impact - has sometimes been reduced to a kind of checklist. Often the starting point has been to write an 'intent statement', perhaps hurriedly and to satisfy Ofsted's criteria. Any genuine changes in curriculum need to start by exploring the persistent problems in a subject and a school's context, and how curriculum might address them. And before any implementation is enacted, enough time needs to be spent thoroughly preparing. It might feel that time is a commodity most schools don't have, but without proper preparation, change will always be surface and temporary.

If a genuine overhaul of the curriculum is planned and the intention is to re-train staff accordingly, leaders need to be emotionally ready for a time that will feel uncertain and challenging. It might seem a strange place to start but emotional context is really important; it might be the most important thing of all. Trying to create cultural change when the people in charge don't feel comfortable or motivated is a recipe for disaster. Not enough attention is paid to this in our opinion. There is often an assumption or expectation that senior leaders and heads of departments will rise to it. That is not necessarily true.

Leaders also have to be intellectually ready to make significant changes. They must have been given enough time to read, research, collaborate and prepare a strategy. Very often, this process is truncated to reading one book and going on a couple of school visits. But moving to a concept-led, knowledge-rich English curriculum is a massive shift for most people. It will be a while before they even realise how much they don't know, perhaps despite having been in teaching for a very long time. It's particularly difficult for your most experienced staff who will have long-held beliefs and habits that will necessarily be challenged.

We must also avoid replacing like with like. For example, many schools have opted to get rid of PEE-style paragraphs (Point, Evidence, Explain), only to replace them with 'what, how, why', seemingly not realising that this is often used the same way. It feels like change. It looks like change. But it isn't. Anyone taking charge of curriculum reinvention needs to be able to rise to the intellectual and emotional challenge well enough to know the difference between surface change and real change and to keep pushing until the real change comes.

If individuals don't feel intellectually ready, sending them on a one-off training course is unlikely to fix it. They need dedicated coaching from someone who knows what they're doing, perhaps from another school, or from an external source. Continuous professional development (CPD) from external providers is highly variable. Having sat through many poor CPD sessions and having failed to benefit in any way from them we know this to be true. There is also good evidence that one-off training has little impact. But the Wellcome Trust has funded a pilot study to try to develop a way of vetting CPD providers which will hopefully improve the situation and provide schools with a list of trusted experts. Their report[9] shows that the project was successful in beginning to create criteria, protocols and procedures for quality assuring CPD providers. We hope there is more to come on this. Furthermore, the EEF have recently published a systematic review and meta-analysis into the characteristics of effective teacher professional development, where 'mechanisms' which facilitate teacher learning are identified.[10] We welcome both studies as offering very clear ways forward for leaders when selecting or designing CPD and ensuring its quality and impact.

All of this has implications in terms of the specific individuals that headteachers or MAT leaders choose to put in charge of overseeing a period of change in English. It needs to be someone they can trust to honestly express their own personal limitations and concerns so they can access support and draw on the collective knowledge of those around them wherever necessary – no one person has all the answers. It also needs to be someone who can rise to a difficult intellectual challenge and someone who has, or can foster, positive relationships with the staff they will lead, educate and support, and on whose knowledge they will draw. If they're in the habit of teacher-blaming or teacher-shaming, they're not the right person for the job. Teachers are going to struggle at times to make this shift in their thinking and their habits. They need to trust that SLT and their HoD have their backs.

Be patient – implementation is a long game

We must consider timeframes. We generally won't see much effect in terms of exam results from any changes introduced for several years. But there will be leading and lagging indicators to look out for throughout the journey that can help us to see if we're on the right track. We discussed this in Chapter 10.

We still see a lack of awareness in a lot of the schools we work with when it comes to implementation. There's a real tendency to underestimate just how difficult it can be to change teacher behaviour, even if those teachers are enthusiastic and fully engaged. Even subtle changes can be tough if it means changing the habits of a lifetime.

And it can sometimes lead to a vicious cycle of mistrust. Senior leaders, and HoDs, want to see the new curriculum up and running. Staff are trying but it isn't quite working. SLT begins to lose faith and may exert some pressure in the hope that it will rectify the problem. But that pressure just makes teachers more stressed and it becomes even harder for them to adapt. The blame game begins.

But, in our experience, piling pressure on doesn't work because it is an attempt to solve a problem which doesn't usually exist. It is, in essence, a well-intentioned misdiagnosis of a situation – the beginning of the cycle of planned failure. The teachers aren't usually failing to try, they're just struggling to change habits because doing so is extremely hard. There is new information to process, absorb, wrestle with, and then we need a lot of practice, with feedback, just like our pupils. It takes time and it has to be appropriately structured and planned for. Poor implementation can mean a genuinely effective, research-informed strategy that *could* have made a real difference to students ends up being thrown out solely because it hasn't been implemented well enough.

Designing and implementing a new English curriculum – one which is rigorous, robust and informed by research – will take significant time. It will be complex, often difficult, and it will involve deep thinking and collaboration. But the rewards it will bring will be plentiful. For many English teachers, the intellectual work will be incredibly fulfilling and allow them to connect with their subject in a more meaningful way. Most importantly, the young people in their classrooms will benefit. We promise it will be worth it.

In summary

- SLT has to honestly reflect on how well they create a space in which teachers feel safe and can flourish so that a culture conducive to teacher learning is created.
- We need to think about time – adequate time to develop as professionals. The focus is long-term, not about quick fixes. Coaching is one very powerful way to affect change, but it must be afforded time and careful, considered thought.

Teacher Insight

Joe Clark, NQT, Marshland High School

Joe is completing his NQT year and part of his training has included one-to-one, subject-specific coaching.

One of the most effective concepts from dedicated coaching for me has been the manner in which information is presented and delivered to students. Not only have I gained a multitude of effective practical tools, but also greater understanding of this aspect of teaching and learning. When I am teaching new information, I now ensure I consider in much more depth *how* it is presented – with relevant diagrams, explanations, annotations and models – to enable all students to access and master new knowledge.

In comparison to typical department or whole school continued professional development, one-to-one coaching has been incredibly impactful on my personal practice. Where more usual types of training only address one specified concept to a large and varied group of staff, coaching allows for the detailed analysis of individual teaching. In our coaching sessions, we would devise an approach to teaching a specific unit or lesson. I would then record my teaching of this lesson and Zoe and I would later examine the video, and she would support me by providing invaluable reflections. Coaching allows for not only relevant development specific to an individual teachers' need, but also for discussion of evidence-informed approaches and how to implement them. This has allowed me to scrutinise my own teaching and to bring my reflections into my lesson planning outside of our coaching sessions.

Although my initial teacher training provided me the tools required to enter the world of teaching, working with Zoe has given me the knowledge and confidence to excel in the world of teaching.

Teacher Insight

Judy Webb, Marshland High School

Judy is an experienced teacher who took part in subject-specific coaching.

The chance to have coaching sessions was offered to me as an experienced member of staff. I must admit to being a little sceptical in the beginning, but I soon realised the sessions were invaluable. Implementing a curriculum that is concept driven, not text driven, was a new and different way of teaching. An analogy I use is, it is like driving a manual car after years of driving an automatic: there are different ways of getting to the same destination.

The coaching sessions were a way of developing my understanding of how pupils learn and the opportunity to bounce around ideas to adapt my teaching. Following the schemes in our teacher booklets does not mean delivering Powerpoints full of bullet-pointed key knowledge. You are the teacher and already have that knowledge: the booklets are there as a guide and the coaching sessions help you impart that knowledge to your pupils in the way that works best for them.

Coaching helped me to understand what I need to do to ensure my pupils develop their own schema – they were not a 'one-way street' where I was being told how to teach. They were also a discussion forum where ideas were shared and implemented in my teaching and then passed on to the department. I personally consider coaching as an important support mechanism that can only improve teaching skills and ultimately pupils' learning.

Teacher Insight

Louise Gill, Assistant Subject Leader for KS4 English at Laurus Ryecroft

Louise is a highly experienced teacher, examiner, mentor and department leader who participated in coaching as part of a whole-school improvement programme.

My initial reaction to the suggestion that I take part in coaching was not overwhelmingly positive. I'm certainly not an arrogant teacher – in fact, I'm very critical of my own teaching and can always find something, in every lesson, that I could improve on. But the idea of being coached in teaching English, the subject I'd been passionately waxing lyrical to students about for the last eight years, where I consistently achieve good results, where my planning is used by the whole faculty, upset and irritated me in equal measure: more CPD being 'done' to me.

And then I met Sam. Time to eat a large slice of humble pie. Being coached by her has undoubtedly been the best CPD I've ever received. The level of detailed discussion we had around pedagogy, subject content and curriculum was unlike anything I'd ever experienced before. It really highlighted and confirmed to me the importance of English teachers working collaboratively and 'observing' each other. Only someone else who teaches our subject and understands it as an art form can truly appreciate the subtle crafting, nuances and sheer depth of knowledge we are trying to impart to our students. I came out of the sessions motivated, enlightened and with a new appreciation for just how complex our subject is, not just for students, but for novice teachers as well: something I'll admit I'd forgotten after years in the classroom.

Being coached around English curriculum and key concepts in particular has allowed me to really understand what my subject-specific teacher training lacked. When I coach other English teachers in future, I'll do everything I can to ensure they don't have the same gaps in their training as I did. Trainee English teachers cannot be expected to just observe others and be able to unpick the layers of what the expert teacher is actually doing – there's simply too much going on both pedagogically and in terms of the curriculum itself. There is so much knowledge we expect pupils to know, and inexperienced teachers to be able to convey. The job of the coach is to guide novice teachers through the minefield of the English curriculum just as much as we guide our classes – perhaps more so. They need direct instruction, smaller 'chunks' or areas to develop, and deliberate practice – all overseen and guided by an expert teacher. The time investment required is massive, but it pays dividends.

Being coached by Sam boosted my confidence and made me comprehend just how much I know, how much of an English expert I am – it also showed me how I've previously expected too much from novice teachers, and how to be a better mentor. It was a humbling experience and one that both myself and the teachers I coach in future will benefit from.

Notes

1 Wiliam, D. (2016). *Leadership for teacher leaning: Creating a culture where all teachers improve so that all students succeed.* Learning Sciences International: West Palm Beach, FL, p. 217.
2 Fletcher-Wood, H. (2017). 'Teacher learning: It's just learning'. *Improving Teaching.* <https://improving-teaching.co.uk/2017/10/08/teacher-learning-its-just-learning>. Accessed 1 October 2020.
3 Education Endowment Foundation (2019). *Putting evidence to work – a school's guide to implementation,* viewed on 10th February 2021, <https://educationendowmentfoundation.org.uk/tools/guidance-reports/a-schools-guide-to-implementation/>
4 Knight, J. (2017). *The Impact Cycle: What Instructional Coaches Should Do to Foster Powerful Improvements in Teaching.* Corwin: Thousand Oaks, California.
5 Sims, S. 'Four reasons instructional coaching is currently the best-evidenced form of CPD'. *Sam Sims Quantitative Education Research.* < https://samsims.education/2019/02/19/247/>. Accessed 22 January 2021.
6 Bambrick-Santoyo, P. (2018). *Leverage leadership 2.0: A practical guide to building exceptional schools.* Jossey Bass: San Francisco, CA, p. 65.
7 Wiliam, D. (2016). *Leadership for teacher leaning: Creating a culture where all teachers improve so that all students succeed.* Learning Sciences International: West Palm Beach, FL, pp. 211-17.
8 Myatt, M. (2020). *Back on track: Fewer things, greater depth.* John Catt: Woodbridge, p. 41.
9 Chedzey, K., Cunningham, M., & Perry, E. (2021). *Quality assurance of teachers' continuing professional development: Design, development and pilot of a CPD quality assurance system.* https://chartered.college/wp-content/uploads/2021/04/Piloting-a-CPD-QA-system-Final-Report_April-2021.pdf. Accessed on 19/05/2021.
10 Education Endowment Foundation (2021). *What are the characteristics of effective teacher professional development? A systematic review and meta-analysis,* viewed on 14 October 2021, <https://educationendowmentfoundation.org.uk/education-evidence/evidence-reviews/teacher-professional-development-characteristics>

Conclusion
A Vision for English

It feels like we are standing at a juncture just now. Recent changes to the inspection framework and to the examination specifications present us with a real opportunity to define how we want pupils to experience our subject. This book is a manifesto for change, yes, but *real* change, sustainable change that isn't based on fads or accountability systems. This is a manifesto for reclaiming our subject through teacher education and improved curriculum design. We wanted to end it by considering an important question:

What do we want the future of English teaching to look like?

We might know more about what we *don't* want English to look like. English should not be reduced to exam preparation or preparation for the workplace, or even to being solely about basic literacy. That's not because those things aren't important. It's because our subject is so much more than that. It is an academic discipline that might be better placed than any other to teach us about each other and about ourselves and our humanity. We need to raise English up and let all of its magic and all of its rigour inspire the next generation. We want teachers to feel immersed in the passion and excitement of authentically sharing a subject that has everything: thoughts and feelings, words and arguments, discipline and technicality, freedom and creative expression.

Some of this might be about us letting go of ingrained habits and old ways of thinking. The cultural lens through which we see ourselves and each other is too often warped by our historical inheritance. Though notions of class may have changed somewhat, they have not entirely disappeared. We still have tendencies to subconsciously divide our pupils into those who can and those who can't; those who are able, those who are not. But, as more is discovered about learning and about intelligence, it becomes clear that these boundaries make less and less sense, as we hope we have shown in this book.

We can teach all mainstream pupils to a high academic level, a very high level. Their journey starts at home and much is learned at primary school, but secondary teachers have a huge part to play in each pupil's journey. We have five years or more to expose pupils to ideas and challenges that will meaningfully shape their lives. We owe it to them to aim high and try to get it right. So, we hope that all pupils, starting in their early years, will be exposed to a broad range of texts, from the past and the present, from the United Kingdom and from all over the world, and in a wide range of styles. We want them to be exposed to ideas, personalities and voices that take them beyond what any of us could hope to encounter in real life in one lifetime. And we hope this gives our pupils nourishment for their souls throughout their lives.

We hope that English teaching will be rooted in high-quality, research-informed continuous professional development (CPD) starting with their initial training and lasting throughout their careers. We hope that every teacher will have an understanding of what might work but, more importantly, that they know what *doesn't* work. We would like to see teachers not just competent but *consciously* competent, knowing why they do what they do.

We also hope that better curriculum design for pupil learning means that far less is left to chance. Teachers cannot control everything. But they can try to provide as clear a path as possible to guide pupils to develop gloriously rich and complex understanding of meanings in English.

We hope for open discourse about, and joyful interrogation of, our wonderful subject and approaches to teaching it.

Most of all, we believe there is good reason for this great hope for a grand revolution in English teaching, now more than ever.

Appendices

Appendix A: A more detailed look at how we might approach an English Language Paper. *Please bear in mind that simply handing this to pupils wouldn't be enough. We would need to model and practice this approach several times. In terms of task complexity though, it's very easy. Pupils only have to write a couple of sentences and do some highlighting as a first step. This could be made more developed and more challenging over time.*

English language - reading extracts and thinking practice

For each text, you're asking yourself three main questions. The reason it's tricky is that the list of possible answers is infinite and it can be hard to put into words. We have to develop our instincts and then learn to pursue them and articulate them. Here is a guide that might help:

1   **First, read the text and gather your thoughts.**
    Does the writing mostly seem to:
    a   present a **subject** (the list of possible subjects is endless - these are just some popular examples)
        poverty
        the class system
        gender stereotypes
        grief and loss
        war
        struggles with growing up
        isolation
        heartbreak
        nature
        family relationships
        memories of the past
    b   present a **social, historical context** (e.g. Victorian England)
    c   present a good example of a **genre** (e.g. gothic, dystopian, detective story, romance, etc.; if you're unfamiliar with the first two or don't know the difference between gothic and horror - do some research)
    d   present an interesting **character**

    NB writers will do a combination of all of the above but choose the one you think is taking priority.

Appendices   171

2   **Next, where appropriate, consider the writer's *attitude* to their subject matter.** For example, there are lots of different things a writer might express about war. They might think *all war is pointless* or they might think *it's a necessary evil*. They might focus on the *brutality* of it or they might focus on the *glory of winning*. Try to work out what the writer thinks and feels about whatever it is they're writing about. This is their attitude.

Keep your answer to number 1 in mind and remember that the possibilities are infinite. Here are some more examples:

- if you think they're focusing on a **subject**, ask yourself:
  - what might the writer be exploring? Human behaviour? Relationships? Feelings?
- if you think they're focusing on **the social and historical context**, ask yourself:
  - is the writer angry about inequality, how people are treated, or are they hopeful for a better future when times might be different?
- if you think they're focusing on a **genre**, ask yourself:
  - is the writer using the genre because it helps them to express feelings of anger or frustration or some other feeling? (For example, *gothic* is a great genre for expressing deep loneliness and rage. *Dystopia* is a useful genre for expressing anxiety and fears about the future.) Or is the writer just trying to create something tense and exciting?
- if you think they're focusing on a **character**, ask yourself:
  - How likeable is this character? How is the character made to sound complex or unique?

3   **Finally, think about where in the text you see or feel your responses to the first two questions.** These 'moments' will become your quotations. Don't worry about techniques yet. Just pick the moments/phrases that capture the big ideas you noticed when answering the first two questions.

So,

- if you think they're exploring a **subject**, find the moments where you see it most strongly. It might be something in the description or something a character thinks or says. It could be anything. Trust your instinct.
- if you think they're exploring a historical period, find the moments where you see the problem with that context being expressed. How is society holding people back or making life difficult?
- if you think they're exploring a **genre**, find two or three moments that help you recognise that genre - e.g. darkness and a full moon might suggest a ghost story. Or write down the moments that are the most tense and exciting, if that is more appropriate.
- if you think they're exploring a **character**, find two or three moments that help you recognise that genre - e.g. darkness and a full moon might suggest a ghost story. Or write down the moments that are the most tense and exciting, if that is more appropriate.

A summary

I've added a series of extracts for you to practice with. For each one,

1. identify the writer's priority and write it down:
   - subject
   - social, historical context
   - genre
   - character
2. identify the writer's *attitude* towards what they're writing about and write it down
3. highlight or underline two or three relevant examples in the text

Appendices

Appendix B: An example of a Year 7 assessment (this assesses narratology and context + the school's chosen key text, *Sir Gawain and the Green Knight*, translated by Simon Armitage).

Yr 7 Assessment   Narratology & Context

Multiple choice

Choose **one** answer for each question.

1. Which statement is true?
   - a   Stories are **always** influenced by the writer's background and real experiences
   - b   Stories are **sometimes** influenced by the writer's background and real experiences
   - c   Stories are **never** influenced by the writer's background and real experiences
2. In which century was *Sir Gawain and the Green Knight* first written?
   - a   16th Century
   - b   20th Century
   - c   14th Century
3. Which character in *Sir Gawain and the Green Knight* is a good example of how a knight should behave?
   - a   King Arthur
   - b   Lord Bertilak
   - c   Sir Gawain
4. What might be the two most important reasons that ancient cultures told stories?
   - a   To explain natural phenomena and to create a shared cultural identity.
   - b   To make friends and to explain why volcanoes happen.
   - c   To make each other laugh and to pass the time.
5. Which of these best explains what students of English do when they read texts?
   - a   See the story as real; think of the characters as if they're real people.
   - b   Remember the story is a construct; think about how and why a writer created it.
   - c   See the story as real because stories are always real.

One-word answers

6. The real things that are happening in the background when a story is written form the _____ of the story.
7. What word refers to a group of people who share a culture? _____
8. What word means to write down your own comments in the margins of a story? _____
9. Who do students of English pay the MOST attention to when they read stories: the **writer** or a **main character**? _____
10. Finish the sentence:
    For each idea we have about a text, we need to provide at least one _____.

Copyright material from Zoe Helman and Sam Gibbs (2022), *The Trouble with English and How to Address It*, Routledge

Short answer questions

11 Give two reasons why modern humans tell stories.
    1 _____
    2 _____

12 Write down two things that might influence a writer.
    1 _____
    2 _____

13 What does the phrase, 'societal norms' mean?
    _____

14 Writers often write about our common concerns. Write down two common concerns that most humans share.
    1 _____
    2 _____

15 Write down two phrases that are useful to students of English when they explain their ideas. (One is provided for you.)
    1   emphasises that
    2
    3

Annotating an extract

From *Sir Gawain* & the *Green Knight*

It was Christmas at Camelot – King Arthur's Court,
where the great and the good of the land had gathered,
all the righteous lords of the ranks of the Round Table
quite properly carousing and revelling in pleasure.
Time after time, kin tournaments of joust,
they had lunged at each other with levelled lances
then returned to the castle to carry on their carolling,
for the feasting lasted a full fortnight and one day,
with more food and drink than a fellow could dream of.
The hubbub of their humour was heavenly to hear:
pleasant dialogue by day and dancing after dusk,
so the house and its hall were lit with happiness
and lords and ladies were luminous with joy.
Such a coming together of the gracious and the glad:
the most chivalrous and courteous knights known in Christendom;
the most wonderful women to have walked in this world;
the handsomest king to be crowned at court.
Fine folk with their futures before them, there in that hall.

Copyright material from Zoe Helman and Sam Gibbs (2022), *The Trouble with English and How to Address It*, Routledge

Their highly honoured king
was happiest of all:
**no nobler knights had come
within a castle's wall.**

16 Highlight a relevant quotation and add the following annotation in the margin: suggests they were having a lot of fun together
17 Highlight a relevant quotation and add the following annotation in the margin: suggests that men had to show courage and physical strength
18 Add a relevant annotation to the line in bold half-way through that says, 'the feasting lasted a full fortnight and one day'
19 Add a relevant annotation to the line in bold at the end that says, 'no nobler knights had come within a castle's wall.'
20 Write one or two sentences explaining what impression you get of Christmas from the extract. DO NOT include quotations.

_____
_____
_____

Extended response

How does the story *Sir Gawain and the Green Knight* reflect the values of the time in which it was originally written?
Refer to examples from the extract in your response.
You can include quotations.
Aim to write one or two paragraphs.

_____
_____
_____
_____
_____
_____
_____
_____
_____
_____
_____
_____
_____
_____
_____
_____
_____

Copyright material from Zoe Helman and Sam Gibbs (2022), *The Trouble with English and How to Address It*, Routledge

Afterword

Throughout this book, Zoe and Sam have urged us of the need to place the conceptual understanding of English at the heart of the curriculum and our teaching. Although there's a lively debate to be had to work out how best to convey these concepts, there's broad agreement on the ways of seeing and knowing that mark out a novice student of literature and language from an expert.

As experts, we can't help noticing the deep reservoir of metaphor at play in language; we have an instinctive feel for the way structural and grammatical choices create meaning; we know, without having to consciously remember, that the way we think about the texts we study is quite different to the ways their writers may have conceived them. Whenever we ponder a poem or write an essay, we bring the accretion of everything else we've ever read or written to bear and this weight of experience guides our interpretations and enlivens our prose. It's easy to take all this for granted, but if our pupils - especially the most disadvantaged - are going to follow in our footsteps and pull up a chair to take part in ongoing literary and linguistic conversations, they need us to break down the edifice of our expertise into manageable, carefully prepared morsels.

But, while this book is a most marvellous manual for helping children see through these conceptual lenses, the examinations for which we are ultimately responsible for preparing our pupils for are not clearly aligned with such a conceptual view of our subject. Here, at the end of this very practical guide to rethinking English in schools and classrooms, seems an appropriate place for something slightly less down to earth.

The suspicion that the way children are assessed in England leaves something to be desired is never far from the minds of most English teachers. Sam and Zoe have explored how, although specifications sometimes change - and although we do seem to solve some problems - things are never quite as we would like them to be. In the wake of the decision to cancel national examinations for a second successive year due to the global pandemic, many have felt that now seems as good a time as any to reassess assessment. However, although there's no shortage of pundits arguing that examinations should be abolished, no one has been able to come up with anything better. Whatever the answer is, we should know by now that it's not to be found in algorithms, or centre assessed grades. Both coursework and controlled assessments were always open to huge abuse and, due to the high stakes nature of league tables, the pressure of teachers to massage results was unbearable. Not only that, all forms of teacher assessment have the unfortunate (and unintentional) effect of rewarding pupils from more privileged backgrounds at the expense of their more marginalised peers. Indeed, in 2012 and again in 2020, the attainment gap between more and less socially advantaged pupils grew significantly.

Surely, if there were a better way to assess pupils' attainment in English we'd have found it by now? Just as democracy is often said to be the worst form of government apart from all the others, examinations are the worst way to assess children's attainment apart from all the other options. But that doesn't mean we can't make our exams better.

Although there are many possible ways to approach reforming the assessment of English, I want to focus here on making examinations better aligned with the ideas Zoe and Sam have outlined. So, here follows a proposal for concept-led examinations. This would require exam boards to produce specifications that focus on the underpinning concepts of English language. These would include the knowledge that:

- writing is an attempt to manipulate readers;
- language is essentially metaphorical;
- structural and grammatical choices affect meaning.

These broad conceptual understandings could, in turn, contain each of the elements proposed by Sam and Zoe in Chapter 3. Let's think about how this might work in both language and literature GCSEs.

English language

I'm not the first – and I'm sure I won't be the last – to point out that the English language GCSE is the most iniquitous of all the exams children sit. In every other subject, children's results are dependent on their teachers teaching the content of the courses, but the fact that English language has *no* specified content means that the broader pupils' cultural knowledge, the better they'll do. Consequentially, children from advantaged backgrounds tend to do better, often despite the choices made by teachers and schools. In contrast, pupils from more disadvantaged backgrounds are so dependent on schools bucking the trend and ditching the myth that English is a 'skills-based' subject that they are statistically much less likely to succeed. The more you happen to know about the unfamiliar texts that pop up in the exam, the better you'll do. English teachers find themselves in a bind. Superficially,† the endless treadmill of making pupils sit past papers and drilling them for a very narrow test can seem like the best bet for exam success but, in fact, it is the very narrowness of this approach that guarantees more socially advantaged children outperform their less fortunate peers.

Perhaps the quickest, simplest solution would be to start specifying content and requiring pupils to discuss and emulate the concepts that make writing 'work'. If pupils were examined on what they'd actually been taught rather on some vague, ill-defined 'skills', the playing field would be substantially levelled. My suggestion would be for exam boards to produce an anthology of texts, carefully chosen for their exemplification of the concepts to be assessed. This should include material on the development of the English language and the ways in which it has changed in recent years. I would also include an opportunity to comment on grammatical and rhetorical choices made by writers. To allay concerns about narrowing the curriculum and teaching to the text, the anthology could be made available mid-way through Year 11.†This would still be far from perfect, but it would at least allow pupils to be assessed on whether they have learned a body of knowledge.

English literature

Unlike English language, the literature GCSE follows clearly prescribed content. Here though the problem is, perhaps, one of too much rather than too little specification. Currently, pupils are assessed on whether they are able to respond to a narrow range of literary texts, arranged around such arbitrary groupings as 'modern texts', 'Victorian novels', poetry (which must include the Romantics) and, of course, a Shakespeare play. It's perfectly possible for pupils to perform well on such a course and yet know little about literature.

My suggestion is that the study of literature would both be more interesting, and more rounded, were it to include some of the concepts that underpin an expert knowledge of the subject. To this end, I would like to see pupils assessed on their understanding of metaphor, their appreciation of narrative techniques, their ability to see the links between structure and content and the extent to which they understand the contexts in which a literary text was written and is read. On top of this, the GCSE should introduce pupils to the broad sweep of literature. We should expect pupils to know something about the origins of literature in English as well as a nodding familiarity with some of the great works and writers. Such a course should still retain some of the close analytic skills which are so inextricably associated with literary criticism, but by opening the subject out to the study of †*literature itself*, rather than just individual works of literature, pupils would be exposed to a far broader – and arguably more useful – domain of knowledge.

Clearly there's not much flesh on these proposals. An awful lot thinking still needs to be done to make concept-led assessment a viable approach to assessment, but, if we agree with Zoe and Sam's analysis of how English should be approached in the classroom, then maybe it also makes sense to begin considering how examinations might better fit such an approach.

David Didau
Backwell, February 2021

Index

Note: *Italic* page numbers refer to figures.

abstract concepts: big ideas, literary texts 36-37; central organising principles, concept-led learning 35-36; central organising principles, literary texts 36-37; dialogic talk 38-39; dual coding 37-38; organising 35-37; pre-reading 39-41; problem and handling 32-33; teacher insight 51; teachers talking about betrayal 34-35; teaching 32-52
abstractions 13, 32, 34, 35, 37, 160
abstract thinking 32, 33
Alexander, R. J. 39
Ashbee, R. 54
assessment 1-3, 54, 78, 82-89, 120, 128, 129, 143, 177
assess pupils 88, 147, 177

Bambrick-Santoyo, P. 159
Bennie, K. 76
Berliner, David 1
big ideas 25, 26, 29, 36, 37, 49, 79, 134
Blunt, Janell R. 85

case study: change, implementation 128-129
Cattell, R. B. 13
Caviglioli, O. 37
challenging texts 40, 58
change, implementation 116-129; applying evidence 123; case study 128-129; cycle of planned failure 118-123; developing plan 125; evidence 116-118; gaps understanding 123-124; leading and lagging indicators 125-126; planning curriculum implementation, key points 127; planning to evaluate 125-126; schema-building 123-124; teacher professional development, Guskey framework 126

Christmas Carol 7, 21, 24, 27, 41-43, 100
Christodoulou, D. 87, 121
chronology 3, 59, 65, 72
Clark, R. E. 14, 92
cognitive load theory 94-98
cognitive science 13, 14
complex conceptual knowledge 10, 103
concept-led curriculum 87
concept-led curriculum, limitations 75-76; challenging 75; hard to assess 76; heavily focused on literature 75; reduces English to list of concepts 75
concept-led English curriculum 77
concept-led learning 35
concept maps 44, 85
conceptual abstractions 6
conceptual curriculum 74, 88, 114
conceptual framework 3, 58, 60, 77
conceptual knowledge 16, 21, 59, 79, 89, 97, 125
conceptual learning 80
conceptual thinking 2, 32, 65
conscious competence 10
Continuing Professional Development (CPD) 1, 2, 10-12
controlled assessments 1-2, 54, 118, 176
curricular deficit 120
curricular knowledge 133
curriculum 10, 51, 53, 54, 56, 60, 66, 71, 72, 77, 78, 88, 116, 120, 128, 130, 147, 148, 150, 161, 163, 164, 165, 166-167, 168, 169; aims 147, 148, 151; assessing English 78-80; assessment 78-89; assessment in English 87-88; assessment look like 82-87;

cognitive load theory 94-98; concept-led curriculum, limitations 75-76; curating 66-77; design 2, 4, 11-13, 51, 53, 54, 118, 124, 152, 154; English as discipline, pupils 66; English Language examinations 82; enquiry-based learning 91-92; evidence-informed approaches 90-115; explicit instruction 91; fiction and non-fiction reading, KS3 curriculum 72-73; guided practice 104; independent practice 104; intentions 3, 90; intermediate steps 104-107; key stage 2 74-75; key stage 3 to key stage 4, transition 74; lesson, planning 108-113; modelling and practice 101-103; models 54, 56, 64; novices vs experts, teaching 91; overall approach, expertise to pupils 90-93; over-arching ideas 66-71; plan 63, 124, 127, 150; planning 3, 11, 150, 160, 161; practice 103-104; progression model and key stages 74; pupils, achieving 98; pupils really access same concepts 96-98; resource design 130-146; retrieval and recap 99-101; retrieval practice, remembering 98-99; second-order concepts 71-72; shape thinking, pupils 66; teacher insight 77, 88-89, 114; teaching essay writing 80-82; texts, choosing 76; traditional differentiation, problematic 96; two ways whole class teaching, pupils needs 93-94; work 153; working to resolve problems, teachers 93-94

department leaders 160, 166
designed curriculum plan 116
dialogic talk 38-39
Didau, D. 71, 87, 93
disciplinary schemas 19-20; building, central organising principles 26-29; inform personal response 22-26
domain knowledge 78-80
dual coding 37-38, 43-44, 47, 51, 98, 112, 132, 134, 158

Ebbinghaus, H. 98, 99
Education Endowment Foundation (EEF) 116, *117*
effective modelling 101
eight strategies 42-51; drawing 42, 44-47; enacting 42, 50-51; imagining 42, 48; mapping 42, 44; self-explaining 42, 48-50; self-testing 42, 48-49; summarising 42-43; teaching 42, 49-50

English curriculum design 2, 3, 29, 53-61, 63-65, 128, 165; chronological approach 59-60; concept-led approach 60-64; implications 53-65; separating literature from language 56-57; text-based approach 58-59; theme-based approach 57-58; topic-based approach 54-56
English language, reading extracts and thinking 170-172
English teaching 2, 3, 5, 10, 12, 22, 130, 146, 168, 169
enquiry learning 91, 101
essay writing 10
expert knowledge 25, 92, 101, 131, 178
expert teachers 22, 53, 78, 156, 158, 167
explicit connections 75, 150, 151

figurative language 34
Fletcher-Wood, H. 155
foundational concepts 64, 78, 120, 121, 135
future, English teaching 168-169

General Certificate of Secondary Education (GCSE): course 1, 54; syllabus 6
generative learning 3, 38, 41-42, 51

high standards, sustaining 153-167; coaching 155-159; curriculum expertise, developing 154-159; effective implementation, lessons learnt 163-165; leading the curriculum, English 154; monitoring learning 161, 162-163; senior leaders support English departments 160-163; subject-specific training 155; teacher insight 165-167; teacher learning, culture 160; teacher learning communities 159

impact 147-148
impact, measuring 147-152; cognitive biases 148-149; correlation and causation 149-150; curriculum not paper document 148; learning is invisible 148; learning taking place 150; limitations of judging 'learning' 151; monitoring vs evaluating 149; reliability and validity 148; rich schema and conceptual understanding, pupils 150; triangulate evidence 151; wider curriculum aims 151; working 150
indicators 126, 127, 150
inferences 24, 120, 126, 148, 151
interpretation 9, 11, 37, 77, 78, 81, 101, 151, 176
intervention 11, 12, 55, 104, 117, 122, 125, 149

Karpicke, Jeffrey D. 85
key stage 3 (KS3) curriculum 66, 72-73
Kirschner, P. A. 14, 92
Knight, J. 158
knowledge 10, 14-17, 21, 22, 24, 26-28, 30, 55, 64, 66, 96, 98, 124, 142, 150, 154, 155, 158, 160, 164, 165, 166-167, 177, 178; domains 14, 21, 22, 35, 78; gaps 8, 17, 124; new learning and *18*; organisers 143-145; pupils 64; schema building and 16; teachers 124
knowledge-based subject 2, 105
knowledge-poor pupils 82
knowledge-rich English curriculum 163
Korn, James H. 40

learning 3, 13, 14, 36, 38, 82, 88, 89, 92, 98, 100, 111, 112, 126, 131, 132, 148, 150, 151, 155; process 32, 59, 63
lesson, planning 108-113; activate prior knowledge, retrieval practice 111; after lesson 113; assume nothing 111-112; checking understanding 112; initial choices, making 108; input phase, exploring concept 111; modelling, exemplification and dual coding 112; overall tips 113; plenary will happen next lesson 113; practice 112-113; start of lesson 108-111
literary texts 26, 36, 58, 75, 178

Making Kids Cleverer 93
meaningful concept-led curriculum 87
meaning making, pupils 13-30; internal schemas to external production 21-22; teacher insight 30; text can teach us, right conditions 20-21; writing essays 21-22; *see also* schemas
medium-term plans 3, 116, 130, 131, 133, 142, 148, 163
memory 13, 23, 37, 42, 94, 99, 100, 132, 144; representation model *15*
mental models 15, 19, 36, 41, 53, 65, 92, 98, 124, 126, 130
metaphors 33, 34
modelling 22, 39, 42, 44, 91, 112, 114, 122, 132, 134, 136, 155, 157, 158; thinking 112
Myatt, M. 100, 160

narrative schemas 18-20, 29, 36, 41, 113
National Curriculum 53
new curriculum 116-118, 125, 126, 129, 130, 153-155, 156, 158, 163, 164

non-fiction texts 57, 62, 75
novice teachers 10, 53, 158, 159, 167

Ofsted framework 54

pedagogical content knowledge 3, 12, 53
pedagogical knowledge 12; teachers 12
persistent problems, English 5-12; autonomy and creativity, top-down approaches 10; CPD and 8-9; English as skills-based, rather than knowledge-based, teachers 10; lack expertise, teachers 10; lack of parity of experience, pupils 11-12; lack of time and headspace 8; poorly constructed and sequenced, curriculum 10-11; pupils forget 8; struggle to make connections, pupils 7; struggle to write in depth and detail, pupils 7; teach English authentically and ruthless assessment system, conflict 9-10
pre-reading 39-41; accountability 40; analysing text 40; challenging texts 40; disciplinary and narrative schema 41; reasons for 40
prior learning 14, 93, 99, 100
procedural knowledge 15, 16, 22, 85, 121, 122
professional learning 126, 160
pupil learning 126, *156*, 159, 169
pupils struggle 7, 41, 49, 94

resource design, curriculum 130-146; central organising principle, staff 134-142; effective planning 131; knowledge organisers 143-145, *144*, *145*; long-term plan into medium-term plans 133-134; nine principles of design 133-134; potential barriers, teacher booklets 142-143; rest of booklet 142; revisiting research 131-133; start a booklet, staff 134-142; teacher insight 146

schemas 14-16; develop in English and pupils 16-17; disciplinary 19-20; knowledge and 16; narrative 18-19
school-age pupils 91, 92
second-order concepts 60-62, 71, 74, 77, 134, 135, *139*
sentences 36, 104, 108, 111-113, 134, 145, 170, 173, 175
shared knowledge 24
social injustice 7, 40, 100, 101
socio-economic status 6
Soderstrom, N. C. 104
storytelling 40

structure 21, 22, 35, 36, 71, 72, 108, 110-112, 120-123, 131, 134, 135, *137-138*, 142, 143
subject concepts 29, 32, 67, 76
subject knowledge 10-12, 53, 58, 64, 124, 131, 133, 146
substantive concepts 60
Sweller, J. 14, 92, 94
symbols 24-26, 71, 72, 102

teacher booklets 133, 134-135, *135*, *136*, 142-143, 146, 163, 166
teacher educators 4, 133, 154, 155
teacher insight: abstract concepts 51; curriculum 77; curriculum, assessments 88-89; curriculum, evidence-informed approaches 114; high standards, sustaining 165-167; meaning making, pupils 30; resource design, curriculum 146

teacher knowledge 145; booklets 133, 134-135, *135*, *136*, 142-143, 146
teacher learning 126, 155, 159, 160, 164
teacher training 2-4, 9, 125, 165, 167
thematic concept 6, 40, 97, 134, 135, *135*
thinking processes 66, 82, 91, 120, 123, 132
thought processes 3, 41-42, 66, 71, 81, 90, 98, 102, 114, 143
threshold concepts 60

Venn diagrams 44, 85

Wiliam, D. 125, 133, 154, 159
Willingham, D. T. 95
Wilson, Karen 40
working memory 37, 91, 94, 95, 98, 99, 104, 132, 156